Zeynep Akbal
Lived-Body Experiences in Virtual Reality

Zeynep Akbal, born in 1986, works as a researcher at the Max Planck Institute for Human Cognitive and Neurosciences in Leipzig. She studied communication sciences, media sciences and media philosophy, and worked on developing her interdisciplinary method. She did her doctorate in philosophy at Universität Potsdam. Her research focuses on the intersection of philosophy of perception and cognitive sciences.

Zeynep Akbal

Lived-Body Experiences in Virtual Reality

A Phenomenology of the Virtual Body

[transcript]

This book is a dissertation submitted to the University of Potsdam in 2022. Advisors (Gutachter): Prof. Dr. Marie-Luise Angerer, Priv.-Doz. Dr. phil. habil. Bernd Bösel and Prof. Dr. Arno Villringer.

Bibliographic information published by the Deutsche Nationalbibliothek
The Deutsche Nationalbibliothek lists this publication in the Deutsche Nationalbibliografie; detailed bibliographic data are available in the Internet at http://dnb.d-nb.de

Cover layout: Maria Arndt, Bielefeld
Cover illustration: Mert Akbal, "Mirror Neurons", still image from animation, 2019
Proofread: Elana Katz

https://doi.org/10.14361/9783839466766
Print-ISBN 978-3-8376-6676-2
PDF-ISBN 978-3-8394-6676-6
ISSN of series: 2702-8852
eISSN of series: 2702-8860

To my parents

Contents

Abbreviations

BCI   Brain Computer Interface
OBE   Out of Body Experience
OOO   Object Oriented Ontology
PPL   Phenomenon of Phantom Limb
PLP   Phantom Limb Pain
RHI   Rubber Hand Illusion
TPJ   Temporoparietal Junction
VE   Virtual Environment
VR   Virtual Reality
HMD   Head Mounted Display
MTBA MachineToBeAnother
VRT   Virtual Reality Therapy

Ethical Consideration

Prior to the experiments, all ethical considerations have been carefully made, including informed consent, confidentiality and anonymity. All experiments were conducted with voluntary participation. Additionally, all participants were informed about the potential side effects of VR exposure (e.g. motion sickness). In some cases, VR can cause cyber-sickness in the shape of general discomfort, dizziness, or nausea. However, this has mostly been reported during VR experiences with a lot and particular types of movement. In the experiments I present in this dissertation, participants have mostly remained (sitting) in one place, which naturally decreased the possibilities of cyber-sickness. Participants were informed about the possibility for cyber-sickness before the start of the experiment and we have emphasized that they can stop the experiment at any moment.

Proposals were approved by the following ethical committees of:

- Max Planck Institute for Human Cognitive and Brain *Sciences* (2018–2019)
- Berlin Graduate School of Mind and Brain (2017)
- "Kultur Macht Stark", Bundesministerium für Bildung und Forschung Berlin (2015–2017)

Abstract

This dissertation aims to answer the question "Can Virtual Reality (VR) technology become a central instrument for the evaluation of the subjective experience of the body?" In order to explore this question, I present three experimental projects in VR which I have conducted. I explore this question through these hands-on experimentations in VR and situate the results in context with existing theories in media sciences and the phenomenology of bodily perception.

The first of these experiments aimed to explore the body image through a live stream between a 3D camera and VR glasses, which enabled the participants to evaluate their body image from a third-person perspective. In the second experiment, I used a device called the "Machine to Be Another" (MTBA)—this time for the participants to visually experience the body of another person within a VR setup—and thus explored what embodiment might mean in VR. Additionally, by manipulating visuo-haptic sensory modalities, I investigate what a body schema might mean within a body swap setup. The third experiment differed in focus from the first two, which were concerned with body image exploration. It delved into the perception of the inner parts of the body within an animated VR atmosphere. This idea of inner body exploration aims to reverse the conventional understanding of technology as an alienating medium. Instead, I suggest we can make use of technological artifacts to overcome the existing gap we have with our bodies. These three experiments represent three consecutive steps of subjective experience of the body in VR, starting from body image as the first outer layer of the body and then developing into the inner experience of the body. Throughout this dissertation, I indicate how the virtual body and the lived body incorporate each other in reflexive cycles that mediate presence, perception, and sensation.

The main contribution of this research is to place VR, as a novel technology, into a transdisciplinary dialogue with theories that provide a subjective understanding of the body. By employing a phenomenological method, among others, I also reveal shortcomings in traditional phenomenology and how certain notions in this field need pragmatic and contemporary reinforcement. In this way, this dissertation can also be considered as a contribution to postphenomenology, as certain insights will be recontextualized within new technoscientific horizons.

Introduction

Aims

This dissertation examines the subjective experience of the body when it is exposed to VR. To do so, it engages with three VR experiments: 1) "Ambiguity in Lived Body Experiences," 2) "Machine to Be Another" (MTBA), and 3) "Sit Behind My Eyes." These three experiments represent three layers of examining the body in VR. The first experiment focuses, as the first layer, on the outer layer of the body, i.e., on perceived body image. The second experiment signifies an exploration oriented toward within the body, while also adding another person in a VR setup. This inclusion of another person points, in the process of embodiment, to the presence of the felt body, which leads to an examination of the body schema. The third experiment, as the final layer, highlights the experience of the inner parts of the body.

In presenting these three VR experiments, I draw connections between what has been theorized as the "lived body" and the virtual body. With the rise of VR technologies, the body has come to play a central role for increasing sensed presence in tele-worlds. In contrast to most scholarly debates today about VR and cyberspaces, which often bypass the importance of bodily perception, I will address how the experience of VR evokes and intensifies the subjective experience of the body. I will furthermore underline why we need to consult media theories, cognitive theories, and insights from phenomenological philosophy, and how these disciplines have an intertwined relation allowing us to make sense of technological developments that attempt to improve the immersive quality of how a virtual body is felt. Furthermore, I suggest that VR technologies can also be used to reverse feelings of self-alienation, by using it as a multifaceted mirror to look beyond what we are used to seeing and eventually becoming acquainted with these unseen aspects.

The shared intention behind the three experiments I present in this work is to present new techniques for the observer, mainly influenced by Jonathan Crary's 1992 book *Techniques of the Observer: On Vision and Modernity in the Nineteenth Century*. Crary underlines how early optical technologies (e.g., the telescope and microscope) enabled access to places that escape the perception of human vision. Such access has produced a vast knowledge and allowed us to recognize how instruments directly operate on the body of individuals. The sense of presence in remote environments can be established via technology. VR technology calls for us to focus more directly on the body and on bodily perception in order to create an even stronger sense of presence. VR makes it possible for us, as observers, to have an altered visual perspective, allowing us to explore the phenomenal character of the subjective experience we have with the body and of the body in space. In order to understand this complex reflexive cycle between technology and the body, we need to consult the formative theories and practices which have led technological developments to this date.

Toward the end of the editing process of this dissertation, we experienced a global pandemic (SARS-CoV-2), which has resulted in millions of people being confined to their houses.[1] During the first national lock down in 2020, I came upon another analogy to explain the main intention of this dissertation. The excessive amount of time I have spent in my own flat has led me to the awareness that I have always observed, and still do observe, my own home from only a limited number of angles. Understandably, this is due to my own height and to the positioning of the furniture in the space, and to the way the objects occupy the space which prevents me from having more places to stand and gaze upon my environment. We may live in the same flat for twenty years, while never be able to see our bedroom from a top-down angle. The irony of this visual deprivation has motivated me to search for possibilities to try to unlock and experience these unknown angles, like an end effect or an inspiration stemming from my past VR experiments. As a result, I installed a thick shelf running right up to the front door of my flat and climbed up on it to stare at the corridor and at the entrance of the rooms. I also climbed up on my wardrobe and stared down from

---

1   During the global pandemic caused by SARS-CoV-2 (which is declared by World Health Organization as a public health emergency of international concern on January 30, 2020) many people have suffered and died, and a number of upsetting consequences have become part of our lives. To summarize such event here is impossible, both due to the lack of scientific knowledge and evidence at this point in time, and also due to the aims of the dissertation.

three meters high to look at my bed; I crawled down under the bathroom sink and looked up from ground level; I entirely emptied one of my bookshelves, placed myself into it, and stared at my room. During all these repositioning of my body in rarely or non-practiced angles in the space, certain memories were unlocked as I had the opportunity to imagine myself within these unusual perspectives. From this example, it also became clear to me that what I could do in our physical reality remains limited, in comparison to what we can achieve by using the plasticity of spatial orientation and cognition within VR. Similar to the unusual aspects of our home space that we never see, both the space in which our body occupies and the space within our body remains partially inaccessible. Each chapter in this dissertation aims to underline how to reverse such inaccessibility with the help of VR technologies. The main motivation was to underline how the affordances of existing media alter the way we explore the subjective experience of the body during a close exposure to technology. Development of immersive technologies require an in depth look into the relations between human beings and technological artifacts. At this point subject's own experience as a feedback for further development plays a significant role.

The nature of this dissertation requires a vast span of evaluation between different disciplines. Media theory engages with an extensive spectrum of media, and I focused on media's capacity (in my case, the medium of VR) and its potential alteration of bodily perception. I explore the interplay between humans and technology, along with the meaning of the causality of this interplay. I look at the reciprocity between the body and the medium, highlighting the considerations of the materiality of these technologies and their bodily techniques of use. This is the baseline for why this dissertation relates to media theory. Media studies employ theories and methods from a variety of disciplines, which also include philosophy, psychology, and cognitive sciences, among many others, but in this dissertation I have mainly oriented my arguments toward these three. Because I am interested in clarifying the medium of VR's effect on human perception, I naturally got involved in studying the phenomenology of perception, as well.

My investigation is phenomenological, as the phenomenological approach amplifies the body as the starting point of perception. In addition to this phenomenological method, I nod toward the implications of cognitive neuroscience, but I will maintain a critical distance from both the traditional restrictions of phenomenology and the isolating explanatory powers of neuroscience. This distance also signifies why I have chosen the term "transdisciplinary," rather than "interdisciplinary," to explain the methodological intention of this dissertation. The goal is not to underline how each discipline might provide the most suitable knowledge but to reveal the connections that exist between these disciplines. Because VR is situated at the junction of issues addressed by these disciplines, studying it requires a transdisciplinary approach. Even more, this analysis especially has the potential to demonstrate how the body has been both the subject and the object of research in media sciences, phenomenology, and cognitive neurosciences. My investigation as a whole will thus amplify the notion of the body in these fields of inquiry and the importance of sensory modalities. As a result, I will underline the necessity of grasping lived body experience in terms of a mediation related to new technology, while also demonstrating how this central position of the body could have remained undertheorized for so long that it seems to have been forgotten altogether. This context-specific application of phenomenology to research oriented technology automatically brought me to the borders of postphenomenology, a term initially coined by Don Ihde in the beginning of 1990s with an intention to highlight the effect of media on human perception. Postphenomenology is a modified, hybrid phenomenology that considers a deeper understanding of embodiment and active bodily perception; as a result it blends technoscientific developments and analyzes the role of technology in social, personal, and cultural life. In this way, the discipline aims to overcome traditionalist and rigid formations of phenomenology. Similar to the approach of Yoni Van Den Eede's 2017 *Postphenomenology and Media: Essays on Human–Media–World Relations*, this dissertation explores how we can study human perception while it is being exposed to technology. By taking a postphenomenological approach, I challenge the basic notion of traditional phenomenology (the deobjectification of the body) by objectifying it within the VR setups I present in this work.

I believe that such approach to an examination of a virtual body can inform media theories while also explaining why VR technology may become a central instrument for evaluating the subjective experience of the body.

Main Research Questions

This dissertation will examine the importance of the cognitive architecture of the lived body as the receiver and manipulator of technology. What are the fundamental aspects that enable one to perceive a virtual body? How do subject-object relations occur and how can they be actualized in virtual environments?

What is it like to perceive a virtual object through the sensed presence of a virtual body? What is the role of a virtual agent for self-narration in virtual worlds? What is the role of subjective experience in these acts? Can we reemphasize the notions of body image and body schema from the framework of technological developments? How do these developments alter bodily perception and cognition? For us to answer these questions, we need a transdisciplinary approach, and this dissertation will exemplify why this is necessary in order to develop an understanding for the virtual body.

VR in scientific research tends to be more at home in the cyber-physical sciences, which explore the connections between computation and physical processes, and informatics, computer science, and engineering, yet it has not been widely acknowledged or implemented in humanities and in philosophy as a tool to study human perception. Only a handful of researchers have taken the phenomenology of the virtual body into consideration, such as Stefano Gualeni (2015) and Roberto Diodato (2018). Both Gualeni and Diodato raise the question of what the philosophy of perception might gain from a theory of perception in virtual environments, given the specific nature of this kind of environment. A virtual environment is experienced through a virtual body, and we must develop a dialogue with this body in order to reveal its ontological structure. The milieu we conquer in reality is defined by the body's spatiality; likewise, the interrogation of the virtual environment and the virtual objects surrounding the virtual body can enable new ways of digging deeper into this ontological structure. How do I see myself in the virtual world? How do my other senses give me access to this virtual world? When deprived of one sensory modality, can we manipulate other senses to create a more cultivated sense of presence?

By including theories and my hands-on experiences in VR, I aim to fill the gap in the relevant literature. My aim is not only to provide a philosophical text that reflects on the outcomes of VR implementations but also to suggest practical solutions for developing a virtual body—to suggest VR as a method to reform phenomenological insights and implement them in media theory, while pointing to the fundamental changes in bodily perception we experience as we become engaged with this advanced technology. In this way, I will contribute to postphenomenology by examining the role of VR in spatial cognition, perception, and human embodiment.

The VR interventions and experiments I present in this dissertation demonstrate how my practice of using can contribute to the practical aspects of the technology. Most of these practices were initially influenced by my interest in phenomenological readings, more specifically by the French phenomenologist Maurice Merleau-Ponty's book *Phenomenology of Perception* (1945). His phenomenological approach, along with his focus on the phenom-enal character of subjective experience and his habituation of the body as the starting point of perception, has served as the primary theoretical framework for my work. In each chapter, I have initiated conversations between Mer-leau-Ponty and his contemporaries within the advent of media technologies. The more I combed through the works of Henri Bergson, Jonathan Crary, Paul Connerton, Shaun Gallagher, Dan Zahavi, Vittorio Gallese, Elizabeth Grosz, Katherine Hayles, Catherine Malabou, Thomas Nagel, Alva Noë, A. V. Ramachandran, Antti Revonsuo, Florian Rötzer, Mel Slater, Vivian Sobchack, Tom Sparrow, Francisco Varela, Evan Thompson, and many others, the more I have found similar modes of thinking in line with Merleau-Ponty's, regardless of whether these authors and thinkers themselves have traced or adopted Mer-leau-Ponty's philosophical intentions. In fact, some analytical philosophers I quote in this dissertation have strictly excluded Merleau-Ponty from their in-vestigation, yet at some point in their work they all seem to refer to subjectivity and subjective experience as the core dynamic for understanding bodily expe-rience, since all of them systematically avoid the Cartesian mind/body split. I enter into dialogue with these "oppositional" thinkers, too, confronting them throughout the work. These dialogues may suggest that we recognize VR as an embodied technological mechanism that renders interactive content. This new interactive content naturally demands a series of new discussions about the subject-object relationship and the ontological understanding behind it.

Organization and Literature

This dissertation has three chapters, excluding the introduction and conclu-sion. Each chapter demonstrates a VR intervention/experiment I have con-ducted and became involved in between the years 2014 and 2020. All partici-pants were informed about the procedures and signed consent forms. In order to protect their privacy, I have changed their names as I report their subjective evaluations related to their post-VR experiences.

In the first sections of each chapter, I explain the practical and technical aspects of VR setups and include fragments from interviews with the partici-pants and users. After demonstrating these practical aspects, each chapter un-folds into relevant theories and insights. To cite each and every author's work here in this section is a difficult task, but below I will briefly list some of the authors and their works I find most influential and explain how they fit together in relation to my approach in this work.

I begin in Chapter 1 with introducing my first VR intervention "Ambiguity in Lived Body Experiences." Here I underline how philosophical inquiries about the perceptional qualities of the body can inspire creative ways to implement VR and then explain the technical aspects of the setup. This VR setup brought an out-of-body experience (OBE) for the participants, similar to Henrik Ehrrson's (2007) setup, a connection between a VR head mounted display (HMD) and a camera enabled the user to visit their body from an external point of view. In my version of OBE, the main purpose was to tackle the dimensions of subjective experience during a visual examination of the bodily self in VR. Together with six participants, I questioned the notions of body ownership, body image, and the importance of active movement in perception, and I investigated how the phenomenological distinction of body awareness can be explored through the lens of VR experience. I draw conclusions from the users' interviews and related these insights to theories of Alva Noë's (2015) action and perception and Elizabeth Grosz's movement-vision, while visiting Henri Bergson's (1896, 2004) dynamic universe where the interaction with the objects is possible only through an action upon them. Additionally, I integrate Vivian Sobchack's (1994) view on embodied presence as a new perceptual mode. Within this chapter I also provide an overview on Katherine Hayles' (1999) comments on the relevancy of neural networks in the human brain and in information processing systems. I am influenced by her recent work *Unthought: The Power of the Cognitive Nonconscious* (2017), and I underline how this issue can be explored and externalized through technical mediation and within the domains of VR. Because of my intention to increase the sense of presence of the virtual body, cognitive architecture and sensory modalities of the body start to become central issues in this first chapter. I underline Francisco Varela's (1993) remarks on the inseparable connection between cognitive technology and cognitive science. He refers to technology as an amplifier for anyone who wants to look deeper into their own experience. The VR intervention I explain in this chapter directly points to this amplification, as the users are exploring their body image and beyond, in a confrontational setup. I then visit Gallagher and Zahavi's (2008) distinction of object body and subject body and exemplify how these modes of body awareness can be traced and distinguished in the personal reports and indications of the participants. Influenced by Tom Sparrow's *The End of Phenomenology* (2014) and Don Ihde's *Husserl's Missing Technologies* (2016), I highlight the shortcomings of phenomenological approaches and how certain phenomenological notions have neglected media devices as embodied instruments. I frequently refer to Brian Massumi's *Parables for the Virtual: Movement, Affect, Sensation* (2002). Borrowing his multidisciplinary approach, I explore his main question: "What exactly does the inconvenient reality that we see things we don't actually see say about the nature of perception?" (Massumi 2011, 42). I compare film immersion and VR immersion, based on the works of Paul Connerton (1989), Vittorio Gallese (2014, 2018) and Jonathan Crary (1992). I end this chapter with an evaluation of Jacques Lacan's (1936) mirror stage, as the OBE setup provides a similar mirrored body image for the observer. This chapter reevaluates the notion of body image through a VR intervention and demonstrates how the body image contains one's own emotional imprints and reflections.

Chapter 2 provides an overview on the outcomes of the workshop series "ich bin du, du bist ich," in which I worked with another VR setup called "The Machine to Be Another" (MTBA). In addition to the previous setups' evaluation of body image, with the integration of MTBA, I included the exploration of the body schema through the manipulation of sensory modalities, such as visual and tactile. After providing the technical details of the setup, I report the observations and conclusions from several interviews I conducted with nearly thirty participants. These reports underline and validate several indications from Hayles' (1999) takes on bodily practices: performing habitual movements communicates an intention to the receiver in a better way, exceeding the verbal aspects of communication. Through a visual body swap illusion, participants actively reflected on their sense of embodiment, and we explored how the sensed presence of body contributed to the definition of the body schema, which seems to be an experience that all people share (contrary to the unique associations each individual attaches to their own body image). As articulated by Francoise Dolto (1984, 22), the body schema is felt unconsciously, preconsciously, and consciously.

In this chapter I also evaluate the previous technical details of previous body swap mechanisms (Petkova and Ehrrson 2000) and reflect on the new body swap setup as MTBA. The body swap setup was initially suggested as a gender swap experience, as the users could visually adopt the physical attributes of their counterparts (Bertnard 2016). I suggest that MTBA's gender swap visualization can magnify what Elizabeth Grosz (1998, 32) indicates with "neighboring sex": rather than being opposites, people can have neighboring sexes, referring to a kind of ontology of entangled bodies, a conurbation of sexes.

Additionally, I criticize Bertnard's (2016, 2018) take on presenting MTBA as an empathy machine, by examining Paul Bloom's *Against Empathy* (2017). I furthermore draw attention to Rafael Calvo and Dorian Peters' (2014) distinction between empathy and compassion, and explain how this distinction may help us to reconsider the dangers of empathy. I approach the discourse of empathy from the mirror neuron research of Vittorio Gallese (1998) and question how reciprocally performed bodily exercises in VR can stimulate corresponding mirror neurons in the brain. Here I also explain mirror neuron research's recent validation of phenomenological insights related to empathic behavior. Throughout the chapter, I deliver insights to support computer scientist Jaron Lanier's (2017) suggestions on simulating the neuronal expectations of the body in order to develop a virtual body. In order to gain a clearer understanding of the cognitive architecture of the body, I present the importance of certain sensory modalities in Chapter 2 (also in Chapter 3), mostly focusing on the visual sense and tactile sense. Furthermore, I underline the role of multisensory integration in media technologies to demonstrate how media devices mirror our cognitive abilities. Within the domains of VR technologies, it is also possible to look beyond our existing cognitive abilities. At this point, I turn to Hayles' (2017) most recent exploration on nonconscious cognition. In her book *Unthought: The Power of the Cognitive Nonconscious* (2017), she explains how nonconscious cognition operates on the cellular level and how it remains inaccessible to consciousness. I suggest that we might tap into the nonconscious cognition by developing the haptic feedback models in VR with datagloves and other sensor tracking systems that could be worn or be attached to the body, since haptic feedback operates directly on the biological body, i.e., on the flesh through the layers of the epidermis. I then compare Hayles' "tripartite framework of (human) cognition" (2017, 17) to Antti Revonsuo's "levels of cognition" (2010, 97) and pinpoint the similarities in their respective approaches to nonconscious cognition. Both point out that while nonconscious cognition is inaccessible to consciousness, it plays a role in subjective experience, whether we are aware of it or not. In my experience, VR technologies may provide us a potential ground to explore nonconscious cognition's additional invisible quality to subjective experience, since we can manipulate, reverse, and amplify the nature of perceived assets.

To clarify, I can give an example how this might be possible. Hayles (2018) explains how nonconscious cognition represses the multilayered noises that exist in the environment so that we can channel our attention to one significant stimulus; we can listen to a friend speaking to us, even if there is a constant loud traffic noise in the background. We hear both the friend's speaking voice and the honking cars in the background, but although the background sound is still vividly present, it is repressed and automatically ignored so that we can direct our attention to the content of what our friend says. We consciously switch in between these inputs in order to tune into one of them. We regulate our cognitive abilities while the conquered milieu happens to us, but we do this on a nonconscious level.

Now, imagine a similar scenery in a virtual environment. There are several visual inputs we can focus on, all of which happen in a 360° depth (while wearing a VR HMD) of visual field and additionally auditory input (headphones). The sound volume and direction can be manipulated according to the user's speed of movement, as they turn around and explore the moving images within the 360° visual exposure. The virtual images can be aligned in a composition, all having the same depth of focus. Unlike the camera eye, which puts one image in focus while the rest remains out of focus, in a VR environment all segments can remain equally in focus. It is up to the interactive observer to choose what to focus on, contrary to the imposed images which have been readily captured by the camera eye and which give us no choice but to gaze at the focused image, inasmuch as all other surroundings remain out of focus. By having extensive control within the environment, we are able to develop an omniperspectival perception and to manipulate the perceived stimulations, which may bring us closer to understanding how nonconscious cognition operates. In this way, in a VR environment we may be able to examine the invisible effects of nonconscious cognition. These aspects also underline the plasticity of VR systems. To exemplify this malleable nature of VR setups, I further emphasize the role of proprioception. Proprioceptive cognition is an important matter in VR, since it establishes the feeling of spatiality by, e.g., moving the body in a space and manipulating objects, even without any perceived body image. Here I refer to Massumi's remark "the spatiality of the body without an image can be understood even more immediately as an effect of proprioception" (Massumi 2002, 58), and I reflect further on his approach to tactile sensibility and visceral sensibility. In connection to this tactile sensibility and visceral sensitivity, I underline why haptic feedback is necessary to develop interoceptive qualities in the virtual body. Furthermore, I explain the difference between interoception and introspection. I indicate the embedded relations between affect and interoceptivity (Varela and Depraz 2000) and how interoceptive cognition of the body may be connected to the sense of affect, as it is preverbal and pre-established within the senses, i.e., we watch them coming into existence. As Bergson articulates "I look closer: I find movements begun, but not executed" (Bergson 2002, 103).

The chapter closes with an emphasis on Thomas Metzinger's (2017) proposal to establish "degrees of immersion" in VR and a comparison of these degrees to Spinoza's definition of affect, as it is sensed as an increase or decrease in the body's vitality. Can we compare an increase of vitality to a high degree of immersion and presence in VR? Or a decrease of vitality to the decrease of immersion in VR? While I am well aware of the precarious nature of this comparison of things that are not immediately related, and that the attempt to bring Metzinger and Spinoza together in a dialogue is a risky attempt, my interpretation stems from both of these thinkers' respective innovative styles of approaching the body conceptually and experientially. For Spinoza, unlike his contemporaries in the seventeenth century, thinking through the body was crucial. As Gilles Deleuze reminds us of Spinoza's approach to the body as a mode: "Everyone knows the first principle of Spinoza: one substance for all attributes. But we also know the third, fourth, or fifth principle: one nature for all bodies, one nature for all individuals, a nature that is itself an individual varying in an infinite number of ways" (Deleuze 1988, 122). Deleuze interprets this further in his *Spinoza: Practical Philosophy*, arguing that mind and body are not substances or subjects but rather "modes," and these modes cannot be grasped merely through a theoretical approach (Deleuze 1988, 130). Similarly, I suggest the fluidity of these modes can be exercised and explored more in depth through different VR frameworks. Following this suggestion, the question arises: how can we integrate technology as a tool to practice philosophical understanding, specifically to study bodily perception, since technological artifacts are in an ongoing engagement with the body? Furthermore, what could such practicality have meant in the 1980s and how can we reform this understanding in 2020s?

My objective for Chapter 3 is to highlight the inner experience of the body and how we, as the owners of our bodies, remain strangers to the inner parts of our bodies. If a perceived body image is considered as what is apparent on the skin, how would the recognition of what lies beneath the skin contribute to the investigation of one's body image? Contrary to the view that technology is a potential cause of alienation, I suggest we can use technological advancements to tackle the structural estrangement of inhabiting a body that we do not know from the inside. If applied responsibly, VR technology can help us to overcome feelings of estrangement, as it can be used to initiate portals to reach and identify what seems to be hidden. Contrary to the cultural pessimism surrounding developing technologies, this work attempts to carve a rather optimist stand. The definition of "irresponsible application" requires precisely such experimentations, in order to understand what a responsible application could mean, as one needs to observe and collect information and effects.

Different from the experimentation-based practical works that were the focus in the previous chapters, Chapter 3 represents an installation called "sit behind my eyes," that was exhibited in 2015 during Transmediale's CTM Vorspiel Festival. In this installation, the user (who is wearing a VR HMD) is encapsulated in an eyeball (imagine you are a Lego man and you are sitting in an emptied-out inside of a watermelon that can represent the inside of an eyeball). As the owner of the eye looks out from a train window, watching the passing images, the user who is situated behind the iris at the middle of the eyeball, watches both the images projected from the iris, while observing the animated blood vessels and nerves surrounding the inner parts of the eye. My intention with this installation was to invite people to cozily sit in a body part and enable them to engage with an idea of what it might look like inside of their own eyeball. If the body is our ultimate "home" (in German: *Heim*), why do we remain estranged to the inner parts of it and avoid visually grasping its totality? Borrowing the term "das Unheimliche" coined by Sigmund Freud (1919) (the usual English translation for "unheimlich" is "uncanny," but I prefer to use to the original German term, since it retains my home/Heim reference), I emphasize the ironic twist that lies in the fact that while the body is our home of existence it also has an inaccessible and abject nature. Why does the thought of our innards evoke the feelings of disgust, since these innards are precisely what we are made of, or that in which we are literally are absorbed? Would it be possible to reverse the abject connotations if we can habitualize a visual recognition of the inner body? How can we make an effort to convert something "unheimlich" to "heimlich"? Drawing insights from Julia Kristeva's (1980) theory of abjection, Massumi's (2002) emphasis on the flesh exceeding Euclidean geometry, and Malabou's (2008) plasticity and autoaffection, I suggest that an investigation of the visual representation of inner parts of the body can reform certain notions behind these theories. Furthermore, I return to Merleau-Ponty's (1964) understanding of the felt presence between the visible and the invisible, and underline how the invisibility of the virtual body can still linger as a felt presence.

I end Chapter 3 by examining the phenomenon of phantom limb (PPL) and phantom limb pain (PLP) from a phenomenological and clinical lens, tracing Merleau-Ponty's approach in *Phenomenology of Perception* and explaining the notions of anasognosia, organic repression, and sensory substitution. All these issues, both in philosophy of mind and in cognitive neurosciences, remain somehow inexplicable as they manifest themselves in the junction of ambiguous and complex perceptional processes. I refer to the phenomenon of phantom limb mainly to explore perceived presence within absence, in that both the phantom limb and the virtual body are about representation. In the case of a phantom limb, there is no visually perceived existence, yet the felt presence lingers. Similarly, the virtual body may exist via a felt presence, even though we may not see it. In both cases, we are dealing with the issues of actual absence and felt presence. A virtual limb and a phantom limb thus have a great deal in common. I also use PPL to tackle the plasticity of the brain and flesh and to reevaluate the notion of body schema. Chapter 3 concludes by arguing for the necessity of further VR development for biotechnological applications and why we need to address disability while evaluating biotechnological reformations. Phantom sensations, disability, and the experience of incorporating prosthesis as embodied objects (technologically embedded, or not)—all these issues point to the need of an evaluation of subjective consciousness, as these issues are initially experienced by the subjects themselves. A prosthesis can be attached to a person, and from a third-person perspective, it is already an extension that belongs to the attached person. But whether this prosthesis has become a felt extension and is adopted into the body schema is something that can only be sensed by the subject, that is, by the owner of the body.

In this dissertation the word virtual is without a doubt the most recurring word and concept. I would like to clarify this conceptual confusion, which stems from the word's technological and ontological connotations. Throughout the text, I use the word virtual as a computer simulated reality, a technologically mediated environment, but also, my usage carries echoes from the post structuralist philosophers Gilles Deleuze and Brian Massumi's definitions of the virtual. The technologically mediated virtual differs from the Deleuzian and Massumian virtual, but on many levels it corresponds to their understanding of virtual. Deleuze's concept of the virtual is a kind of surface effect which is a result of a series of interactions which occur at the material level. The virtual has a generative nature and conceived as a kind of potentiality that becomes fulfilled in the actual. "It is still not material, but it is real" (Deleuze, 1968, 169). Which also corresponds to Massumi's (2002, 133) definition of the virtual, that is something "inaccessible to the senses" but "can be felt in its effects". The virtual, as such, is inaccessible to the senses. This does not, however, preclude figuring it, in the sense of constructing images of it. To the contrary, it requires a multiplication of images. The virtual that cannot be felt, also cannot, but be felt, in its effects" (Massumi 2002, 133). I think when we look at the definition of virtual from these aspects, the technologically mediated virtual body does not stand too far away from Deleuzian and Massumian virtual, or even the philosophy of the virtual body could be constructed upon such definitions. In addition to my usage of technological mediation, I laid parallel conceptualizations from such insights, not to identify with them but to underline the possibilities of constructing a philosophy of the virtual body upon such definitions. My intention here is to envelope them as I use the word 'virtual' in technological mediation.

My greater aim with this dissertation is to suggest VR technology as a tool, similar to a microscope, that can be used to more closely examine and study the fundamental intersections of the humanities and the natural sciences that explore the nature of perception. When VR is used as a method, both approaches to knowledge seem to agree on the importance of subjective experience: on the need to examine how subjective experience influences behavior and physiology, the perception of one's environment, and the interconnectivity of these issues in order to establish a virtual body and an immersive experience. Distancing myself from cultural pessimism, I intend to create a position against alienation that is potentially caused by technology, by demonstrating how VR technology might become a central instrument for evaluating the subjective experience of the body. Contrary to the potential alienation effect of technology, such evaluation can result in a way of overcoming the feelings of alienation, precisely through the usage of novel technologies. This stand also signifies technology being a liberator rather than a threatening factor in our lives, especially for women. As it was stated by Laurie Spiegel (1994), technology blows up power structures and allows women claim a brand new digital space, in which we can explore new dimensions of subjectivity.

Chapter 1. "Ambiguity in Lived Body Experiences"

"As soon as we see other seers [...] henceforth, through the other eyes we are for ourselves fully visible...For the first time, the seeing that I am is for me really visible; for the first time I appear to myself completely turned inside out under my own eyes" (Merleau-Ponty 1968, 143–144).

This chapter is explores the theoretical and practical aspects of the first experiment "Ambiguity of Lived-Body Experiences." After providing the details of the technical setup and reflecting on the conclusions from the interviews, I draw connections between these insights and the existing theories. In this VR experiment, together with the participants, I actively studied how the perception of one's own body image alters as we get to observe it from different angles. With this intervention, it was highlighted that the body image contains subjective experiences and that there are significant shifts in our understanding of these imprinted subjective experiences as we disconnect from our habitual gaze upon it.

The idea behind this VR experiment occurred during my masters thesis research. The theoretical aim of this thesis was to investigate the first chapter "The body" of Merleau-Ponty's *Phenomenology of Perception* (1945). In this part of the thesis, I dealt with the body as a mechanical object and analyzed the author's criticism of mechanistic causality. Following, I provided an overview from a psychological perspective and argued why both physiological and psychical inquiries remain insufficient to describe the ambiguous nature of the body.

In the practical section of my masters dissertation titled "Empowering The Perception," I conducted a VR experiment with six people as my respondents. These six people were mainly from my friend circle, people who were interested in exploring similar questions relevant to the initial idea behind the experiment, which is the alteration of self perception during an interactive technological setup. As indicated in the ethical consent section above, they have signed the necessary consent forms and were informed about the potential side effects of VR exposure (e.g. motion sickness). They were not informed about certain details of the process, so that they could remain unbiased and naive to the experience itself.

Figure 1: Cover of master thesis, 2014

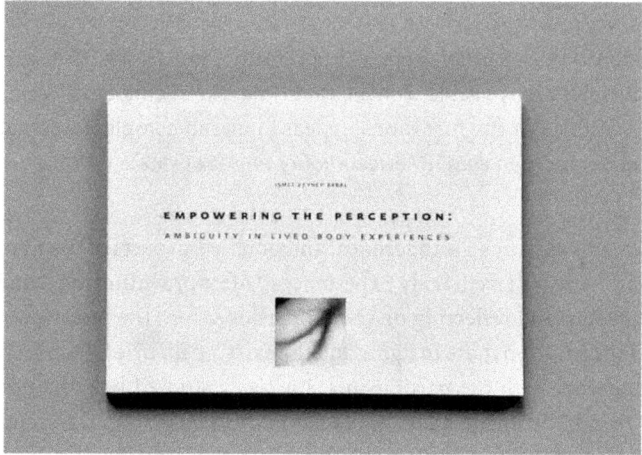

Figure 2 & 3: Sample pages from my masters thesis, 2014

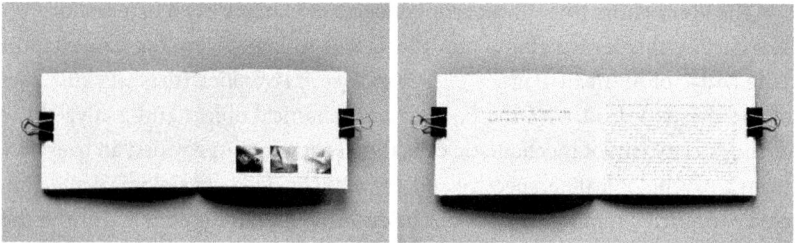

As an initial attempt to point out how the reflective dimension of bodily perception can be explored with the use of this new technology, I created a very simple setup which included a 3D camera (Minorou 3D Webcam, and a single

HMD (Oculus Rift DK2). It has been an intriguing task to bring VR out from its most common usage in the entertainment industry and to introduce it as a research tool.

In this setup, I connected the camera to the VR HMD, and held the camera, moved around the participants in the direction they requested. In this way, I was being an external eye upon them as the recorded images simultaneously played in the HMD. This quasi primitive setup enabled them to explore their body image in VR. According to their verbal reports during the interviews, it was clear to me that such interaction with the bodily self through new mediums of technology may lead to vast deconstructive arguments in technoscience, specifically related to the reflexive cycles between new technology and their implementation as our extension.

The notion of "ambiguity" was central to this experiment. Merleau-Ponty indicates that humans experience and tolerate ambiguity (Vieldeutigkeit), such as the ambiguity of the experience of touching/being touched. That is, we can touch one hand with our other hand, but we cannot touch the act of touching; therefore, the act of touching remains an ambiguous experience. We have to interoceptively switch between the perception of being touched and touching, in order to experience the act of touch. Ambiguity, as a common quality of human experience, was present in the title of the experiment because akin to the ambiguous nature of the experience of touching/being touched, we experience a similar ambiguity as we look at our own bodies from different angles. When we watch our bodily self, we watch someone watching his/her own body. Similar to the necessity to switch between the sensations of touching and being touched, we have to switch between "me as the watcher/observer" and me as "the thing being watched." This virtual setup enabled the participants to indulge in this ambiguity, but at the same time, they experienced the possibility to decrease the sense of ambiguity by having an unusual eye extension with the help of a 3D camera and a VR HMD. Such practice is not habitually integrated in our day to day living, therefore we welcome an entirely new way of seeing ourselves and the world contained within. In this experiment, I investigated whether these six participants could experience a shift in their idea of an objective body or in their objective world when they were exposed to their own body image from an outsider's point of view.

1.1   Technical details and Setup

For this setup, I used an HMD and a 3D camera. The VR HMD was initially designed to create a more life-like virtual experience for gamers. However it can be adapted for the use outside of the video game context. The product resembles ski goggles, where a 7-inch cell phone screen replaces the window, displaying two images side by side (one for each eye). A set of lenses is placed on the top of the screen, focusing and reshaping the picture for each eye, creating a stereoscopic 3D image. The goggles have sensors that monitor how we turn or tilt our head and adjust the image accordingly. The result is the sensation that we are looking around a 3D world. In this experiment, instead of a computer generated 3D content, I used real time video in 3D. As a result the participants were able to watch a live stream of 3D video image (see figure 4).

Figure 4: Still image from the "Ambiguity in Lived-Body Experiences" group experimentation

With this experiment, I aimed to develop an awareness of how perception begins with the body and is affected by our ability to see it as a whole in relation to other objects—in this case the observed object becomes our own body, since the HMD projects the body image as a 3D object in front of our eyes. Creators of similar experiments (which will be discussed in depth in the following chapters) expect these VR methods to be applied more in research, and even as a potential therapeutic tool in certain research fields. In this experiment, my intention was to use this setup for a subjective intervention of self image, by enabling a different way of seeing the body. My expectation was to bring the participants to a state where they could observe their own bodies from outside and thus introspect the layers of their own body image from different angles.

1.2   Interviews

The participants were asked different questions before and after the experiment. In the first interview, I asked for their general opinions about their body and what the notion of body implies for them. Some of these pre-VR exposure interview questions were asked to capture specific details which would then be useful during the experiment. For example, I asked each participant which aspects of themselves they like or dislike observing, and apart from the aspects multifaceted mirrors enable us to see, which other angles they would wish to see themselves from if they could. According to those answers, I tried to make specific arrangements in order to create the angles they wanted to see or wished to avoid seeing. In the second interview, which came right after the experiment, they reflected back on their subjective experience in VR. I asked them to remember the content of the VR experience, and asked about their emotions and thoughts as they encountered their body image. Four out of six people experienced dizziness at the end of the experiment.

Before and after the experience, they were also asked to touch their own hands and express feelings of ambiguity in their own ways, in order to bring the complex semantic field of "touching-touched" into the course of the experiment. After the VR exposure, the individual answers to these question were different than the pre-exposure ones, which we can consider as a significant end effect of the exposure.

Below, I will address some of the most significant answers from both pre- and post-VR interviews. These answers contain certain reflections which have influenced my VR works in the following years. Certain notions the participants raised were in line with several insights from perception theories, which I will consecutively discuss throughout the body of this dissertation.

1.2.3   Pre-Intervention Interviews

Throughout the first interview, I intended to raise the participant's awareness on the feeling of body-ownership, particularly aside from the awareness of extreme sensations, like pain or pleasure (e.g. "Do you recognize your body's existence in daily life? If yes, is it a comfortable feeling or rather awkward?, "Do you experience feelings of self-alienation when you look in the mirror and does this feeling affect your interoceptive feeling of the body?"). One answer was particularly in line with Alva Noë's indication of relation between action and perception (Noë, 2005 76); she experiences her body and feels connected with her body the most when she walks and runs. Another participant said that he is mostly absorbed by his environment and does not pay attention to himself much. He did, however, indicate that he is aware of his bodily state when his body is in physical contact with something (i.e. when his hands explore his own skin or the surface of other objects around him). This response underlines the importance of exteroception, meaning, how environmental stimulation is central to perception in general, but here specifically, perception of bodily self. This same participant also reported that, as a child, he had a totally different concept of who he was and who he was seeing in the mirror. He always thought he looked different and never identified with what he saw in the mirror. In time, he adapted to the reflection in the mirror, but sometimes he still catches a glimpse of that self-image he had of himself as a child. This indication, which reflects back on his first encounter with his body image as a child, calls to mind what Jacques Lacan (1960, 1997) refers to in the "mirror stage." I will discuss this issue further in this chapter. I was exhilarated to hear his reply but also worried that he might feel confused and upset, since he was going to experience a very similar self-recognition pattern through the mirror experience in VR. One other participant said that he feels his body through the recognition of his heartbeat, which is also worth mentioning, as interoceptive heartbeat recognition is widely considered as a physiological parameter for the feeling of body-ownership (Tsakiris et al., 2011).

Following this stage of questions, I brought the participant in front of a mirror. When they looked in the mirror, I asked which part of their body they look at first and which part they would want to look at but cannot because of physiological constraints. Through such questions, their specific preferences would allow me to modify the camera angles when they are in VR. Three participants said that they usually avoid eye contact with people, so they instinctively avoid looking at their own eyes in the mirror. One participant explained that he is overwhelmed with the information that comes from eye contact, so he tries to avoid it.[1] For this participant, his confession of the relation between his social anxiety which derives from eye contact, mirrors the avoidance of meeting himself in the eye in the mirror. Another participant remarked that if she focuses on her eyes for too long, explained "...as if her entire body was going to come out of her eyes." Contrary to the eye-avoidant participants, one other person said he likes to stare into his eyes from a very close distance, and that he could keep staring for long durations of time. Another participant said he avoids looking at his feet and that he doesn't have a connection with them, which signifies a disassociation with this body part. But he explained that he keeps staring at his chest with pleasure. Another participant complained about her haircut, specifically how she is not content with the way her hair looks from behind, realizing that she did not catch that specific glimpse at her hair when she looks at the back of her hair with double mirrors, as she usually does.

My intention with asking these questions was to equally evoke discomfort and admiration about the body image, and to highlight how both of these aspects naturally coexist in our perception of body image. I also wanted to explore whether it would be possible to reverse these habitual associations people have with their own body image in a VR setup. The body image stores the emotional aspects of lived experience, as if these subjective experiences are imprinted in the body image (Dolto 1984, 22). Is it possible to reverse these habitual connotations and replace them with a series of different emotional experiences with the assistance of new technology? Can we constructively consume the habitual gaze and proliferate the ways we see ourselves beyond our traditional associations and viewpoints?

I also asked the participants about the other angles they would watch themselves from, if they could. The collective answers could be summarized as "from above, from both left and right profiles, the transitioning moments from the sides to the frontal image of the face, and from behind" (one person specifically underlined from behind, because he wanted to have an idea of how he appears to others as a bystander at a party). One other person indicated that he would like to see the blind spots on his back, in between his shoulders and around his

---

1   This indication overlaps with Emmanuel Levinas' (1961, 66) understanding of how the eye resembles a portal to the universe. Due to its vastness of this portal, a pitch-dark void into the pupil, the avoidance of eye contact with ourselves, and consequently with the others, is not very unusual to hear. "The eyes break through the mask—the language of the eyes, impossible to dissemble."

spine. All these desired angles of the body cannot be achieved in a visual tour around our bodies in daily life.

What is stored in our body image also carries what contributes to our social anxiety. One person explained that, when he sometimes looks at his ears, he remembers how people made fun of them as he was in primary school. "Looking at my ears," he continued, "still, instantly reminds me of those times." This is another point where we can stop to remember how the lived experiences are embedded in the body image and the body image reflects them back to us in retrospect. The same person also implied that due to his big beard, he is usually categorized under a specific socio-political group and he dreads the extra effort he has to pay in order to defy this stereotype. Although he enjoys to have a beard, he often considers to cut it because of this conflicting image he creates in people's mind.

At the end of the pre-VR exposure interview, I asked them to touch their own hand with their other hand and asked them to interoceptively explore this feeling: do they feel like "touching" or do they feel "touched"? Five out of six people said that they feel like "touching".

1.2.4 Post-VR Intervention Interviews

After the VR intervention, the participants were seated exactly in the same position for the second part of the interview. All of them looked calmer but also more in thoughts, compared to the pre-VR experience. One person reported that the image of himself he encountered made him think about his social identity conflicts. Another participant noted a specific awareness she felt related to her personal relationships. The shift in perception of their bodies caused an eventual shift in their evaluation of their personal histories.

During this second interview, which came right after the VR exposure, the participants reflected on their experience and verbalized several feelings such as confusion, irritation, the fear of aging but also tranquility and self-acceptance. When I asked them how they would more specifically articulate the sensation during the experience, the common answer was that the unusual perspectives made them feel very present. Additionally, the common saying was that they perceived their own body similar to an object, as if they were not in control of the body they saw.[2] One person said, it was similar to seeing his

---

2   As Florian Rötzer (2000, 156–157) explains, 3D exposure brings an inevitable loss in the sense of autonomy, which I will discuss in depth within the next chapters.

"doppelgänger" on the street. The most recognizable part of the intervention for most of the people was the 360° exposure of the body image. This was possible as I held the camera and slowly walked around them in a full circle, so they could stand still and see themselves from a 360° angle in slow motion. During this 360° exposure, one person indicated that he did not like his posture; he perceived himself as a hunchback. I observed his facial expression during the interview and seeing his concern left me skeptical about whether such confrontational intervention was a good idea.[3] Although all the experiments were ethically approved, there was always a part that could not and would not be predictable in terms of confronting such exposure. Do their voluntary participation allow me to stage such prismatic confrontation and expect them to adjust to the perception of such unexpected corners of their body? Where do I stand in this paradigm and why did I specifically chose to stand at this point, as an observer to those who observed? Although I was conscious of my multiple roles (a conductor, an interviewer, in the case of this specific experiment—isolating myself from my role of being their friend), was there a part of me desiring a transference into their experience? If something is ethically approved, do we need not to speculate further, but then who can state we do not need to? If the fundamental formation of ethics stems from not hurting anyone and if no one is hurt, where do I need to stop? This was the question mark I had to return to in my mind, as I was asking about their experience during the post-exposure interviews (which will be summarized within the next section). This work did not carry artistic concerns during its production, neither the documentation video work (which was made of video images recorded in VR and of the video documentation of the entire experiment procedure) was edited with an artistic motivation. Since I am not a therapist and have no background education in psychology, the drive was also not therapeutic. The main motivation was to explore the user's subjective experience during a close exposure to technology in order to inform relevant theories about alteration of bodily perception, by examining the causality of this interplay. Development of immersive technologies require an in depth look into the relations between human beings and technological

---

3   When I told a colleague/friend about this intervention, she questioned whether I enjoy to perceive myself as Mary Shelley who yearns to understand Frankenstein (1818)—My friend questioned if I want to be in charge of a perceiving living-entity, influencing the way they want to see themselves. This is the most creative criticism I have received about this specific part of my work.

artifacts. For the further development of technology, the subject's own experience as a feedback plays a significant role. In a more general sense, we often consult the metaphorical representations and seek formulations such as "as if" (e.g. "I felt dizzy, as if I was falling down") to communicate the lived experience to the receiver, to the listener. Establishing technology and the modes of technology as communication models need an in depth understanding of the reciprocality between the user and the technology, for technology to perhaps become a medium to pass the vividness of the experience to the receiver. In this respect, it could be possible to approach technology not merely as an instrumental object, but also as a living mediator. Furthermore, such exploration embarks on the influential connections between human beings and these new technology products as our extensions.

Aiming for a contribution to such developmental phase, I suggest, the subjective reports and insights of the users should be carefully implemented for an immersive experience to become more rich. While such idealist notions promise a fruitful ground, what kind of risks await us? Are we supposed to sharpen our critical stand before we pour the ideas into a practical mold, or do our critical edges sharpen as we get to coherently observe and endure the consequences of practical formations? In the case of this specific experiment I present here, the inevitable question arise: are we supposed to see our body in its entirety? Can we all willingly experience and deconstruct the mismatch between the perceived body image and the body image from a third person perspective? Does egocentric perspective actually keep our sanity in check while we question our physical existence? Could such omni-perspective stretch in our visual perception challenge and destruct our feeling of being grounded in the body itself? Additionally, in the post-VR interview, a couple of people articulated their general emotional state as "confused." One person indicated, "I kind of lost the feeling of the body, the one I'm actually in, not the one I was seeing." This articulation points out to the exact opposite of the underlaying motivation of this work, which suggests to use VR exposure to overcome self estrangement.

But at the same time, having experienced an exposure other than the habitual perception of body image with the help of mirrors, one person explained how he was fascinated by seeing his own body "as a full corpus, recognizing the volume of the body, like an object." He further indicated that usually he has a feeling of "the backside of the body is sort of opening up to a space"[4] and as he observed his body from outside, he thought that it is not and indicated "...actually I'm trapped in this body, I'm not opening up to an outer space." While an out-of-body experience may distance the people from their own body and cause feelings of depersonalization, it may also provide a grounding sensation which can increase the sense of self-containment.

At the end of the second interview, I asked them to touch their own hand again. I included the touch-touching exercise again to see whether the virtual out-of-body-experience would create a shift in their self-perception of touching. Three people said they now feel like they are "being touched" (at the pre-VR interview all three of them answered "I feel like [I'm] touching") and the other three of them said they did not feel a change in the feeling of 'touching', just as before. One of the participants said that as she was in VR, she instinctually felt the need to touch her own arms more than usual, in order "to ground herself in her own body."

Two weeks after this intervention, two of the participants called me to address certain shifts in their self-perception which occurred over the course of time. I did not request such a re-evaluation, so I was both surprised and excited to hear about certain ripple effects they experienced due to the exposure. Their post-revelations became the most significant reasons for me to continue using VR as a medium in my own research. I gathered two important reports from this third interview. First, one of the participants reported that a couple of days after the VR experience, he dreamt of seeing himself from outside. He said he has never experienced this perspective before in a dream, which is why he assumed that this effect was due to the VR experience. After the dream, reflecting back on his experience, he had an epiphany. When he saw himself from a certain angle during the experiment, for the first time he detected a similarity between his smile and his brother's. He indicated that the realization of such a simple yet fundamental similarity between him and his brother indirectly affected their ongoing emotional conflicts. He stated that while talking to his brother, he is not as angry nor as stubborn as he was before. The rigidity

---

4   This articulation aligns with Brian Massumi's indication of "the oneness of the body is back-flow" (Massumi 2002, 150). The participant's impression underlines an elevated look on this circular way of self-containment, by catching up with the back-flow of the body, one might come close to experience the totality, the oneness of the body (more on this subject will be discussed in Chapter 2).

of his judgment against his brother was slightly diminished. Another participant with a very short haircut, reported that as she observed her haircut from
behind, she realized that the cut was uneven. For months, her partner was repeatedly telling her that her haircut was not straight. Each time she shrugged
it off and internalized it as a critique and an emotional attack on her confidence. After having seen it herself, she started to reconsider her judgments.
From a variety of similar reports from participants after being exposed to this
experience, it is possible that observing our own bodies from an external point
of view in VR can alter our self-perception and may consequently alter our in-
terpersonal relationships. Furthermore, it was evident that such a viewpoint
of the body image has effected their ability to self-reflect. These alterations in
self-reflection show us how emotional and subjective experience are imprinted
on the body image, and points out that the body image is potentially malleable.

1.3   Conclusions to draw from the Intervention

Departing from a close reading of *Phenomenology of Perception*, I reflected on the
exploration of psychical and physiological aspects of the body in my VR experiment. *Phenomenology of Perception* is composed of an enormous pattern of examinations between the individual and society, language and expression, science
and common experience, philosophy and the concept of time and our place in it
as a living subject. Of course, this singular attempt was just about the inclusion
of a technological apparatus and to see whether such inclusion can explore the
subjects' relation to other objects and their relation to body experience; specifically by altering the body's spatiality and motricity.

This initial VR intervention has carved the way for my interest into different disciplines: from media sciences to phenomenological philosophy and to
cognitive neurosciences. By using a visual perception altering medium to reflect on the notion of body image, I happened to examine the theories I had
been reading throughout my media studies, which I will reflect further in the
following chapters. Furthermore, with a hands-on intervention, I saw how media functions like a mirror, by showing us the capacity of our cognitive abilities
and amplifying the possibilities beyond these abilities. Such media like VR can
magnify these existent but not-yet-evoked abilities. Working with the introspection of these six participants has led me to reflect upon and further explore the notion of body image and how it differs from the body schema. I will
discuss this issue further in the following chapters, as well as the theoretical

aspects of this experiment such as: the role of active movement in perception, subject-object relations and the manipulable nature of these relations in VR, confrontation with the mirror image and its relation to Lacan's "Mirror Stage."

The experience of one's lived body and corporeality is not a fixed one. It is adaptable to a variety of objects and to products of technology that can be embodied. Self-perception goes through a transformation during an engagement with technology. As Vivian Sobchack (1994, 87) states, "Insofar as the cinematic and the electronic have each been objectively constituted as a new and discrete techno-logic, each also has been subjectively incorporated, enabling a new perceptual mode of existential and embodied presence." This approach supports the underlying phenomenological claim that our body is not limited by the boundaries of the skin, but that we are in a continuous exchange with the lived world's instruments.

1.4   Cognitive science and cognitive technology

> "Invention of the mind as a mirror
> of nature"
> *(Richard Rorty 1979, 7).*

Before I introduce the underlying connections between my VR experiments and certain phenomenological and media scientific theories, I want to inform the reader that my research has been influenced by several methods rooted in cognitive neuroscience. In the midst of difficulties which transdisciplinary study brings along, I have had the chance to acknowledge the obvious connections between computational media and cognitive sciences. After all, cognitive science by itself is already a multidisciplinary approach which combines the study of mind and slightly underlines that "cognition is information processing or computation" (Mandik 2010, 25). My aim with including notions from cognitive science in this work was mainly to argue how modalities of bodily perception constitute sensory experiences and how VR can be used as a magnifying glass to explore such experiences. When we speak of sensory experience, it is almost impossible to bypass the topic of cognition, more specifically the role of neural networks in the body for cognitive processes to occur, which signifies the sensory experience.

The connection between neural networks in the human brain and information-processing systems was recognized in the early 1950s. Katherine Hayles

(1999) summarizes the significant outcomes of the so-called "Macy Conferences on Cybernetics"[5], as

> "...the construction of theory of information (Shannon's bailiwick), a model of neural functioning which implicated how neurons worked as information-processing systems (McCulloch's lifework), computers that processed binary code and that could conceivably reproduce themselves, thus reinforcing the analogy with biological systems (von Neumann's specialty), and a visionary who could articulate the larger implications of the cybernetic paradigm and make clear its cosmic significance (Wiener's contribution). The result of this breathtaking enterprise was nothing less than a new way of looking at human beings. Henceforth, humans were to be seen primarily as information-processing entities who are essentially similar to intelligent machines" (Hayles 1999, 22).

More recently, neo-empiricist psychologists have asserted that the "cognition is inherently perceptual, sharing systems with perception at both the cognitive and neural levels" (Barsalou 1999, 577). This intertwined connection between neural and informational networks progressively influenced the theories of cognitive neuroscience and techno-science. As Bruno Latour emphasizes, this connection has altered the essential understanding of scientific activity (Latour 1988, 12).

In the specific case of VR, addressing each sensory modality of the human body is fundamental to create a sense of immersion in virtual worlds. In other words, for the instantiation of the virtual body, elements like sensorimotor contingencies are required. Therefore the use of VR in new technological applications and the aim of understanding the effect of it on our perceptual processes require an in-depth understanding of our cognitive abilities. In this line, we can take VR to study human perception more specifically as a way to study the interconnectivity of subjective experience, environment, behavior and physiology. All of these merge together to create an immersive experience. As a tool, VR can significantly underline the nonexistent hierarchy of these, as

---

5   "Macy Conferences on Cybernetics" was sponsored by the Josiah Macy Foundation, 1943–1954, the aim of the conference was to develop a communication modal that could be eventually applied to entities like humans, animals and machines. For more information see "Cybernetics. The Macy Conferences 1946–1953" The Complete Transactions by Claus Pias, 2004.

they are all equally fundamental and explanatory features of our perceptional processes.

Moreover, in VR it is possible to detect certain abilities which exceed conscious cognition. In Hayles' terminology, nonconscious cognition pertains to "the cognitive capacity that exists beyond consciousness" (Hayles 2017, 9). An early example is Franz van der Helm's "MeMachine" (2012) project, where the subject's body was mirrored in an animated anatomical figure, via multiple tracking sensors on his body. The animated display was without skin, traditionally used as a medical demonstration of muscular and skeletal systems in the human body. Although van der Helm hinted at the potential ethical and social dangers of "somatic surveillance," Hayles further reflects on the MeMachine project as

"a missed opportunity for productive collaboration between the sciences and humanities. In another sense, the MeMachine demonstrates the extent to which the workings of the cognitive nonconscious can be externalized through technical mediation, creating situations in which the human cognitive nonconscious, technical cognition, and human consciousness interact in real time through multiple feedback loops and recursive circular causalities to create a cognitive assemblage of unprecedented surveillance potential" (Hayles 2017, 131).

For Hayles, nonconscious cognition occurs in the body in an uninterrupted flow: "Removed from the confabulations of conscious narration, nonconscious cognition is closer to what is actually happening in the body and the outside world; in this sense, it is more in touch with reality than is consciousness" (Hayles 2017, 28). This relation between nonconscious cognition and reality exceeds conscious understanding. The meaning of "reality" in this context can be understood as the reality of what happens in the body (interoception) and the reality of how the external environment affects the sense of body (exteroception)[6]. Both of these realities may escape our recognition in nonconscious cognition. We do not interoceptively recognize each phase of digestion (whether our lunch has already reached our intestines or not). In the same way, we also do not allow all external stimuli to dominate our cognitive

---

6   Exteroception is the "Input of information about stimulation from outside the body" (Mandik 2010, 8). From this definition it is possible to say the exteroception highly influences interoception, since we are continously identifying, filtering and processing the information which is exteroceptively perceived.

process; we can continue to listen to a friend talking to us although there is a traffic noise in the background. In a virtual realm, we have the opportunity to explore these connections, as the virtual configurations may allow us to recognize what escapes our cognition. If we can consider the importance of nonconscious cognition while evaluating the experience of a lived-body in the physical reality, we may also draw steady connections to strengthen the ties between the virtual body and the virtual reality. Therefore, in this dissertation the reader should expect frequent analogies between the cognitive architecture of the human body, perception theories in phenomenological philosophy and media theories. Furthermore, I will emphasize how these juxtapositions can be applied to developments and consequently, I aim to contribute the development of these technologies.

Cognitive science and cognitive technology, as Francisco Varela (1993, 5) asserts, have a vital, complementary and inseparable nature. He marks that the necessity and relevance of these concepts is based on their interdependence. "Technology, among other things, acts as an amplifier" he continues, "Through technology, the exploration of mind provides society at large with an unprecedented mirror of itself, well beyond the circle of the philosopher, the psychologist, the therapist, or any individual seeking insight into his own experience" (Varela 1993, 5–6). This interdependent and reflexive quality of the relation between technology and scientific approach is also underlined by Hayles in her famous formulation "What we make and what (we think) we are co-evolve together" (Hayles 2005, 164). Or as Culkin (1967, 51) similarly articulates "We become what we behold. We shape our tools and then our tools shape us."

Similar to Varela's "technology as an amplifier" notion, postphenomenology takes the technology as a tool to look into the human perception. In the next chapters, I will explore the limitations of phenomenological methods and exemplify how certain approaches can be reformed in the frame of technological developments, contributing in this postphenomenological attitude. Technology's amplifying function in this interplay between man and the world around him can be seen as a central point in post-phenomenology. But before writing about the potential contributions of this work to post-phenomenology, I should first visit the main phenomenological approaches on the body.

1.5   Phenomenological distinction of Body Awareness: Körper and Leib

Phenomenology is "the study of things that appear", gr. phainómenon, "thing appearing to view", from the verb φαίνω-phaínō, "to show itself, to be manifest" and λόγος (lógos, "the study of) (Smith, 2018). There is a basic phenomenological distinction of what "body" can mean in German: 'Körper' and 'Leib' (Husserl 1973a, 57). In French, this was translated as the "corps objectif" and the "corps propre" (Merleau-Ponty 2002, 192). This distinction between the "object body" and the "subject body" (or the lived body) helps us to understand the experience of the body. We experience the object body as we consider it from an outsider's perspective: "an objective description of the body understands the body from an observer's perspective, where the observer can be myself, examining my own body in the mirror, or another person, such as a scientist or physician" (Martiny 2015, 18).

The subjective body is not analyzed as an object body since we are in continuous alignment with it. Dan Zahavi (2018) writes: "We experience the lived body as we feel the wind in our hair, when we immerse in pleasure, when we have a toothache." Such experiences belong only to the subject; it is qualia; conscious experience is difficult to articulate, although it is certainly shared among all humans.

We engage in a series of actions throughout the day and can disconnect from conscious recognition of its fluent operative functionality. When I prepare to get on a train while waiting on a platform, I do not look at my legs and observe how the mechanistic causality will help me to take the next step to get on the train. My intention carries me forward and I get on the train. Meanwhile, I consciously operate on a different cognitive level—thinking of what I will discuss with my boss when we meet in half an hour. Or when I feel the breeze in my hair, this is an experience of the subject body, a lived experience. I feel the breeze in the hair roots and allow myself to introspect what the sensation of wind recalls from my memory, experience the intentionality further. Such subjective experience of the body is not transferable but articulable. Drew Leder (1990, 34) underlines that in our day-to-day lives, our body is experientially absent but it "pre-reflectively" goes on. This distinction between objective and subjective understanding of the body is ambiguously contained within the human experience. As Shaun Gallagher and Dan Zahavi (2008) articulate, we cannot perceive the subjective/lived body of other people around us, we perceive their bodies as objects. But we can perceive our own bodies as subjects and as objects simultaneously. [7]

1.6   Own-body-perception and Out-of-body experience (OBE)

The division of bodily awareness in the phenomenological sense (the object body and the subject body) seems to be united in a self-explanatory term in natural sciences, namely what psychologists and neuroscientists call "own-body-perception." When we perceive our own body, we develop a self-awareness in its different attributes, such as interoceptive and exteroceptive awarenesses. On self-awareness of the own-body-perception, Mandrigin and Thompson (2015, 515) explain:

> "Besides own-body perception (this body is mine), bodily self-experience includes agency (I'm the one making this movement), self-location (I'm in my body), and egocentric perception (I see the world from here). Notice that these aspects of bodily self-awareness normally coincide—you feel that the body in which you are located (self-location) and through whose eyes you see the world (egocentric perception) is your own body (ownership) that you control from within (agency)."

Through an altered visual experience, these specific attributes of the body can be revisited and the understanding of one's bodily awareness can be altered as well.

In the "Ambiguity in Lived Experiences" setup, we observe the body from an outside perspective as the third person and therefore we may get to question our own agency (I see myself making this movement), self location (I see that I am out of my body), and egocentric perception (I see the world from outside of my body). These altered perceptions of self-awareness can strengthen the understanding of body. An OBE can in this way enable this altered self-awareness.

---

7   "Epistemology often makes a distinction between self- and other knowledge; between the knowledge that I have of my own states and dispositions, and the knowledge that I have of everything else. The observational/non-observational dichotomy appears to map onto this: my knowledge of myself is non-observational and my knowledge of others is observational" (Wiseman 2016, 85).

Mandrigin and Thompson (2015) reflect further on the neural correlates of OBE and explain that OBE occurs in the temporoparietal junction (TPJ) in the brain, where temporal and parietal lobes meet. They imply that the TPJ is "[...] crucial for multisensory integration—for integrating signals from the different sensory modalities of sight, sound, touch and self-movement—for being able to switch between taking a first-person perspective and a third-person perspective in mental imagery" (Mandrigin & Thompson 2015, 519–520). They emphasize that with the inclusion of a VR setup, it was possible to see (by observing the magnetic resonance imaging of the person while being exposed to VR) the relevancy of TPJ in multi-sensory integration. In an OBE setup in VR, it is possible to detect how the TPJ responds to visual, tactile and proprioceptive cues.

"[W]hat these virtual reality experiments [referring to VR experiments in which multi-sensory integration was investigated] have done is to use the power of vision over other senses to manipulate bodily self-awareness in systematic ways that reveal different aspects of our bodily sense of self. We locate ourselves within our body, but we can be made to feel that we are located at places outside the borders of our body. We experience the world from the visuo-spatial perspective of our body, but we can be made to experience the world from perspectives outside of our body with different 'up' or 'down' orientations. We feel an ownership of our bodies, but manipulating both our visuo-spatial perspective and the sensory cues we get from vision, touch, and proprioception can make us feel ownership for an artificial or a purely virtual body" (Mandrigan &Thompson, 2015, 523).

These principal findings from empirical studies highlight the possibility of constructing a virtual body through sensorimotor contingencies (using sensory cues to create a sense of bodily self in VR).[8] Yet, the phenomenologically significant modes of bodily awareness (the body as a subject (lived body) and the body as an object), are not sufficiently considered while evaluating these empirical findings. Mandrigan and Thompson conclude that an inclusion of phenomenological and conceptual understanding of the bodily awarenesses can enable a broader sense of clarity while considering empirical outcomes.

---

8   Reconfiguration and modification of intentional objects in VR influence the scope of sensory modalities in a drastic manner. It is fascinating to read similar lines from Aristotle: "Sensory modalities, are to be individuated by their intentional object" (Aristotle, *de Anima*, written c.350 B.C.E., translated by J. A. Smith, 2016).

Here we can see once again that the complementary forces of both humanities and empirical sciences can assist each other's knowledge. It is intriguing to know that it is possible to visually detect an area in the brain related to multi-sensory integration (TPJ), but without an application of phenomenological distinctions in bodily awareness, the interpretation of such empirical knowledge could be convoluted.[9] Furthermore, without an application of subjective experience, we cannot develop our understanding of consciousness and conscious experience. Multi-sensory integration and its consequences for bodily awareness is an important issue for post-phenomenological studies, as it is concerned with technological reformations and with the potential changes on the bodily perception.

1.6.1 Henrik Ehrsson's Out-of-Body Experience (OBE)

Three years after conducting the "Ambiguity in Lived Experiences" intervention, I came across with Henrik Ehrsson's research "The Experimental Induction of Out-of-Body Experiences" (Ehrsson, 2007). I realized that I had unknowingly re-created his OBE in VR experience. An OBE, Ehrsson explains, is defined as the experience where a person who is awake sees his or her body from a location outside of the physical body (Blanke et. al, 2004). Although OBE is classified as a neurological condition that can result from an abnormal brain function, Ehrsson claims that this illusory experience can be induced in participants who do not necessarily have a disturbed brain function (Ehrsson, 2007). Supporting his hypothesis with empirical and subjective data, Ehrsson's motive was to identify how the first-person visual perspective can determine "the perceived location of one's own whole body." As a neuroscientist, Ehrsson raised the question about whether multi-sensory mechanisms play a role in OBE in a VR setting. As he indicates in his personal website "By clarifying how the normal brain produces a sense of ownership of one's body," he suggests, "we can learn to project ownership onto artificial bodies and simulated virtual ones." Ehrsson and his co-author Petkova conclude,

> "The present findings could have groundbreaking industrial and clinical applications. Experiencing swapping bodies with other individuals could provide a valuable tool for research on body image disorders or self-identity

---

9   Although Brian Massumi (2002, 21) comments that humanities need natural sciences more than the natural sciences need humanities.

in social psychology. Likewise, experiencing 'becoming' a humanoid robot in tele-robotics and feeling ownership of simulated bodies in virtual reality applications would probably enhance user control, realism, and the feeling of 'presence" (Petkova & Ehrsson, 2008).

In addition to Ehrsson & Petkova, several researchers have experimented with different body swap setups in VR by manipulating multi-sensory and motor stimuli in the first-person perspective of an avatar.[10] While there has been different innovative attempts at inducing OBE and body swap setups, Thomas Metzinger (2018) points out that a significant OBE effect has not been yet established, since the users are still missing the ability to look from the eyes of the avatar, therefore the experience resembles the clinical phenomenon of heautoscopy (Metzinger 2018, 4). Similar to a confrontation with one's own Doppelgänger, Karl Jaspers (1973, 77) defines heautoscopy as a situation where the subjects perceive themselves separate from the body and see the appearance of their body from an outside perspective.[11]

As a philosopher who attempts to draw significant connections between the humanities and empirical sciences, Metzinger claims that the self does not exist; it is a construction of models within the consciousness, and that this constructed sense of self is merely a process in the consciousness. He calls this model the "Phenomenal Self-Model" (PSM) and the interrelation between this phenomenal self-model and other models (other subjects) the "Phenomenal Model of the Intentionality Relation" (PMIR) (Metzinger 2003, 265). Hayles (2017) argues against Metzinger's claim that the experience arises from these models,[12] and states "[...] by positioning the self as epiphenomenal, he [Metzinger] reduces the phenomenal experience of self back to the underlying material processes" (Hayles 2017, 42). But, just because something

---

10   As Bertnard (2018, 3) summarizes, these methods range from "using computer generated imaging (Maselli and Slater, 2013), body swapping with a plastic mannequin (Petkova and Ehrsson, 2008), as well as a swap with a Barbie doll (Van der Hoort et al., 2011), a digital avatar (Maselli and Slater, 2013), an invisible body (Guterstam et al., 2015), and even in a body located in front of them (Lenggenhager et al., 2007)."

11   I translated from the original text. In german, Jaspers defines heautoscopy as "die Erscheinung, daß der Mensch seinen Leib in der Außenwelt als einen zweiten wahrnimmt, sei es in eigentlicher Wahrnehmung, sei es in bloßer Vorstellung, in leibhaftiger Bewusstheit" (Jaspers 1973, 77).

12   Hayles (2017, 42–43) notes that, alongside Thomas Metzinger, William James (1890: 2017, The Principles of Psychology, Vols. 1–2), Owen Flanagan (1993) and Antonio Damasio (2000) hold somehow similar view that the sense of self is constructed.

is constructed, does it mean that it is unreal or epiphenomenal? This could be debated from a social constructivist's point of view in a totally different way, as they state that our emotions and thoughts are socially constructed but they are also very real and affective.

Metzinger emphasizes why a constructed OBE lingers as an heautoscopic experience and explains, "it [OBE] fails to provide an alternative unit of identification because the user's interoceptive self-model is firmly locked in the biological body; it cannot be simulated in an avatar yet" (Metzinger 2018, 5). The possibilities of increasing the sense of presence in VR through the examination of interoception and its potential effects on the virtual bodily self will be explored within the next sections.

The confrontational nature of the "Ambiguity in Lived-body Experiences" setup can influence the self-identification pattern of the minimal/phenomenal selfhood, which refers to the process of "perceiving our own body here and now, within the existing time frame" (Blanke & Metzinger, 2009, 7). Such a visual shift in VR may contribute to changes in top down (longer lasting aspects of our body) and bottom-up (self perception in current situation) information processing. While this new perspective of the bodily self in VR may open new gates for cognitive neuroscience, it can also contribute to fields in metacognition (the state of being aware of self-awareness). We may shift the focus on the understanding of the objective body: "is this me who is watching myself?" This is similar to one of the interviewees' answer during the post-intervention interview of the "Ambiguity in Lived Experiences" intervention: "I kind of lost the feeling of the body, the one I'm actually in, not the one I was seeing." When we look at the mirror and see our body image, we are certain that the reflected image belongs to our body, because that is the image we are used to seeing. There is no in-depth recognition or a need to dig beyond what is seen. Throughout our lives, we have habitually practiced a couple of angles and only from those limited amount of angles we define and develop the idea of our body image. When we can gaze at our own body from a third person perspective, we may grow curious to catch ourselves in different angles and expand the understanding of our phenomenal selfhood. By examining a new bodily self through VR, we may lean towards vast deconstructive arguments in techno-science, specifically concerning the reflexive cycle between new technology (their implementation as our extensions) and our perception.

1.6.2   OBE in phenomenology: A recreation of OBE

"The perceiving and sensing
body is always also a lived-
body—immersed in and mak-
ing social meaning as well as
physical sense."
(Vivian Sobchack 1994, 139)

The phenomenological approach traditionally (by traditional phenomenology,
I indicate Husserlianian epoche and reduction methods) distances itself from
empirical insights, and instead sides with the perspective of consciousness
and the phenomenal character of subjective experience. Conversely, empiri-
cists typically exclude phenomenological understanding due to its speculative
and subject-centered orientation. But recent research points to a growing
influence of phenomenological accounts in natural science paradigms (e.g.
mirror neuron research, Gallese, 1998). Since Hermann Schmitz's[13] "new phenomenology" (Die Neue Phänomenologie) in the 1960s, theory of subjectivity
has been progressively and fundamentally integrated into medical and psychological research. This field later expanded into a specific approach called
"neurophenomenology," which was initially suggested by Francisco Varela
during early 1990s.

Charles Siewert (2015, 137) explains that phenomenology has found its
place in a philosophical culture which has been mostly dominated by experimental science and technology. As an example of a related contemporary
phenomenology, he indicates that Hubert Dreyfus (2001) draws insights from
Merleau-Ponty "to bear on contemporary cognitive science." Furthermore,
Siewert illustrates the importance of Gallagher's (2005) body schema, Thompson's (2007) phenomenological 'embodied' view of perception and Noë's (2004,
2012) sensorimotor contingencies in perception and of the 'problem of presence', as significant phenomenological insights into cognitive neuroscience
(Siewert 2015, 149).

These attempts to include phenomenological methods in natural sciences,
confronts the alleged opposition between "the perspective of consciousness"
and "the perspective of science" (Merleau Ponty, 1945/2008: xxi – xxii). The perspective of consciousness has to be consulted after years of being disregarded

---

13   See Hermann Schmitz, Die Neue Phänomenologie, Bouvier, 1980.

as "loss of time" as the empirical findings seem to be insufficient to clarify the ambiguous nature of mind and body problem. "The process of constantly providing new pieces of the puzzle of the object-body risks obscuring the non-objectifiable, experienced lived-body" (Eriksen 2019, 101). VR can function to elaborate how both the objective and the subjective body can be explored from both the perspective of consciousness and from the perspective of science, since "technology increases the scope of our access, and so it increases the extent of what is or can be present for us" (Braidotti 2002, 83). In my version of OBE, the main purpose was to tackle the dimensions of subjective experience with a phenomenological method during an external revisitation of bodily self in VR. Jochem Zwier and his co-authors (2016, 4) alluded to the basic principle of phenomenology as "to investigate the things themselves as they show themselves." A VR setup provides an altered perception in order to investigate what is shown, which in physical reality remains beyond our grasp.

Ehrsson (2007) used a VR setup to create an OBE for an investigation of multi-sensory mechanisms, whereas, as mentioned before, my unknowingly reproduced paradigm came upon me as a result of an intensive reading of Merleau-Ponty's (1945) *Phenomenology of Perception*. According to Merleau-Ponty, the main concern of phenomenology is to examine the essence of things through their appearances.[14] Bringing the body into the focus of our gaze and to see the appearance of itself in detail is an essential starting-point for integrating a phenomenological perspective into technological apparatuses. Phenomenology, in the Merleau-Pontian and Husserlian sense, emphasizes the body as an essential source of knowledge and as something that reveals our primary connection with body, as the body is in an ongoing perceptual exchange with the external entities. Both Merleau-Ponty and Husserl "develop a latent phenomenology of instrumentation and thus lay the potential groundwork for a promising reconfiguration of agency in relation to high technology" (Richardson & Harper 2002, 13). Luna Dolezal (2009, 12) states "the phenomenological understanding of the lived body as investigated by theorists such as Husserl, Merleau-Ponty, and their commentators, is instrumental to understanding how new technologies work and how interaction with them

---

14   On the definition of "appearance" Pete Mandik (2010, 12) notes, "a way in which something seems, as distinct from the way it really is. Issues surrounding the distinction between appearance and reality have been crucial in many areas of philosophy, but of special interest to philosophers of mind are issues surrounding sensory or sensible appearances: the ways in which things appear to sensory perception."

can be successful." By implementing a phenomenological perspective during lived-body experiences in VR, it is possible to address phenomenological ideas such as corporeal schema, body image, lived body, bodily presence and virtual embodiment. Moreover, it can detect which phenomenological accounts so far are neglected and overlooked.

Merleau-Ponty stated "true philosophy consists of re-learning to look at the world" (Merleau-Ponty 1945/2008: xxiii). He continued to apply this notion further in his work with extensive examinations of patterns between the individual and society, language and expression, science and common experience, philosophy and the concept of time and our place in it as a lived-body. The central insight of Merleau-Ponty's philosophy evolves around phenomenology, a field that examines essences and existence. Phenomenology encourages us to reconsider our unquestioned communication with our own subjective worlds and meanwhile take the "lived world" as a point of departure, where, after our examination of many lived experiences, we will eventually return to. He was influenced by many philosophers, such as Martin Heidegger, Henri Bergson, Immanuel Kant and most importantly Edmund Husserl, but his distinctive withdrawal from empiricism and intellectualism was crucial for protecting the phenomenon-centric method of perceiving the world and one's own subjective experience. For the intellectualist, the structure of experience is imposed by our minds, and for the empiricist, our consideration of the "matter" influences our sensations. Both the empiricist and the intellectualist assume that experience cannot form its own structure "in itself" and that it is conditioned to the mind. Thus both fail in explaining our pre-theoretical experience, "it [phenomenological approach] is an illumination and an elucidation of a pre-philosophic experience" (de Boer 1989, 152).

Therefore, we are first asked to liberate ourselves from how both of these disciplines taught us to think, in order to delve into understanding the phenomenological approach. Merleau-Ponty encourages us to explore our lived body, its structural existence, and the living world our body inhabits. The living world grows beyond our reach, therefore neither scientific fixations nor philosophical innovations are fully capable of outlining what is perceived.[15]

---

15   The problem of perception cannot be only the problem of philosophy and other disciplines such as neurology, psychology, as it is widely assumed. We should be able to understand that there is a cross pollination in between (what may seem like "irrelevant") disciplines and theories, which can aid us to understand the complex nature of perception. As Heinz von Foerster (1989, 27) articulates: "Zunächst glaubt man, das Problem

In its vastness, the world reveals itself to us in its condensed forms; the subject body, as our worldly anchorage. This is the starting point of perception and where we primordially feel how 'I' and the world are inseparable. *Phenomenology of Perception* can be taken as a guide to realigning our philosophical understanding of perception and recognizing what we already know but seem to have forgotten. Merleau-Ponty urges us to redefine our contact with our body and to rearrange our perception by reminding ourselves that we perceive the world with our bodies. He reminds us that perception, by its very nature, places itself in the background, as it pushes us into the happenings of the world: it is in the essence of awareness to forget its own phenomena thus enabling things to be constituted.

The experience of "being in the world" requires attention to the concepts of the lived space, the lived time, and the lived world. Our body takes place as a worldly anchorage which observes, lives and drifts in a continuous manner. By its nature, a phenomenon-centric perspective is difficult to recognize in our everyday existence. No matter how precise and convincing we think it is, our subjective awareness suffers from a general failure to be recognized and classified; we find ourselves unable to articulate the process since what we perceive cascades fast and recurrently. Merleau-Ponty (2002, 35) marks that phenomenology allows itself to be practiced as a style, prior to one's possession of a full philosophical consciousness. This style urges us to explore the world through our own perception and as long as our consciousness pulses through our body, there appears to be no final resolution, nor is there a need to find one. That is precisely why phenomenology expects us to explore our consciousness using such a method, since it already exists in us. However, we are immensely absorbed in our world, along with the products of social presuppositions and personal histories. We certainly cannot break away from these patterns, but we can delve into the ontological structures beneath them, which are essential for the phenomenological method in general.

Regarding the role of technology in altering perceptions and magnifying our rediscovery of appearances (of things and realms), philosophical phenomenology and neuroscience intersect on this quite often, despite the

---

der Wahrnehmung sei ein physiologisches, oder ein neurologisches, oder ein neuro-anatomisches, oder ein psychologisches etc., Problem; aber es sind gerade die Resultate dieser Wissenschaften, die immer wieder zeigen, daß Wahrnehmung ein logisch-philosophisches, ein sozio-kulturelles, manchmal sogar ein politisches Problem ist."

contemporaries of Husserl preferring "to reroute it down a less scientific, more existential path" (Sparrow 2014, 4).

In the mid-1990s, this existential path seemed to have taken a turn back to scientific shores, or perhaps phenomenological methods were unknowingly being applied in their research. In *The end of Phenomenology*, Tom Sparrow lists Francisco Varela, Evan Thompson, Dan Zahavi,[16] Shaun Gallagher as people who "attempt to naturalize phenomenology or otherwise synthesize it with the hard sciences" (Sparrow 2014, 11). As subjectivity and the world (in scientific understanding, world could be emphasized as "the matter") are tightly embedded, it would remain counter-intuitive for a scientist to exclude phenomenology's style of digging into subjective experience and intentional consciousness. In order to understand the matter (or the world), we need to look at the subject's stand, who interprets, who is in an ongoing exchange with the givenness of the matter, who could report to us what it is like. "The subject is a being-in-the-world and the world remains 'subjective' since its texture and articulations are traced out by the subject's movement of transcendence" (Zahavi 2003, 73). Zahavi (2018, 19) divides phenomenological analysis into categories of perspectival givenness, horizon and context, embodied spectator, action-perception, temporality and sociality-intersubjectivity. All these categories strictly underline the importance of a subjective body/lived body.

Perspectival givenness, also central to body-ownership and lived-body experience in VR, is the revealed side of the object to the subject's eye; as Zahavi mentions in his online lecture (2018) although we never see the entire bottle[17] at once, we know that there is more to the bottle than what is currently presented. "Husserl uses the terms protentions and retentions for the intentionalities which anchor me to an environment. They do not run from a central I, but from my perceptual field itself, so to speak, which draws along in its wake its own horizon of retentions, and bites into the future with its protentions" (Merleau-Ponty 2002, 487). Horizon and context determines the interplay of presence and absence, which also naturally alludes to the perspectival givenness.

---

16   Zahavi (2018) himself calls this turn of phenomenology as "the renaissance of phenomenology with a focus on embodied, perceiving, feeling agents." This is precisely the relation I aim to code between VR and phenomenological approach by recontextualizing the traditional methods.

17   Zahavi's bottle, Raymond Aron's (1969) "investigation of the cocktail glass," Merleau-Ponty's (1945) "house," Husserl's (1913) "hammer"—all points out to the same method of investigation of the perspectival givenness.

Even when certain sides of the bottle are absent in our visual field, the totality of its presence lingers in mind. Patterns of action-perception allow the subject to explore the bottle. The body with its mobility becomes a central source for a myriad of ways to engage with the bottle. This exploration is also temporal and registers a temporal reconfiguration of consciousness. In the category of sociality-intersubjectivity, when we think of the bottle, it remains as a public phenomenon. Zahavi (2018) distinguishes the bottle as a public entity from a toothache: whereas the bottle may belong to anyone and everyone, the toothache can belong only to me.

While Merleau-Ponty emphasized phenomenology as a manner of thinking, more than a method to adopt, Husserl insisted on the method of bracketing (Einklammerung/phenomenological reduction) as a central method to disentangle the objects from their manifested physical nature; we can go back to the things themselves; "Zurück zu den Dingen selbst" (Husserl 1977, 20–21). Husserl famously concluded that only through this reduction can one have the subjective analysis of the lived-world. Anything in our perceptual field can be carefully studied, until their taken-for-granted appearances[18] peel off and eventually reveal their unique attributes to our consciousness. The world and all things exist with or without us, therefore registering "true knowledge amounts to a kind of flawless mirroring of a pre-existing reality" (Zahavi, 2018). We can try with an attitude of suspending automatic belief, by going back to the epoché and acknowledging the objects' chronic need of validation. By focusing on the objective reality of our surroundings and remembering their independent existence, we automatically omit our subjective gaze upon them. The quality of our subjective affordances would gradually and then suddenly appear to us, even clearer than before. In this way, not only can we respect the given nature of things around us, regardless of our gaze on them, but we can also gain a bird's eye view on our own pre-conscious patterns (being objective about our own subjectivity).[19] In my version of OBE in VR, one's own body is placed in front of the eyes as an object to be observed and

---

18   Zahavi gives a literary example from Gustave Flaubert (1869, 2004, 122): "We have fallen into the habit of remembering, whenever we use our eyes, what people before us have thought of the things we are looking at. Even the slightest thing contains a little that is unknown. WE MUST FIND IT. To describe a blazing fire or that tree until they no longer resemble for us any other tree or any other fire."

19   "Subjectivity is not an impediment to but a precondition for objectivity" (Zahavi 2003, 23).

acknowledged. In Husserlian terms, the body is present in each and every perceptual experience (this state of the lived-body was emphasized as "zero-point of orientation" (Stein 1916, 2010, xvi). What would happen if we could visually experience our body from outside? Could we see the body, as a departure of perception while still being contained in it? Could we then have a better objective glance of our subjective existence? Klaus Held speaks of the "Welthaltigkeit" of objects: "the sense of every single object contains a complete view of the world" (Held 1986, 5). The objects contain a something greater than what they appear to be, a potential lucidity of the world itself. The object and the world have structural similarities, mirroring the parallels between micro- and macrocosmos.

Vilém Flusser, also being occupied with the aesthetic constitution of a cumulative truth and knowledge reproduction of old and new media, underlines a similar notion from the aspect of philosophy of technology: "We are not programmed to see the world through the images, but we are programmed to see the world within the images. As soon as we become conscious of this programming, it collapses."[20] Images, as objects of perception, carry a representation of the world. Their multilayered consistency brings the perceiver a deeper and more unconventional way of relating to the world itself. This brings us back to 'the study of things that appear' and to one of the underlying motivations of the phenomenological world.

These perceived objects naturally reserve a perceptual horizon in our consciousness. At the same time, they have an extending horizon in the outer world. This object-horizon relation fortifies one's own sense of body spatiality. Furthermore, this perceived spatiality enables the perceiver to more efficiently differentiate the qualities of objects. In this way, spatiality also determines the extent to which the perceiver can interact with them, such as in Henri Bergson's (2002) universe, where spatiality is not static but dynamic: "The objects which surround my body reflect its possible action upon them" (Bergson 2002, 106). Spatiality determines the limitations of such interactions.

Between the physical and psychological layers of perceptional experience, the bodily existence is a central component, as it remains as the starting point of perception. The body as a subject-object coexists alongside objects and other

---

20   I translated it from the original in german (Flusser 1996, 117): "Wir sind programmiert, nicht durch die Bilder die Welt zu sehen, sondern die Welt als einen Kontext von Bildern zu sehen. Und sobald wir uns dieses Programms bewußt werden, bricht es zusammen."

subject-objects, and these are all reflecting each other in space and time.[21] Object and subject horizons, with their attribute of motion, are tightly knitted in existence. Their stationary distances from one another influence our perceptual processes. For example, if I see the chair positioned in front of a table, the table influences my perception of the chair. Without the chair, the table would look different as well. Due to my viewpoint of these objects, the total perspective is never graspable; the partial-hiddenness of objects is always there, certain viewpoints of the object always escapes from my gaze. "Merleau-Ponty regards this indeterminacy of appearance as a 'positive phenomenon'" (Siewert 2015, 144). The positioning of the objects surrounding the body and the body's positioning around them define and proliferate the quality of individual perception. In this case, we can say "motor activity of the body is prior to perception" (Merleau-Ponty 2002, 165). Indeed, if we were to move, our awareness of the perspective shifts, likewise there are different ways things look at us. "The ways that things look from one perspective sometimes have for the different ways that things as we look from other perspectives" (Gregory 2013, 214). In an interview, Sobchack (2017) reflects on the relevance of movement and perspective: "When you look at something, what you visually gain from one perspective, you lose from another. There is finitude to perception because it is materially embodied, and so movement indicates choice-making which gives everything meaning." In the virtual world, subjective experience and cognitive science can be merged to describe the sense of presence and broaden the sense of subjectivity. As Sobchack (1994, 87) implies, "It should be evident at this point that the co-constitutive, reversible, and dynamic relations between objective material technologies and embodied human subjects invite a phenomenological investigation."

1.7   Importance of Active Movement in Perception

In *The Embodied Mind*, Varela et al. (1992, 173) comment on the relationship between a perceiver's action and their local situation: "Since the local situations constantly change as a result of the perceiver's activity, the reference point for understanding perception is no longer a pre-given, perceiver-independent

---

21   "Objects and phenomena are not separate entities that pertain to separate realities, but projections that are derived from univocal phenomenality and can have different impacts on an infinite continuum" (Eriksen 2019, 111).

world but rather the sensorimotor structure of the perceiver (the way in which the nervous system links sensory and motor surfaces)." They refer to the crucial role "embodied action" plays in the process of cognition: "Sensory and motor processes, perception and action, are fundamentally inseparable in lived cognition. Indeed, the two are not merely contingently linked in individuals; they have also evolved together" (Varela et al. 1992,173-174).

Varela et al. additionally recognize Merleau-Ponty's insight (mostly based on *The Structure of Behavior*, 1942) about "the organism both initiates and is shaped by the environment" years before it gained empirical support.[22]

> "Since all the movements of the organism are always conditioned by external influences, one can, if one wishes readily treat behavior as an effect of the milieu. But in the same way, since all the stimulations which the organism receives have in turn been possible only by its preceding movements which have culminated in exposing the receptor organ to external influences, one could also say that behavior is the first cause of all the stimulations" (Varela 1992, 174).

Similarly, Alva Noë (2005) underlines the importance of active involvement in "Action in Perception." Perception does not happen to us, rather "it is something we do." It is an active endeavor, rather than a passive one. Although, as I previously interpreted from Hayles' (2017) approach to nonconscious cognition, perception is heavily bombarded with external stimuli, even when we are not actively engaged. Therefore, one should reconsider how Noë's definition of "action" can be understood within the nonconscious cognition.

During a perceptional process (when we speak of the body's spatiality and motricity), it is up to us to choose a stand point, and to explore which side of the object's givenness we prefer to absorb. The spatiality of the body is a determinant factor in this perceptual experience. In his article "Action Based Accounts of Perception," Pierre Jacob (2015, 225) supports Noë's understanding of "enactive conception" (O'Regan & Noë, 2001; Noë, 2004, 34) and explains how the

---

22   Similarly, Catherine Malabou (2008) reflects on how perception is shaped by external stimuli and by the environmental feedback. On the importance of how visual perception develops in time: "A great deal of the development of the human brain is accomplished in the open air, in contact with the stimuli of the world, which directly influence both the development and the volume of connections. The visual system, for example, is not entirely functional at birth. The synapses connecting fibers coming from the retina to neurons in the visual cortex are not yet entirely formed. Information received from outside activates the synapses and encourages maturation" (Malabou 2008, 20).

content of perceptual experience is determined by one's innate knowledge of sensorimotor contingencies. He [Pierre Jacob] continues:

> "Noë (2004) has argued that enactivism solves the puzzle of perceptual presence: in perceiving an object whose back surface is occluded from my view (e.g. the back of a tomato in front of me), I am perceptually aware of the occluded part that does not reflect photons on my retina. On the enactive account, the reason I am perceptually aware of the occluded part is that I tacitly know that were I to pick up the tomato and turn it over, I would see the back of the tomato."

We are sure that there are more sides to perceive, which at the moment, are not apparent to us. In our mental imagery, relevant perspectives complement each other. When you are reading this, you know what the next page (at least visually) will look like, compared to previous pages, it is highly unlikely that there is a hologram waiting for you when you turn the page. Noë's example of the unperceived side of a tomato resembles Merleau-Ponty's example of the perception of a house; the visually unperceived sides of the object in our horizon are already tacitly embedded in our understanding. If I stare at a house from the front, I would define the house based on this specific aspect. To someone else who looks at it from an airplane, it would seem different. Therefore we must consider all possible perspectives of the house that we haven't yet perceived, that is "the house itself is the house seen from nowhere" (Merleau-Ponty 2002, 79). And is it possible to say that the house exists, even if it is not visually grasped? Perhaps this question should lead us to reconsider the existence of objects regardless of our gaze. Or in other words, we cannot take our own gaze as the absolute determination of the objects, since we continuously attach our subjective perspectives onto the related object. Therefore, we do not really identify and acknowledge this object as is, but rather define what it is for us; ontologically speaking, we do not recognize the object's phenomenal existence.[23]

Although these aspects will be closely examined in the following sections, I have to take a moment to highlight the importance of the spatiality of bodily existence in phenomenology, as it is significant for my characterization of OBE.

---

23   This detached and dispassionate way of interacting with objects was described as "high altitude thinking" (pensée de survol) by Merleau-Ponty (1942), also known as "held captive" by Wittgenstein (1958), and "desertion" by Gabriel Marcel (1967).

As embodied virtual identities in a virtual environment, we have an extraordinary capacity to switch between horizons, unlike in reality. Therefore we are introduced to a brand new subject-object relationship; a new virtual subject as us and the surrounding virtual objects. The inspection of the virtual objects' givenness requires a different attitude of observation in comparison to a 2D exposure and to reality, mainly because of the "motion parallax," (Jaron Lanier 2017, 53) which is a significant visual quality of 3D perception. Lanier (2017, 53–54) explains the importance of these features in VR: "Move your head absolutely as little as you can, and you will still see that edges of objects at different distances line up differently with each other in response to the motion." Consequently, through the proliferation of this givenness of the objects, the spatiality of the body is once again amplified. This unfamiliar causality in movement and perception does not perfectly match with the one we habitually practice in physical reality, thus a reconfiguration of bodily senses becomes inevitable. Such reconfiguration can also influence our understanding of the subject-object relationship in the phenomenological sense. On the incorporating practices of cinematic vision, Connerton (1989, 78) articulates that spectators are not puzzled when the camera tilts and pans between images. They do not need to move their heads as the angles change, and they still can adapt to the shifting images without being perplexed. Because the audience ingrains the camera eye as their own,[24] they become all-seeing subjects. In a movie theater, I am both inside the action of the visual story and outside of it, "I am everywhere and nowhere" (similar to "the house is seen both from everywhere and nowhere" Merleau-Ponty 2002, 72). He [Connerton] continues, "The inscriptional practice of cinema makes possible, and is in turn made possible by, the incorporating practice of the cinema spectator" (Connerton 1989, 78). When we think of motion parallax in VR, this cinematic experience differs exceptionally, since the images continue if we tilt and move our heads in 360 degrees, unlike the cinematic experience in a movie theater. The VR audience inscribes and incorporates the moving image in addition to the self-narrative aspect of virtual agency. In doing so, we tend to get an optimal grip of the things around us. This optimal feeling is readily available to us and it is a given thing. In *On the*

---

24   "...cinematic loved-body: the camera its perceptive organ, the projector its expressive organ, the screen its discrete and material center. In sum, the cinematic exists as a visible performance of the perceptive and expressive structure of lived-body experience" (Sobchack 1994, 99).

Internet, Hubert Dreyfus (2001, 56) emphasizes this Merleau-Pontian intercorporeality and argues that in order to create a sense of presence in the world of telepresence, this optimal grip has to be established. Dreyfus argues that this optimal grip is a pre-reflective domain of our daily embodied interaction, and is not yet clearly defined in cyberspace. Therefore, the integration of all stereoscopic imagery and altered sound systems remain "useless" due to the lack of this sense of grip. The body, with all of its sensory modalities and related physical feelings and desires, is central for creating this sense of grip. "We are not only conscious beings, but also carnal beings" (Sobchack 2000, 140).

In VR, this optimal grip is not properly established and we still do not know what optimal is. Because of this, the flow of skillful coping is interrupted. The innate skills needed for achieving this optimal grip for a sense of presence is scattered. Finding the appropriate ways to master everyday skillful action in VR would require an alteration of understanding subject-object relations. As Grosz (2017, 43) implies "sense is not subjective, nor is it the quality of objects, but the way in which each is capable of being separated yet fundamentally engaged."

1.8   Subject-Object Relations in VR

Simone de Beauvoir (1945, 363) notes that phenomenology's greatest achievement is the abolition of the subject-object dichotomy. Reflecting on the method of "élucidation phénoménologique," she argues "it is impossible to define an object by cutting it from the subject through and for which it is object; and the subject manifests itself only through the object with which it is involved." Similarly, according to Merleau-Ponty, the body is the starting point of perception rather than simply an object within the field of perception (Merleau-Ponty 2002, 108). These views understand the body as a multidimensional medium—one of self-awareness that manifests itself as an embodied object. The visual discovery of this multidimensional fleshy object is limited for each individual, as we are absorbed in our own bodily existence.

Although from a top-down angle, many of my body parts are within my reach, I am both visually and tangibly unable to attain a full grasp of my own body. Can I ever hold and lift my own body? This is not really achievable. Pierre Jacob explains: "Humans have dexterous hands that enable them to grasp targets in their peri-personal space with either precision grip or full prehension. For the purpose of teaching a target of prehension, an agent must represent its spatial position in an egocentric coordinate system centered on her body" (Jacob 2015, 221–222). My body can never be placed as a target in my peri-personal space for me to grasp. But in contrast to this tangible impossibility, Jacob implies that the visual experience of objects brings two complementary functions:

> "selection and recognition (or identification). Selecting an object consists in both segregating a complex visual array into several separable objects and in attributing to each item its own set of appropriate visual attributes (this is the so-called 'binding' problem)" (Jacob 2015, 222).

Raymond Barglow describes the hiddenness of the bodily being thus: "What a strange object to find: oneself. Something vital and central remains absent and hidden" (Barglow 1994, 92). The body, as our constant in space and time, tries to adapt to all sort of changes; and as Frank Biocca points out, "... before paper, wires, and silicon, the primordial communication medium is the body. At the center of all communication rests the body, the fleshy gateway to the mind" (Biocca 1997, 13). We are observers, movers, and users of our bodies as we engage in different actions. Without containing the self in the body, it is not possible to reflect on the problem of perception. But to what extent are we able to visually explore this mass of flesh? We live in it, we own it,[25] and yet ironically it is not totally in our reach, unlike the other things we own. Surely, I can reach one hand with the other, and my hand can reach other parts of my body, and I can visually and tactically manipulate their existence to an extent, but not as much as the objects around us. We relate to ourselves as thinking subjects and reflect upon the objects around us. We orient our limbs around the objects around us and our actions accordingly develop as we make use of these objects. It is worth recalling here the first VR experiment I elucidated above as an example in which the participants hold a 3D camera in their hands and observe the real time video in their VR headsets. The images they perceive change according to their hand movements. Most of the participants at first experienced disorientation, leading them to move about in a clumsy manner. In time, however, they developed a very specific sensitivity toward the equipment and became acquainted to the equipment's relation to the body. Additionally, it must be said that this setup did not include truly hyper sensitive high-tech products,

---

25   We may not even get to say we "own" it, if we recall Wittgenstein's remark about the paradoxical nature of this issue: "If someone says I have a body, he can be asked, who is speaking with this mouth?" (Wittgenstein 1972, 244).

which made it even harder to practice finding an equilibrium state between the subject and the technology. But even then, after a certain amount of time, participants accepted the camera as an extension of their hand and switched to a more fluent coordination with it. The movement of their hand was not clumsy, and the moving images became steady as they chose to perceive at their own self-modified pace.

The 3D camera itself is an end product of human intelligence and skill. Here we can recall Marshall McLuhan's fundamental dictum "We become what we behold. We shape our tools and thereafter our tools shape us" (McLuhan 1964, 19). Yet the way in which media (from photography to audio records) function as an extension of our physical and nervous systems has been entirely neglected in the philosophy of perception. This was one reason for why media studies took off during the 1960s—a development that underlined the notion of technology as an extension of the body. This is especially the case with McLuhan's (1964) "Electric Age," which highlighted the importance of the central nervous system in engaging with media devices. McLuhan suggested that we perpetually seek to understand the ongoing correspondence between media and the nervous system enable equilibriums (McLuhan 1964, 76), similar to the equilibrium between the hand and the 3D camera I mentioned above. McLuhan emphasizes "the electric technology as organic and non-mechanical, because it extends, not our eyes, but the entire central nervous system as a planetary vesture" (McLuhan 1964, 201).

In the 1980s and 1990s, the increased engagement of scholars with the phenomenon of cultural articulation led to a conception of praxis as a central medium for understanding the relationship between the bodily self and its cultural articulations as its extensions. This tendency sparked a turn in phenomenology, which originally focused on the philosophy of consciousness and subjectivity. Don Ihde (1993), Hubert Dreyfus (2014), Graham Harman (2011), and others combined phenomenology with technoscientific developments. The field of postphenomenology then mainly carved out a contemporary standpoint for phenomenologists to consider technology that has led to a deeper understanding of embodiment and active bodily perception. This reformation became possible through a recognition of how technological instrumentality immensely alters the subjective experience of the body. Without McLuhan's breakthrough recognition of the sensorium of human subject, postphenomenology's technoscientific horizon would cease to exist. The technological artifacts as objects that surround us have thus come to enable an in depth understanding of subjectivity and influenced the ways we can connect to our body as an "object" as well.

Objects are there for us to observe because we can walk around them, or stare at them from above and below. Yet our own phenomenal body is not accessible to us in the same way that an external object is. "I objectively confront every object. But not the I" (Wittgenstein 1979, 80). As Merleau-Ponty underlines: "I can see my eyes in three mirrors, but they are the eyes of someone observing, and I have the utmost difficulty in catching my living glance" (Merleau-Ponty 2002, 105). In this same vein, Bernhard Waldenfels (2000, 518) also notes that Husserl questioned whether it is possible to see everything from one's own lived body, and if it is possible for one eye to see the other eye. Waldenfels (2000, 529) notes that when we are sitting in a cabinet of mirrors, what we see is someone watching himself/herself; we watch the act of watching. Therefore, positioning one's self at the center of a multifaceted mirror does not provide a sufficient environment to revisit our bodily self, since what we try to see is also paradoxically watching us. This inevitable hiddenness of, and inability to grasp, the body as a whole entity is what Husserl would indicate as an example of how the representational content of objects remain inadequate due to the horizon problem. Because I do not have the capacity to visually apprehend the totality of an object in my horizon, it is only defined within the moment of my position to the object itself. It remains inadequate to have a glimpse of one's bodily existence in its totality, as is practiced in the phenomenological object-horizon context.

Postphenomenology's role here is to reframe the subject-object relation, as we engage with the affordances of media technologies which have already influenced us. In this chapter's experiment, "Ambiguity in Lived Body Experiences," the living glance which escapes the eye was often captured within the VR setup. The 3D camera became an extension for the eye and the arm, which in return overcame the subjects' limited span to see themselves in a mirror cabinet.

1.8.1 Phenomenology's Neglect of Objects as Embodied Instruments

To a certain extent, Husserl proposes that to grasp the totality of an object, one needs to have an omniscientific stand, which highlights the impossibility of such a total capture. Due to Husserl's negligence of the instrumental nature of objects (unlike Heidegger and Merleau-Ponty), he could not consider how new technology might one day allow for such "impossibilities" to be revisited and further questioned. This comes as no surprise, since his methodological approach systematically excluded the role of multifunctional instruments as extensions of the bodily self.

In *Husserl's Missing Technologies*, Don Ihde (2016) elucidates Husserl's lack of interest in technology in the twentieth century. Although Husserl reflected on the instruments such as telescopes and microscopes, he overlooked the idea that such instruments have already altered human perception. By providing a gaze into physically inaccessible environments, it is possible to manipulate perception. Ihde indicates that Husserl mostly focused on "the analogue-isomorphic limits of instrumental technologies," and that he dismissed the recognition of how external objects can be embodied (Ihde 2016, 76). Husserl's dismissal of instrumental technologies and their role in intensifying our bodily skills may explain why different criticisms have been raised against the phenomenological approach. Ihde accordingly proposes a postphenomenological reformation of common notions in phenomenology. "With each new technology there are interrelated embodiment skills that implicate us embodied humans and for which there is a possible post-phenomenological analysis" (Ihde 2016, 76). This approach also signifies Ihde's inclusion of technological trajectories in his analysis, which he uses to distance himself from traditional subjectivism of Husserl, and from the romanticism which is associated with Heidegger.

Husserl's neglect of technology has also been emphasized by Michael Kelly: "Husserl himself says very little (indeed almost nothing) that directly concerns technology" (Kelly 2005, 227). Kelly underlines that existing phenomenological insights carry great potential for exploration in technoscience and the philosophy of technology. He argues that this could also establish new postphenomenological understanding: "In order to create a space for a Husserlian contribution to the philosophy of technology, much work remains to be done" (Kelly 2005, 230). Similarly, Varela remarks that Husserl did not use any other method other than his own philosophical introspection, which resulted in an avoidance of direct embodied aspects of experience. Unsurprisingly, Varela adds, this caused several European philosophers to distance themselves from traditional forms of pure phenomenology (Varela 1992, 17).

Likewise, Joona Taiple (2014, 76) highlights the significant influence of Husserl's phenomenology on theories of embodiment in a broader sense, and how Husserl remains unchallenged. Writing about how the horizon of technoscience can be expanded, Dimitri Ginev (2016, 222) states: "From a postphenomenological perspective, the stabilities of technological embodiments and natural-technological hybrids are always already open to be transcended and re-contextualized within new techno-scientific horizons." Furthermore, Zwier underline how postphenomenological method must be approached as mediation theory (Zwier 2016, 313). He continues: "This leaves undiscussed how mediation theory about ontic beings (i.e., technologies) involves a specific ontological mode of relating to beings, whereas consideration of this mode is precisely the concern of phenomenology" (Zwier 2016, 313). Additionally, Introna and Ilharco (2004) suggest that the phenomenological method of investigation can be applied to the understanding of screenhood, which is a phenomenological approach to explain how screens now permeate sensory experiences and human experience in general (Introna & Ilharco 2004, 225).

Mediation theory's central idea is to consider technology as mediator of subject-object relations, rather than seeing them solely as material objects, as entities in opposition to human subjects. This understanding goes back to McLuhan's (1964, xv) teaching of how media are agents of change in our experience of the world, in our use of our physical senses, and in our experience with each other as individuals. Media studies have carefully considered the impact of media as agent for their effects, that is, for us to effectively use the media itself. McLuhan's approach oscillates over a vast range between society and culture, but his fundamental warning was to study media's effect on the individual, since he considered the media to be an extension of the body. Thus, postphenomenology's digging into the body's sensorium to explore the effect of technology has been a topic for media studies since the beginning of 1960s.

As a reply to a modification of traditional phenomenology (postphenomenology requires a pragmatic and contemporary reinforcement), this project explored bodily existence (as a potential milestone to reintroduce flesh into informational processing) by positioning it in front of the owner of the body in an OBE VR setup. Working from a postphenomenological attitude, it challenged the basic notion of traditional phenomenology (the deobjectification of the body) by objectifying the body within a VR setup. This materialization of the body into the category of a "thing" is derived from the intention to apply Husserl's: "Wir wollen auf die 'Sachen selbst' zurückgehen" (Husserl 1984, 10). This is a postphenomenological attitude, realized through a novel approach to new technology. Technology, in this sense, will continue to alter the phenomenal quality of subjective experience, because as Lanier puts it, "VR is the technology of noticing experience itself" (Lanier 2017, 55).

In his essay "At the Discretion of the (a-) thing: Derrida and German thought," David Appelbaum (2015) examines the importance of "(a-) thing."

He revisits the notion of the "thing" by reflecting on Jacques Derrida's work: "Derrida is particularly interested in the virtual or spectral manifestations of things and the affective power they possess" (Appelbaum 2015, 3). As we tend to see the world in every image (Flusser 1996), the objectified and perceived 3D image of one's own body may push us to reexamine our bodily existence and reform its contained sense of self and world. Furthermore, Appelbaum implies that "there [is], at the enigma of an origin, an *Ursprung*, where we need to look for the thing." In this sense, observation of the body as an extraordinary enigma with its unconquered sides and their unrevealed givenness allows for an in-depth exploration of the constitutional self.

As Catherine Malabou explains in her foreword "After the Flesh" in Tom Sparrow's *Plastic Bodies: Rebuilding Sensation After Phenomenology*:

> "the necessary de-objectification has been clearly accompanied by a de-materialization. If the flesh was essential as the future of the physical body, now we need to question the future of the flesh. For this reason, the materiality of the body must be rethought" (Malabou 2014, 15).

Malabou explains how Husserl stressed the notion that we cannot apply Euclidean geometry to the perception of the reality of one's own body—just as we cannot perceive the six faces of a cube at once, in the same way we cannot perceive the totality of our own body. This "perceptual creation of a dynamic image of the body" became the starting point of my version of OBE, "Ambiguity in Lived Body Experiences."

In *Parables for the Virtual: Movement, Affect, Sensation*, Brian Massumi (2002) approaches the body with a refined consideration of sensation, movement, and affect. He considers these to be the fundamental components of bodily existence, which highlight the experience of embodiment. The importance of bodily existence has been traditionally articulated within linguistic theories, but we should reconsider obvious but neglected significations of the body as a carnal being. His way of reemphasizing virtual and bodily existence at the proximity of cognitive science (interoception and exteroception) and philosophy (mixing William James' "intentionality" instilled from empiricism, together with a reassessment of Bergsonian theory of perception) indeed resembles an attempt to formulate a response to Husserl's call for an omniscientific approach. Charles J. Stivale (2004) comments on Massumi's "creative contagion" method and multidisciplinary insights:

"[Massumi is] [w]ell aware of being charged with 'shameless poaching,' of 'theft from science for the humanities,' [and he] happily but not naively embraces such charges. His interest is in radical relevancy of concepts, the very ways in which rhythm, relay, arrival and departure' (i.e., affect) enable a two-way transmission between science and the humanities" (Stivale 2004, 148).

Indeed, Massumi's tendency to make these radical connections between disciplines clarifies how each discipline in itself is compelled to arrive at a dead end within their scope. Massumi's interest lies in tackling the aspects of things we don't actually see (illusion). "The question is: what exactly does the inconvenient reality that we see things we don't actually see say about the nature of perception?" (Massumi 2013, 41).

An experience of the totality of the body not is not only enabled by a long-lasting practice of interoception (alongside a continuous introspection) but also consists of grasping an external and visual understanding of it, since this totality includes the material nature of the body. The givenness of the body is attainable, as we have a sense of being contained in it (or by it?), but it is also unattainable, in the sense that its totality is concurrently ever-escaping our gaze and grasp. It chases its own "back" in a continuous manner, as in Massumi's formulation, "the oneness of the body is back-flow." This "back-flow," as he describes, is "always at a lag. The body's relative slowness returns to it, after a habitual detour, as its own objectifiable unity. Thus, back-formed, the body may now appear to itself as a bounded object among others" (Massumi 2002, 150). The "Ambiguity in Lived Body Experiences" experiment underlines the importance of "the objectifiable unity of body," which becomes apparent as we become able to detour around the body in VR.

I think that a reinvestigation of the body, as our own fleshy mass, and a close-up on one's own back in VR could support reformations of the traditional phenomenological body. By manipulating a new media technology, this VR paradigm could also contribute to the necessary technoscientific revolution of postphenomenology. This pragmatic reformation and advancement owe their ground to initial media theories that considered media as an extension of the body. Media alters the ratio between our senses, just as the ratio between the mediums enables another set of new effects to study. Such effects can be traced in the case of the VR paradigms I present in this dissertation; the connection changes between the cameras, head mounted displays, the positioning of the body between VR motion trackers, and how with a slight movement of equipment and/or the body the configuration of the entire system.

Something that might be considered physically inaccessible (i.e., total graspability of one's own body) can be explored as we get to detour around the body itself in a virtually accessible dimension. The finitude of the visual perspective I direct on my own body, such as the vague gaze of my body via multifaceted mirrors, can be expanded and explored within a virtual environment. At this point, it is crucial to describe what I mean by the "virtual body" in the context of an OBE. This does not refer to an animated body image developed in a realistic 3D fashion; rather, I use it to refer to a peer-to-peer simultaneous connection of a 3D camera and a VR HMD. With this installation, the user is encapsulated in an HMD, watching his/her body in a 3D video projection of himself/herself. One other way to do this is through 3D modeling of the human body. One of the most compelling attempts at a realistic 3D modeling of body image has been launched by the Fraunhofer Institut (HII), with their work on "3D Human Body Reconstruction for VR." Researchers at the institute have developed a system that captures a computer-generated person or object, providing the user with a chance to virtually navigate the 3D model from a variety of angles. Both of these methods (computer-generated virtual body and real-time 3D video capture of the body) can be used to test new ideas in connection with Hayles' distinction between the natural self and a "cybernetic posthuman"—to make an attempt to bring decomposed flesh back into the cognition of cybernetic subjects (Hayles 1999, 23).

1.9   Self-Narration and Action in VR

The system I adopted from OBE could be useful in terms of stepping into an understanding of how perception begins with the body and is affected by our ability to see the body as a whole in relation to other objects—in this case, to see our own body as an external object, ready to be closely observed. The insights that can be derived from such a practice of awareness might be influential in defining phenomenon-centric uses of VR setups. A VR setup contains a fast and an interchangeable configuration of perspective; e.g., while gazing at our virtual body, we can first switch to a bird's eye view of ourselves and then immediately blink to a view of our own neck.[26] Unlike the imposed narration of mov-

---

26   This can be proposed as a potential response to Husserl's (Hua XXI) above mentioned assertion about the impossibility of applying a Euclidean geometry to the perception of one's own body, just as we cannot perceive the six faces of a cube at once.

ing pictures, in a virtual environment the perceiver has the freedom to switch between desired perspectives, generating a distinct flow of self-narrated perception. Early immersive media installations, such as perspective paintings, panoramas, 3D films, and photography, aimed for a similar effect. They amplified the experience of being surrounded by the visual medium while being at the middle of the image (Rötzer 2000, 158). The sensation of corporeal engagement stimulated by such paintings, sculptures, photograph, and architectural forms, as well as works of cinema and literature, augments our emotional responses to those same objects (Gallese 2019).

Lev Manovich (2001, 16) emphasizes that media technology does not necessarily adopt a "linear march" in its cycle, explaining: "The introduction of every new modern media technology, from photography in the 1840s to Virtual Reality in the 1980s, has always been accompanied by the claims that the new technology allows to represent reality in a new way." But in fact, within the use of computer and network-based technologies, we can retrace these "new" realisms. "Just as the photograph did in the last century, so in this one, cinematic and electronic screens differently demand and shape our "presence" to the world and our representation in it. "Each differently and objectively alters our subjectivity while each invites our complicity in formulating space, time, and bodily investment as significant personal and social experience" (Sobchack 2016, 84). Perspective photography shaped ideas behind digital 3D imagery in the same way that stereoscopic vision in early inventions influenced the VR HMD structure. Hayles (2017) emphasizes that the initial intention of technological artifacts was often appropriated for another use (e.g., the typewriter was mainly invented for blind people). She underlines "the unexpected effects of technological innovations, arguing that technological systems almost always modify and transform the ends envisioned in their original designs, opening up new possibilities and, in the process, entangling means and ends together so that they can no longer reasonably be regarded as separate categories" (Hayles 2017, 36).

Similarly, we are now witnessing how VR is moving past its initial intention for military training and is being integrated into scientific research, entertainment, and rehabilitation. Inventions exceed their microdimension and proliferate their means when they end up in the hands of polyphonic minds. This can of course be both constructive and destructive. For example, in the 1980s Friedrich Kittler strongly opposed McLuhan's idea of media being extensions of man. On the contrary, he underlined the autonomy of technology and thus sharpened the edges of techno pessimism. As it turned out, VR, among nearly all novel technologies, was initially "misused" in the hands of militaristic training. This applies to every communication medium throughout the history, e.g., media technologies have been strictly in control of the state during the World Wars and the Cold War. This strategic manipulation of technology was the main concern behind Kittler's (1980) central thesis of the "driving of the human out of the humanities" ("die Austreibung des Geistes aus den Geisteswissenschaften"). One questions why such dangerous potential of technology did not quite weigh in McLuhan's understanding, while McLuhan himself was born just before World War I and lived through World War II? While Kittler's concern has to be taken in consideration at all times, humanity will continuously produce conditions that will be both simultaneously threatening and thriving. As Kittler (2012, 387) writes, it is inevitable that "[e]very system of power has the enemies it produces." Focusing on the media as a potential threat serves the opposite intention of this dissertation and would only disable the thriving my work aims to establish.

Early immersive media installations started to evoke, in their participants, the urge to reach out and touch the visuals in order to catch a closer or cross-angled glimpse of the exposed image, bringing the body into a restless state of moving back and forth. 3D exposure gave spectators an instinctual awareness of their hands, inducing a naive and irrational expectation that they could penetrate the borders of the image. These raised-up hands, of course, then sank down in disappointment after encountering a bug in proprioception. Such media installations, as well as telecommunication devices, require visual and auditory attention. The receivers of these signals are harnessed in our bodies. The body coexists with the source of the sender, as it is exposed to the materiality of the device, which magnifies the materiality of the body. In a VR environment, this materialistic coexistence demands cooperation and co-playing, exceeding the borders of conventional communication mode. In an email correspondence I carried out with Alva Noë about our constitutional and habitual relation to telecommunication tools, he raised a question:

> "When you and I drive together our conversation does not distract me, the driver, from the road. When we talk and listen to the radio, I am still not distracted. But the moment I make a phone call, my attunement to where I am is disrupted. (I discuss this briefly and give some references in *Strange Tools*) Why is the phone so disruptive? And what does this have to do with the body?"

My answer was:

"Could it be because the person who we talk to on the phone is not present in the car, their body is in a remote environment, and maybe we thus feel the need to give a full attention to the one and only medium, their voice? And in the case of listening to the radio, this is not reciprocal, so our attention is not as compromised as it would be during an interaction. If I sat next to you while you were driving, you wouldn't necessarily turn and look at me during our conversation. But I would still be in your field of perception; you could still detect my gestures and mood, so the weight of the *auditive only* communication would be partially lifted. Perhaps this would give you a level of confirmation and provide a sense of comfort which enable you to multi-task. It is moreover a matter of ergonomics. Are we talking as we hold the phone close to the ear? Or are we talking via integrated microphones and loud speaker in the car? Are we equally distracted in both cases?"

1.10 Responsible Subject in VR

In VR, spectators are not only passive receivers; they are given the intense role of influencing, manipulating, and directing the visual composition to which they have been exposed. The hypnotizing/paralyzing effect that comes with a steady observation of the teleworld is replaced with a hands-on attitude which requires an alert responsibility for self narration. Another difference between cinematic experience/presence and virtual experience/presence is articulated by Sobchack (1994, 98): "Cinema's animated presentation of representation constitutes its 'presence' as always presently engaged in the experiential process of signifying and coming-into-being. Thus the significant value of the 'streaming forward' that informs the cinematic with its specific form of temporality (and differentiates it from the atemporality of the photographic) is intimately bound to a structure not of possession, loss, pastness, and nostalgia, but of accumulation, ephemerality, and anticipation—to a 'presence' in the present informed by its connection to a collective past and to a future." Contrary to the switching back and forth between past and future that happens during cinematic experience, virtual experience requires a persistent attention to be present in the environment, since without an active influence of the spectator/user, the story cannot continue. Felt presence has to be defined in the present. The rigidity of the fixated body in front of the screen loosens because one feels the need to jump into the screen to take a part in the course of events. The fragility of a nonmoving body is replaced with agility and the urge to embody the new, virtual body. The attempt to identify and explore the vague contours of the virtual body somehow requires a continuous investigation of one's own lived body. For example, when we see a virtual object, we anticipate how it would feel in our hands if we were to grasp it. Bergson highlights the specific embeddedness of perception in consciousness and questions: "How come everything happens as if this consciousness were born of the internal movements of the cerebral substance?" (Bergson 2002, 115). He asserts that perception rapidly accumulates memories. Similarly, Malabou (2008, 24) indicates: "Neurons somehow remember stimulation. Everything happens as if there were no stabilization of memories except on the condition of a potential destabilization of the general landscape of memory." Concerning the relationship between perception and consciousness and how perception is ingrained within cerebral substance, Bergson writes: "In fact, there is no perception which is not full of memories. With the immediate and present data of our senses, we mingle a thousand details out of our past experience" (Bergson 2002, 115). Virtual images may thus represent "signs" or "representations" of former images which are (in Bergsonian terms) illusions as a result of a rapid perception. Bergson even describes representation as virtual, meaning it requires no interaction, thus preserving its neutrality in contrast to presence. A representation is one of the thousands of flickering images erupting from memory. Could we say that by introducing a haptic sensory modality to a virtual image, we are slightly subtracting from the neutrality of the representation? Specifically, by enabling a sense of tactile stimulation and bringing forth an achievable interaction to the user's experience, can we confirm the parallel qualities between the presence and its related representation? Tactile stimulation requires action, and can this action alter what representation means? If we follow Bergson in underlining the importance of action in perception, then without action, perception does not really occur.

Hence, when we see a representation, such as an image of a virtual object, we recall the tactile memory of this specific object from our lived experience and we anticipate how this virtual object would feel in our hands. In *How Societies Remember*, Paul Connerton asserts that in order to remember and execute a specific action, we do not even need representational activity since consulting a mental picture of bodily movement would be enough. He writes: "In habitual memory the past is, as it were, sedimented in the body" (Connerton 1989, 72). This treatment of a mental picture is similar to what Vittorio Gallese (2014, 369) calls a "neural reuse." Following John Dewey's consideration of the important

role insistent desire has on habitual behavior (Dewey 1922, 24–25), Connerton
further elaborates:

> "All habits are affective dispositions: that a predisposition formed through
> the frequent repetition of a number of specific acts is an intimate and fun-
> damental part of ourselves, that such habits have power because they are
> so intimately a part of ourselves" (Connerton 1989, 94).

Connerton (1989, 94–96) categorizes memory sedimentation in the body under two types of social practice: incorporating practice and inscribing practice. Incorporating practice is the use of bodily gestures and activities to transmit a message to the receiver, and this is possible only when both bodies are
present together (e.g., an instantaneous smile as a habitual response to a specific person in our circle of friends). By contrast, during an inscribing practice
we use the body as an interactive vehicle to communicate with the devices that
trap and hold information. Even when the body is not any longer present in
the space, the information that is inserted by a bodily action remains stored.
Hayles (1999, 200) reminds us that this implicit distinction between incorporating and inscribing practices can be first recognized in Merleau-Ponty's *Phenomenology of Perception* (1945). Following Merleau-Ponty, Connerton observes
that learning to type is an incorporating practice, and that with persistent practice, the act of typing gets ingrained in bodily memory. Hayles specifies that we
do not cognitively detect and press each key location, but instead the habitual
memory gives the act of typing a flow quality, as if the keys have become extensions of the users' fingers. It is no longer a conscious attempt: "by their nature,
habits do not occupy conscious thought" (Hayles 1999, 204). She clarifies:

> "When changes in incorporating practices take place, they are often linked
> with new technologies that affect how people use their bodies and expe-
> rience space and time. Formed by technology at the same time that it cre-
> ates technology, embodiment mediates between technology and discourse
> by creating new experiential frameworks that serve as boundary markers
> for the creation of corresponding discursive systems. In the feedback loop
> between technological innovations and discursive practices, incorporation
> is a crucial link" (Hayles 1999, 205).

Technology as an extension of the body and the importance of incorporation is
a crucial link in the embodiment process, and this will be discussed in detail in
the next chapters.

1.11 Lack of Flesh in Virtual Body and Coexistence in Both Realms

In VR, as well as in interactive processes with other technological devices, we need an inevitable reconfiguration of bodily existence and a reevaluation of the spectrums of different bodily senses. In owning a virtual body, the perceivers shift toward an active awareness of their own sensory spectrum and of what surrounds the body. They reinvestigate their own physical capacity and interoceptively reregister their perceptual qualities in order to explore whether such qualities coexist within the virtual body. As Lanier (2017) writes: "Through VR, we learn to sense what physical reality is. We learn to perform new probing experiments with our bodies and our thoughts, moment to moment, mostly unconsciously … Encountering VR refines our ability to discern and enjoy physicality" (Lanier 2017, 49–50). This interrelationality reminds us of our firm connection to physical reality. The other flashing absence we experience is the lack of vulnerability, which would habitually evoke our primordial caution to protect our flesh. Since in a virtual body, there is an impaired perception of bodily integrity and an impaired sense of being incarnated in flesh, a primordial caution is not clearly recognized. Still, when we are exposed to a threat in VR (e.g., in a scary scenario or in a phobia rehabilitation design), our reflexes react and we tend to protect the virtual body.

These new experiments oscillate between sensations of the virtual and the lived body, reminding us of what we primordially are given but seem to have forgotten within the day-to-day use of our body. In this way, the recognition of such fundamental awareness liberates us from the usual association of bodily senses. Florian Rötzer emphasizes that in virtual worlds, we are given the opportunity to break through the conventional sense of the body and to leave the "Gefängnis des Körpers" ("prison of the body"), even if it is just for a short period of time (Rötzer 2000, 158). Sobchack (1994, 103) similarly articulates that electronic space causes a "constant action and busyness, replac[ing] the gravity that grounds and orients the movement of the lived body with a purely spectacular, kinetically exciting, often dizzying sense of bodily freedom (and freedom from the body)."

In his famous article "What Is It Like to Be a Bat?," Thomas Nagel (1974, 435) emphasizes the impossibility for human beings to embody a bat's perception of the world. Specifically, he distinguishes between the experience of "I want to know what it is like for a bat to be a bat," rather than "What it would be like for me to behave as a bat behaves" (Nagel 1974, 435–450). With a similar focus on tackling the phenomenal character of sensory experience and its qualities, Stefano Gualeni (2015, 194) argues that we can get close to adopting the avatar's perspective through personification in video games (whether it be as a human, a dragon, a mouse, or a bat). He uses the game *Haerfest* (2009) to challenge Nagel's assumption and suggests that this game gives the player a glimpse of what it would be like to be a bat. In their recent research, "The Illusion of Animal Body Ownership and Its Potential for Virtual Reality Games," Andrey Krekhov (2019) and his coauthors also highlight how virtual body ownership can be applicable for nonhumanoids. With the integration of different body tracking systems, such modes of embodiment "can even outperform human-like avatars in certain cases" (Krekhov et al. 2019, 1).

In a VR environment, just as we are drawn out of our ordinary visual perception, we are pulled back into our predefined self-conception and given the chance to explore possible alignment with a virtual body. There is a significant, automatic attempt to conquer and fulfill the incomplete and fleshless architecture of the virtual body using the features of the real body. We are filled with a sense of satisfaction and intrigue the moment we embody the virtual body. There is an opportunity to experience the multi-spatial cognition of the body since we remain perceptually active in both reality and virtual reality. As Waldenfels (2000, 230) notes, media technology and its products loosen our rootedness here in reality and extend the possibility to emerge in different realms. This attempt of double existence eventually feels like nonspatial cognition, which brings to mind Massumi's indeterminacy of the body, with "its openness to an else-where and otherwise than it is, in any here and now" (Massumi 2002, 5). He describes this paradoxical nature of the body as being "real, material, but incorporeal" with its indeterminate quality. The title of his book "Parables for the Virtual" was influenced by this paradox, as the "real but abstract incorporeality of the body is the virtual" (Massumi 2002, 5–8).

The virtual body's presence is there for us to experience, but it is too abstract to determine. In VR, we are neither fully in the physical world, as the face is wrapped in an HMD and our senses are tricked into adapting to another dimension, nor we are fully immersed in a virtual world. Concerning the environment of new technology, Waldenfels states that the nonsituatedness of the lived body in "here in reality" will certainly bring a derealization effect, which will diminish the totality of the body and reduce it to just an observable and registerable feeling of "being there" (Waldenfels 2000, 231). He further elaborates on Lucien Sfez's (1990, 412) warning of modern media's "reality generating derealization (déréalisation réalisatrice)" effect. Reality is perceived as hyperreal, and the lived body is limited in its movement, as it does not move like a real body. Even more dismissively, Paul Virilio (1996, 66) indicates that techno-logically governed environments reproduce conditioned minds and alienated bodies that are deprived of self-motion.

Although absolutist views that are derived from techno-skepticism are not fundamentally constructive for the main motivation of my research (nor is it useful to fully indulge in a techno-utopian view), it is necessary to consult such views in order to identify the main developments in media communication devices and their effects on human sensory modalities. The products of con-temporary technology are now requiring bodily interaction and demanding self-motion. Contrary to Virilio's comment on how environments governed by technology lead to "a reproduction of conditioned minds and alienated bodies which are deprived of self-motion," the mind and the body in virtual environ-ment are occupied with chasing self-referentiality, practicing self-narration, and redefining the borders of bodily being. As mind and body are substantially interconnected, a mind certainly cannot remain conditioned while exploring the borders of sense and sensibility.

Nevertheless, such a realization of interconnectivity together with a vig-ilant sense of self-narration can be frustrating since we lose our familiar stance of being a static observer.[27] We are no longer a passive spectator of the exposure. On top of tolerating the state of being both "here" and "there," and dealing with different degrees of derealization and depersonalization within this quasi-limbo, we are given the responsibility to interact with/within the exposed visuals. As Rötzer argues: "To find oneself in an interactive and im-mersive image also means to lose the distance and autonomy" (Rötzer 2000, 156). In a film theater we are exposed to preselected images, so we sit and absorb the visual and auditory input as spectators. As a receiver, we are not entirely passive, since our sensory spectrum is continuously active; this means we are not only spectators. But still we remain as a spectator, more than an ac-tor, as we do not become engaged in the happenings and convergence of events

---

27   See Jameson (1992, 76): "The liberation [...] from the older anomie of the centered sub-ject may also mean, not merely a liberation from anxiety, but a liberation from every other kind of feeling as well, since there is no longer a self present to do the feeling. This is not to say that the cultural products of the postmodern era are utterly devoid of feeling, but rather that such feelings—which it might be better and more accurate to call "intensities"—are now free-floating and impersonal, and tend to be dominated by a peculiar kind of euphoria."

throughout the visuals. In contrast, in an immersive image that requires inter-action, we are no longer only spectators; we are embodied spectators who have lost the secure distance that once brought us a sense of control and autonomy. Confidence is ripped from us because our new virtual body is incomplete, wrought with undefined assets and underdeveloped configurations, barely existing like a phantom sensation. Similar to the existential anxiety we expe-rience in reality, our virtual body is in its infant stage of facing this angst; only recently recognizing its own capacity, borders, strengths, and—even more-so—its inadequacies. While chasing a sense of freedom (through claiming autonomy of movement, sensuality, and spatiality) within this new platform, dizziness is a predicted price to pay in both a physical (motion sickness) and in psychological (depersonalization, derealization) sense. This is needed in order to understand and develop our reflexive relationship with the virtual body.[28] We might be able to stabilize the virtual body's existence, as we enhance its sensory spectrums and learn to evaluate many representations within this medium.

1.12 Subjective Vision and Productivity of the Observer

In VR, each individual is confronted with a new narrative. The traditional nar-ratives in films, videos, and different forms of visual story telling are replaced with a self-narrative. This is the untransferable quality of self-narration of vir-tual agency. In a broader sense, the narrative aspect of virtual agency can influ-ence (and be influenced by) a reconsideration of Marya Schechtman's theory of the narrative aspect of self. She claims, "... selves are inherently narrative enti-ties" (Schechtman 2011, 394). Shaun Gallagher further elaborates on narrative self as "a more or less coherent self (or self-image) constituted with a past and a future in the various stories that we and others tell about ourselves" (Gallagher 2000, 15). Parallel to this, there is a firm connection between self-narration and the sense of self in VR.

In "Is Perception Cinematic?," Mohan Matthen (2015, 461) discusses percep-tual experience from a cinematic perspective and raises the importance of the

---

28   This literal dizziness and the search for a sense of autonomy (freedom of movement) in VR resembles Kierkegaard's statement that "anxiety is dizziness of freedom" (Kier-kegaard 2004, 188).

dynamic aspects of perception. "The cinematic account of perception: perception of events consists of a series of 'snap shots' of the world, that is, is a series of perceptual states each of which has as its object an instantaneous state of the world. On the cinematic account, perception has tightly defined temporal boundaries." Similarly, Vittorio Gallese (2019) explains "the genesis of film immersion" as "the experience of immersion with moving images [that] can be decomposed into its bodily and neurobiological grounding elements: Better understanding of what the concepts referring to film aesthetics are made of." Gallese (2019) concludes that the cinematic experience does not just depend on concepts and propositions but relies on sensorimotor schemas, "which get the viewer literally in touch with the screen, shaping a multimodal form of simulation, which exploits all the potentialities of our brain-body system." In his work on embodied simulation, he underlines how movements and actions highly influence our identity and connection with the outside world. Cinematic experience brings an intensity with camera angles which enables a strong synchronization. "Of the various camera angles, steadicam is perceived to be the most natural" (Gallese and Guerra 2015, 23). The cinematic eye attempts to imitate the retina and the angles we gaze upon from the first-person perspective, and the experience of visual perception indeed resembles a shuffled cinematic experience, where we systematically and intentionally direct each and every moving image. Camera movements are a "persuasive surrogate for our subjective movement through an objective space" (Bordwell 1977, 23). For VR, we can re-articulate this by saying that subjective movement through subjective space can be implemented and designed according to the desired subjective movement. In VR, the subjective movement is even more central than in cinematic vision, as it is liberated from cinema's predefined images. In a virtual narration, the story continues as long as the users change their perspective, tilt their head, and turn around within the given virtual sphere. Within these instantaneous environments, there is not much room for nostalgia since we are bound to be present and alert as we narrate, influence, and direct. All of these contribute to a sense of grounded presence. However, Sobchack warns that such an investment in the senses could deprive us of our human body and that an "enworlded action" (meaning, to be rooted in a teleworld which destabilizes the body) could cost us all a future. "However significant and positive its values in some regards, the electronic trivializes the human body" (Sobchack 1994, 105).

In our physical reality, we already have the freedom of a self-guided perspective; it is the perceiver's choice to gaze upon a specific area with any speed of motion one desires. However, in our physical reality we do not have the capacity to instantly switch our gaze; we cannot change to a bird's eye view in the blink of an eye, nor we can instantly put a five-meter-distance in between us and the perceived object.[29] Within a virtual environment, it is possible to detour around the perceived object beyond our given capacity. Grosz (2014, 115) emphasizes: "It's not as if our body is a fixed thing. But it is a fixed perspective from which we see things." The fixed perspective is obviously due to the position of our eyes in the skull, as Massumi (2002, 60) states: "Movement-vision is sight turned proprioceptive, the eyes reabsorbed into the flesh through a black hole in the geometry of empirical space and a gash in bodily form." This fixated perspective can be transformed within virtual environments. The installation becomes an eye extension, providing a wide and multi-layered visual experience.

In *Techniques of the Observer, on Vision and Modernity in the Nineteenth Century*, Jonathan Crary (1992, 7) describes the significance of optical apparatuses (in his case the stereoscope and pre-cinematic devices) as the "sites of knowledge and power that operate directly on the body of the individual." He also emphasizes that these apparatuses fostered entirely new physiological knowledge in the nineteenth century. Crary's exploration of "subjective vision and productivity of the observer" focuses on the importance of experiments in visual representations, because they helped to uncover the intertwining nature of scientific and technological developments. Similar to Crary's (1992, 7) articulation of the "responsible subject as a productive observer," the interactive process in VR requires the subject to be operative, alert, perceptive, and adaptive, because of the fast and frequent changes in the virtual environment. These traits are not considered as add-on qualities for the observer, but as fundamental for virtual body ownership, virtual agency, story development, and task-based interaction. This applies even to non-interactive virtual exposure (e.g., watching VR journalism, panoramic view gaze, etc. ...).

---

29   "The virtual is a lived paradox where what are normally opposites coexist, coalesce, and connect; where what cannot be experienced cannot but be felt—albeit reduced and contained. For out of the pressing crowd an individual action or expression will emerge and be registered consciously ... Since the virtual is unlivable even as it happens, it can be thought of as a form of superlinear abstraction that does not obey the law of the excluded middle, that is organized differently but is inseparable from the concrete activity and expressivity of the body. The body is as immediately abstract as it is concrete; its activity and expressivity extend, as on their underside, into an incorporeal, yet perfectly real, dimension of pressing potential" (Massumi 2002, 30–31).

VR as a new optical apparatus can be seen as a modern example of tele-scopes and microscopes, in terms of how such devices brought physically in-accessible environments closer for observation (this is in line with Manovich's previously mentioned argument on how new technology allows us to represent reality in a new way and that each piece of new technology reforms a previous "new" realism). This may bring us to a point, even momentarily, to cast our gaze beyond finitude, as we uncover the hiddenness of perceived entities, in-cluding our own bodily self. What is considered as imperceptible can indeed be modified with the help of new technological instruments. The manipulability of these environments can allow us to bypass the boundaries of bodily exis-tence, and "the boundary must not be regarded as a limit to be transgressed so much as a boundary to be traversed" (Grosz 1994, 131). The expanding bound-aries we begin to reveal may provide new ways for the subject-body to recog-nize and experience itself also as an object-body—not with an intention to split subject and object but to witness how the body is an entity which contains both subjective and objective features. Through this observation, we may generate new considerations for the mind-body problem.

Mandrigin and Thompson (2015, 526–527) emphasize that the body-as-subject is an embodied and subjective perspective of perception while, at the same time, the body-as-object is perceived as one object among others. Although illusory body ownership (in case of OBE and similar setups) brings a recognition to this distinction of subject-body and object-body, they comment that "most discussions to date of own-body perception have been limited by a failure to make this distinction and apply it to the various clinical and ex-perimental findings" (Mandrigin and Thompson 2015, 526). The manipulated visual perspective in VR provides evidence that sensorimotor integration reveals the body as the subject and the "agent of perception."

> "In an OBE, one sees one's body as perceptually presented from the outside and as being in a location that does not coincide with the felt location of one's visual and vestibular awareness. In other words, one sees one's body at a place that does not coincide with the felt location of one's awareness as a bodily subject" (Mandrigan and Thompson 2015, 526).

1.13 VR as a Lacanian Mirror

Jacques Lacan's (1936) "mirror stage" is a useful framework for revisiting body image in an OBE setup. Lacan contributed an influential and creative reassessment of the psychoanalytical approach. Influenced by Sigmund Freud (and later on intensively questioning Freud's theories in a poststructuralist way, that is, by questioning Freudian privileging of the ego), Lacan explained that the tangled connections between language and unconscious are crucial, and that their interconnectedness remains central to the theoretical and practical problems which appear during the psychoanalytical process. Lacan's theory of psychoanalysis differs from Freud's, specifically on the issue of what Lacan calls the symbolic order (Lacan 1997). Freud asserts that the symbolic indications can be analyzed only in relation to repressed representations of symbols, while Lacan argues that representations can be analyzed regardless of their connection to the unconscious. Beyond this, while the Cartesian subject validates his/her existence through the cogito, the Lacanian subject "cannot conceive of the whole body until the entire entity is visualized—a primitive media interaction" (Hansen 2013, 85–86).

Lacan introduced his concept of the mirror stage in 1936, at the Fourteenth International Psychoanalytical Congress at Marienbad, and since then it has been considered as "one of the most influential contributions to clinical psychoanalysis since Freud" (Eyers 2012, 18). According to Lacan's theory, the mirror stage is a developmental stage of infants (from six to eighteen months) in which they recognize themselves as a separate being as they discover their self-image in a mirror (whether in an actual mirror or in the reflection of mirror-like surfaces). Laplanche and Pontalis draw attention to the relation between the mirror stage and the ego:

> "The establishment of the ego can be conceived of as the formation of a psychical unit paralleling the constitution of the bodily schema. One may further suppose that this unification is precipitated by the subject's acquisition of an image of himself founded on the model furnished by the other person—this image being the ego itself. Narcissism then appears as the amorous captivation of the subject by this image. Lacan has related this first moment in the ego's formation to that fundamentally narcissistic experience which he calls mirror stage" (Laplanche and Pontalis (1988, 256).

Mirror stage theory was initially proposed by psychologist Henri Wallon (1930). To construct his own account of a mirror stage, Lacan further reflected on the empirical findings of Wallon (Barzilai 1995, 50). [30] Tamisa van Pelt (2000) writes that the earliest discussions on the mirror stage appear in the 1938 *Encyclopédie française*, edited by Henri Wallon himself. [31] In this edition, "a discussion of the 'intrusion complex' illustrates the mirroring theme of recognition of the self out-side itself" (van Pelt 2000, 36). Toward the end of 1950s, Lacan suggested the mirror stage not only as an existing phase within the years of childhood, but as a permanent structure of subjectivity ('imaginary order') throughout one's adult life (Lacan 1960, 2006). On the division of his main construction, namely "the Imaginary," "the Symbolic," and "the Real," he stipulated: "I began with the Imaginary, I then had to chew on the story of the Symbolic [...] and I finished by putting out for you this famous Real" (Lacan 1960 2006, 49).

In terms of using media devices for further exploration of subjectivity and as a tool in the Lacanian mirror stage, we automatically arrive at Marshall McLuhan's (1994) establishment of media tools as extensions of the body and human senses. In the case of virtual exposure, and more specifically in OBE, we may speak about the enhancement of our sensory spectrum through the mirror image (as the system literally exemplifies an extended mirror imagery). McLuhan indicated that the Lacanian mirror is already a media tool, functions as "an extension of self, like a physical prosthesis" (McLuhan 1994, 123). As media devices stretch the visceral borders of bodily sensation, we may state that each advanced media device joins the circle of tools to be integrated in the Lacanian mirror stage. However, concerning intensive modulation, Marc Poster (2001, 16) warns that McLuhan focuses on the "'sensorium' of the receiving subject" and does not focus enough on the subject as an interpreting being. The medium is not merely a mirror, it also contains information. The receiver does not only absorb the mirror-quality of the medium through their sensory modality but also engages in informational flux and interprets it accordingly. Poster (2001, 17–18) states that this informational flux, beyond the "reshuffling of the sensoria," may result in a "destabilization of the subject."

---

30   These empirical findings, however, have been critically examined by Norman N. Holland (1998) in "The Trouble(s) With Lacan" and similarly, by Raymond Tallis (1988). Tallis notes (1988, 153): "If epistemological maturation and the formation of a world picture were dependent upon catching sight of oneself in a mirror, then the mirror stage theory would predict that congenitally blind individuals would lack selfhood and be unable to enter language, society or the world at large. There is no evidence whatsoever that this implausible consequence of the theory is born out in practice."

31   Henry Wallon's initial recognition of mirror stage was in 1930 but the related discussions and publications came toward the end of 1930s.

An overlapping meaning is produced when we position our body in front of a mirror or in front of a screen. The mirror reflects the skin, which covers and protects the more vulnerable parts of the body, one epidermic layer after another. One etymological analysis of the word "screen" is proposed by Fernando Ilharco (2015, 197) as "a word 'probably akin' (MW 1999) to the Sanskrit (1000 BC) words 'carman,' which meant 'skin,' and 'kränti,' which signifies 'he injures.' These meanings, possibly, are those from which the Middle Age words evolved. The Sanskrit origins suggest that the notions of protection, shield, barrier, separation, arose as metaphors of the concept of skin, possibly human or animal skin." When we think of the screen in this definition, it resembles a protective layer for the represented information, which forms the electric circuits and makes the information perceptible to the human eye. How could we then elaborate on the screen as the skin of transmitted information?

Similar to Poster's explanation about the medium's informational input beyond its sensory modulation, Lucas D. Introna et al. (2000, 310) highlight the distinction between the mirror effect and screen effect thus: "Mirrors reflect, screens present." At the same time, Lacan's mirror has an obvious element of self-image projection and the emotional connotations surrounding it. It is not a mere reflection as it presents and constitutes the Imaginary. In this sense, can we say that Lacan's mirror is also a screen? We tend to interpret information presented on the screen similar to how we interpret the body image in the mirror and associate that with certain emotional imprints.

Lucas D. Introna et al. (2000, 310) continue: "This means the kind of information displayed by these different objects have diverse origins. In the case of mirrors it is merely reflecting back what it receives. In presentation there operates a fundamental process of ordering." Mirrors show the existing image, while screens transmit representational content and establish relevancy between presented images, which eventually must be interpreted. This is the screen's timeless feature, regardless of the advancement of media technologies. Here we can remember Manovich's famous assertion (2001, 114–115): "A screen is still a screen...We still have not left the era of the screen." Regarding the representational quality of images, Introna (2000) reminds us of Wittgenstein's argument: "Words do not refer to something because we agreed it, rather they already have meaning because we share a form of life" (Wittgenstein 1958, 88). In this sense, screens present selected data which are pre conceptually organized and aim toward representing a form of life. Likewise, the perceived body image from mirrors already carries selected information which we have imprinted on it throughout the years.

Chapter 2. The Machine To Be Another (MTBA)

"Ambiguity in Lived-Body Experiences" was the first VR intervention in which I explored the body image and how an altered observation of this self-perception can lead to shifts in our understanding of it. "The Machine to be Another" (MTBA) is another virtual setup that I have extensively worked with. The software is developed by the "BeAnotherLab," a research group based in Barcelona. Their interdisciplinary approach in VR includes, as described in their official web page[1] "understanding, communicating and expanding subjective experience, as well as exploring the relationship between identity and empathy from an embodied perspective." The MTBA system provides two participants with the visual experience of exchanging first-person perspectives, meaning, each both companies see the other's body image when they look at their own body. Each person wears headphones, and the auditive narration includes brief instructions about how to move and where to focus (e.g. "keep your movements slow, and look at a specific limb, such as the hands or the feet"). These instructions are played for both participants synchronously, so that they can align and pace their movements. In between these short instructions, there is a soothing, white-noise in the background, in order to diminish the external sounds in the room and heighten their concentration on the audio and on one another.

While my OBE experiment involved observing one's own body image, MTBA brought in an exploration of the body schema, in addition to the body image exploration. The MTBA facilitates an interaction where one can experience the malleable nature of one's body schema, and to see how the borders of the body can extend when visual and tactile sensory modalities are manipulated. Sensory modalities of the body are perpetually embedded together and they smoothly coexist (in this specific case, visual and tactile modalities

---

1   https://www.beanotherlab.org

are manipulated for elevating the feeling of embodiment), therefore a technologically designed multi-sensory integration reveals the plasticity of our senses. Another main motivation of the body swap setup was to facilitate the development of empathy and suggest the model as "a theme for discussion and behavioral changes related to issues such as racism, altruism, inclusion and anorexia, among others" (Bertnard 2016, 4).

2.1 "Ich bin du, du bist ich": A Workshop Series With MTBA

Between the years 2016–2018, we, as the collective "autoscopie,"[2] ran the MTBA with over 30 people in different body swap workshops with the title "Ich bin du, du bist ich"[3] (see figure 5). This gave us the chance to closely observe the effects of such an embodiment exercise. Some of the participants were from a housing project for unaccompanied refugee minors, called "Neues Wohnen im Kiez GmbH" in Berlin. We have welcome the minors in groups. Throughout their stay in Germany, they became close friends with each other after sharing the same household and spending a significant amount of time together.

---

2   "autoscopie" is a VR research group founded by Filiz Avunduk and Zeynep Akbal 2015 in Berlin. The focus of our research lies on alteration of mind states through the use of emerging virtual reality and HCI devices. We conceptualize and realize installations and devise hands-on workshops to gather qualitative data with an artistic and philosophical approach for our individual research purposes. We work on topics like the body, notions of virtual time and space, virtual body swapping, self-perception in virtual worlds and dreams as a biological form of VR.

3   The project "Ich bin du, du bist ich" was supported by "Bundesministerium für Bildung und Forschung Berlin" (2015–2017), under the "Kultur Macht Stark" collective, with the aim of providing different contexts of cultural and social integration for minorities. The focus of the workshop was to bring young adults (14–18 years old) from different ethnicities together and enable them to swap bodies in MTBA. How would a white euroasian person would feel when they themselves as a black person or as someone from the middle east? Would such visual replacement of physical attributes influence the way we see each other? Could such awareness lead to have less prejudice towards each other and eventually pave new ways to communicate with a more delicate attitude? Prioritizing the aim of creating a playful and fun environment, together with the participants we have tackled such questions.

Figure 5: Flyer image for the workshop series "ich bin du, du bist ich,"
2015

Ich bin Du, Du bist Ich:
Eine Virtuelle Realitätserfahrung

Hast du dich jemals als eine andere Person gesehen? Wir meinen es wörtlich!
In unserem Virtual Reality Workshop können Teilnehmer_Innen die Körperlichkeit
des Anderen und das Phänomenen empathischen Verbundenseins erleben.
Alter 13 bis 18 Jahre. Keine Anmeldung notwendig, einfach vorbeikommen!

Apartment Project

Kultur
macht STARK
Bündnisse für Bildung

MeinLand
Zeit für Zukunft

tgd

30.10. & 1.-3.11.
15:00-19:00
13:00-19:00

0160 2070913
Schloßstraße 19, 14059 Berlin
Computerraum @ Schloss19 Jugendclub

I am You, You are Me:
A Virtual Reality Experience

Have you ever seen yourself through the eyes of another? Literally!
In our Virtual Reality workshop participants can experience the feeling of
being in another's body and explore the notion of empathy.
Ages 13 to 18. No prior registration necessary. Just come by!

Within the following weeks after their VR experience, these minors who have paired up in the MTBA setup, have reported that they started to negotiate in a less verbal way with the person they swapped bodies with. Instead, they adopted a more hand gesture based interaction, increased eye contact before simultaneous decisions and they realized that they started to walk together in a similar pace. This could be interpreted as embodiment exercises in VR could perhaps influence our habitual ways of socializing. Moreover, such experience can be considered as another phenomenological exercise, and as a way to understand the connection between mirror neurons and intentionality. As Lawrence Barsalou (2008, 623) formulates "mirror neurons... respond strongest to the goal of the action, not to the action itself. Thus, mirror circuits help perceivers infer an actor's intentions, not simply recognize the action performed." In the MTBA setup, it was central that both people recognized the intention of one another in order to execute a synchronous movement. Here with the usage of MTBA, I suggest, the ability to read the bodily intentions of the other may be exercised in depth and from such alteration of communication models I mentioned above, we may gain a more grounded (and more comprehensible) understanding of how the mirror neurons operate.

The developer Philippe Bertnard (2018) explains: "MTBA has been broadly presented in over 25 countries in artistic, cultural, and academic contexts, and is used as a tool to promote mutual understanding." In addition to the standard MTBA protocols (flow task, synchronous-asynchronous stroking on the face and hands of the participants by the assistants), in "Ich bin du, du bist ich" series we have developed exercises to stimulate other senses. One example was to tackle the sense of taste by representing a cocktail tomato and a grape to the participants, as the texture and shape of a tomato and a grape are very similar, but they have totally different tastes. To make it more clear: If Person A and Person B were swapping bodies, Person A was given a grape, and Person B was given a tomato. Person A sees a tomato in her hand (because Person B's camera shows her a tomato in hand) and the tomato feels real because of the bouncy texture of the grape she is actually holding. As we tell Person A to eat it, she is disturbed by the unexpected taste of a grape. In this case, there appears to be conflicting sensory information: a visual signal (seeing a tomato) and the taste signal (tasting a grape). The majority of the participants have reported to have a jolted sense of irritation because of this mismatch. One person experienced a taste suppression, claiming to have eaten a grape, even though he had eaten a tomato.[4] Such perception altering exercises aimed to increase the sense of embodiment in the other by stimulating different sensory modalities of the body.

---

4   This example can be explored alongside the "Colavita visual dominance effect," (Posner, et al. 1976, 157–171) which states that the vision is the most dominant sensory modality for human beings.

2.2 Technical Details and Setup (2015's Body Swap)

The setup included following hardware; a VR HMD, namely an Oculus Rift DK2, two motion capture cameras (monoscopic) and a pair of stereo headphones. We used the MTBA software and we closely followed the protocol which was initially developed by BeAnotherLab.[5] MTBA is a virtual setup, in which 2 VR HMDs are cross-connected to individual stereo-cameras, and attached on the headsets. As can be seen in figure 6 below, the 'green person' sees his hands as yellow, and the 'yellow person' sees the hands of the green person as hers. This cross connection enables each person to see themselves in the body of the other.

The users are asked to move slowly and in some cases, are given a certain choreography to enhance a more synchronized movement, which usually raises the possibility of embodiment in VR setups. Following the body-swap moments, when the curtain between both users lifts, a confrontation, similar to the experience of a confrontation with the doppelgänger occurs. The participants see their own body in the other (see figure 7).

---

5   "MTBA software was built using the OpenFrameworks (OFx) version 0.7.4. The OFx software received the orientation data to be sent via OSC (Open Sound Control) messages to a software built on PD extended for controlling the servo motors using an Arduino UNO electronic platform. Both were run in the same computer using Windows 8.1. The system is built to send the orientation input from the HMD worn by the user to the servomotor controlled camera worn by the performer; it also displays the image of that camera in the HMD. The software allows for a digital zoom of the camera input as well as its rotation. It runs the camera at 60fps and has a digital dimmer to turn on and off the video shown on the HMD. As the camera is monoscopic, the software replicates the image in each of the lenses of the HMD. The OFx software is also able to trigger audio files containing instructions and personal narratives of the performers by pressing the computer number keys" (Oliveira et. al, 2016).

Figure 6: Sketch for MTBA structure

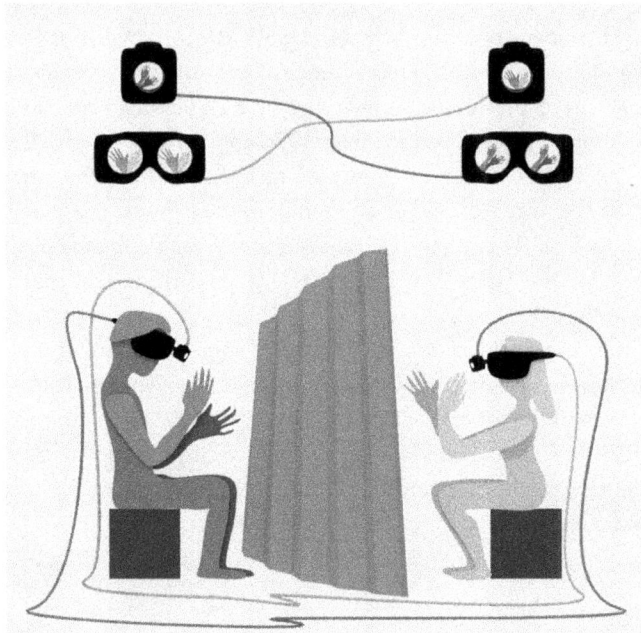

Figure 7: Body swap moment during the workshop series "ich bin du, du bist ich"

2.3 Conclusions from MTBA and Further Insights

In addition to the earlier body swap setups, it is recognized that the head-body agency in the MTBA had brought a high impact on the virtual immersion and the sense of presence. While seeing another person's body as their own, the participants were still in control of their own body (head and bodily agency), unlike the one in the remote-controller based (e.g. joysticks) computer simulations. The challenge is to preserve the autonomy of movement, but also to align the movement of the encounter. This configuration has made it clear how fundamental synchronicity and the mutual recognition of bodily movements are, if we want to achieve a more fluent feeling of embodiment.

Although the standard model of the body swap setup requires a performer/avatar to imitate the participant's movements, in the several sessions we conducted, both parties were free to move the way they desired. In this way, without a leader-follower pattern, a mutual and natural choreography of movement was established without a prior agreement. Although this improvisational and leaderless version of synchronous body swap took a longer time for the users to reach, once the flow of the movement was established, a more persistent and motivated embodiment was observed. During one experience, two friends between the ages of 13–14 swapped bodies in MTBA. A couple of days after the embodiment experience, one of them explained that during the times they spent together, he spoke less and felt more in sync with his playmate. The silence they experienced together did not lead to an awkward feeling, on the contrary, he felt more comfortable and less likely to explain himself during the course of play. He said they started to negotiate in a more instinctual way, through bodily gestures, which could be considered as an effect of this embodiment experience. Hayles (1999, 204) indicates: "bodily practices have this power because they sediment into habitual actions and movements, sinking below conscious awareness [...] Verbal aspects of communication are actually a result of sensory responses, motor control, and proprioception." Only, in MTBA these bodily modalities (motor control, proprioception) were observed and practiced without having the verbal aspect. As an end result, the sense of embodiment, without having a verbal communication, was established. The felt embodiment can be strengthened due to the liberation from the potentially intimidating misunderstandings of verbal negotiations. Hayles adds, "Because these ceremonies [bodily practices] are embodied practices, to perform them is always in some sense to accept them, whatever one's conscious beliefs" (Hayles 1999, 204).

Bertnard and co-experimenters (2016) have reported on the significant expressions participants gave after the body swap experiences, e.g. "It felt confusing to be me and, at the same time not to be me!", "Wow, who is me right now?!", "I'm shaking hands with myself!" In 30 body swap sessions we have conducted, I have repeatedly heard similar expressions, specifically as the users proceed to shake hands and hug their own body. Another participant, at the age of 17, wanted to try the MTBA with his mother. This was an unusual coupling, since none of the participants I had worked with before had any familial connection. A mother and a child's connection is symbiotic, since the child was once already in the mother's body. Observing the correspondence of a mother and her child in a VR setup was an emotionally overwhelming experience (for them and for myself) and exceeded my expectations of the workshop.

These observations support the arguments of Harrison J. Smith and Michael Neff (2018) in their research *Communication Behavior in Embodied Virtual Reality*, highlighting media impact on both verbal and non-verbal communication. They suggest that embodied VR will lead to a significant shift in social presence to something "that [is] very similar to face-to-face interaction" (Smith et. al 2018, 6). During an interview which was broadcasted in EL PAIS TV (GloboNews, 2018), Bertnard further commented on his MTBA experiences with people, underlined the potential use of MTBA as an exercise for social interaction and added that further studies have to look into developing more effective protocols to achieve a better usage. On the challenge of embodiment and social interaction in VR, Xueni Pan & Antonia Hamilton (2018) emphasize the importance of visual recognition of the body. When the users put on the HMD, they lose sight of their own physical body and although the sense of body ownership is constructed with "visual-proprioception synchrony (i.e., the virtual body or body parts are where you expect your body to be), visual-motor synchrony (as you move your body, the virtual body moves the same way), or visual-tactile synchrony (as you experience touch on part of your body, you see the same virtual body parts being touched at the same time)" Pan & Hamilton (2018, 395). Yet, a realistic experience of body ownership in VR remains to be a widely accepted problem across different disciplines. Pan & Hamilton (2018) further suggest that increasing the quality of motion capture and integrating innovative software could lead to progressive solutions.

One other positive aspect of the MTBA is that users are not exposed to the disruptions posed by the uncanny valley effect. The notion of the "uncanny valley" was first identified by robotics expert Masahiro Mori (2012) in the 1970s. Derived from Freud's (1919) "The Uncanny" (Das Unheimliche), the uncanny

valley effect "is a negative emotional response experienced when encountering entities that appear almost human" (Lay et. al, 2016). Ayse P. Saygin and her
coauthors (2012) suggest that such uncanniness might arise from perceiving
a photorealistic human-like figure moving in an unnatural and faltered way.
Such image becomes more agitating, more uncanny in comparison to a car-
toon imagery of a character. In other words, if the perceived virtual character has human-like features with a non-human-like representation of movement, the possibility of uncanny valley effect increases. With the use of real
time video capture instead of computer generated imagery, the MTBA experience bypasses the possibilities of being distracted by the uncanny valley.

Although the MTBA setup is a highly innovative and inspiring configuration to work with for myself and the younger generation of researchers, the
history of virtual body-swap research goes back to the early 1990s. In a sense,
what we have considered as a "new technology" is not actually that new. Researchers from a variety of fields have already been experimenting with and
debating the effects of VR in perception altering experiences. In the next sections, I will provide an overview of the first virtual body-swap attempts, compare the technical details of an earlier setup (Ehrrson, in late 1990s) to a new
setup (MTBA in 2015). Furthermore, I will debate how the MTBA can enable
a new discourse on the role of mirror neurons in empathy, and how media
technology provides an opportunity for extended multi-sensory integration,
therefore providing an in-depth exploration of human cognition. Can technologically governed setups help us to reconsider these established theories of
perception? Can we use VR to translate all these considerations? Or is the gap
between what we consider possible and what is really possible still too big? As
Lanier (2017, 50) puts it, "...human cognition is in motion and will generally out-
race progress in VR." I suggest that the attempt should not be about outracing
human cognition; but rather to evaluate our own perceptual capacity along the
way.

2.4 Empirical Methods for Measuring Presence in VR

In order to quantify the bodily responses of VR users for increasing the feeling
of immersion in the future, researchers measured or at least clustered certain
psychophysiological data. Such measurements can contribute to broadening the sensory spectrum of the virtual body. These measurements can be
classified as objective and subjective. Subjective measurements consider

behavioral methods, such as questionnaires. These are used to identify observable changes in the user when they experience their body in VR. Objective measurements quantify the sense of presence by measuring certain bodily responses when exposed to a VR environment. Some objective measurements include heart rate, SCR (skin conductance response), blood pressure, muscle tension. Additionally, neural correlates are measured using different neuroimaging technics such as fMRI, EEG, NIRS.[6] Such neuro-technologies can be fundamental for the development of media technologies in long term, as they provide physiological data which later on can be interpreted and appropriately implemented in the software/hardware development.

Rötzer (2000,163) reflects on how neuroscientific progress can influence the development of virtual technologies, "When neurotechnology reach its maturity, it may even be possible to stimulate the brain in a very specific way, triggering certain effects, sensations or perceptions."[7] Now, 20 years after his prediction, there has been a large progress in brain research which has been steadily influencing not only virtual technologies, but also biotechnological developments and beyond.[8]

2.5 Body Swap and Body Ownership in VR

In their pilot experiment, Bertnard et. al (2016, 2) describe their design as "[...] a low budget system that reproduces a person's head movements as if one's own head were in another body viewed through a head mounted display (HMD) while having body agency, i.e., controlling the movements of another real body as if it was a 'real avatar'." Both the user and the real avatar experience synchronous and asynchronous touch on their hands or faces (see figure 8). The most central element to this experience is the speed of movement, which needs to remain slow. "The activation of motor or visual areas during mental motor or visual imagery, qualify as forms of embodied simulation, likely defining the experiential backbone of what we perceive" (Gallese, 2019). In this sense, the

---

6   fMRI: Functional Magnetic Resonance Imaging, EEG: Electroencephalogram, NIRS: Near infrared spectroscopy.

7   I translated it from "Wenn Neurotechnologien ausgereift sind, wird es vielleicht sogar möglich werden, das Gehirn ganz spezifisch zu stimulieren und so bestimmte Wirkungen, Empfindungen oder Wahrnehmungen auszulösen" (Rötzer 2000, 163).

8   For similar notions which were emphasized earlier, see Stanislaw Lem's Summa technologiae (1964) and Robert Nozick's Anarchy, State, and Utopia (1974).

MTBA can be suggested as a method to practice embodied simulation, and provide an opportunity for users to corporeally engage in altering their motor and visual attributes.

Figure 8: Synchrnous touch during MTBA

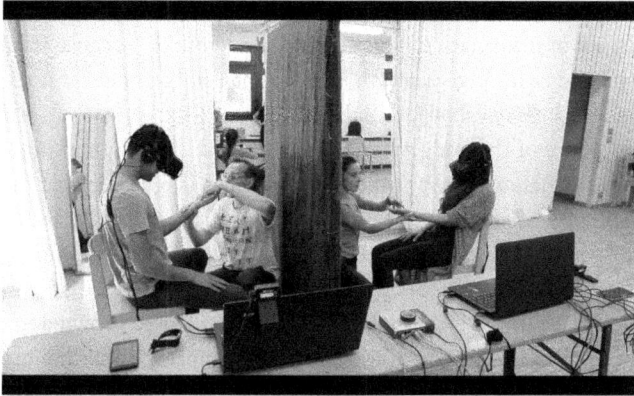

The MTBA provides a more realistic embodiment exercise, since it combines "real time video capture instead of computer generated images and enables the user see it in virtual reality." Bertnard et al. (2018, 5) continues, "Combining physical interactions to stimulate touch, swapping perspectives (under visuomotor and visuo-tactile synchronicity), body-swap is used to present real narratives from different individuals acting as performers."

2.5.1 The First Body-Swap Attempts

Although the MTBA is a low-budget immersive technology design, it has created a significant effect while revisiting the embodiment practices and experiments that go back to the early 1900s. Petkova and Ehrrson (2008) pioneered the body swap experiment after a series of attempts with both an artificial body (a mannequin) and later with an actual human body. They have reported (2008, 6) that the "manipulation of the visual perspective, in combination with the receipt of correlated multi-sensory information from the body was sufficient to trigger the illusion that another person's body or an artificial body was one's own." Similarly Mel Slater et al. (2010) have focused on the body transfer illusion in VR, as well as Lenggenhager et al. (2007). However these first swap attempts lacked head movement and the possibility for gestures. These initial setups have been adopted by cognitive scientists to bring more awareness to the idea that the cognition is not merely a process in the brain; bodily existence and the perceptual field of the body has a dynamic impact in cognitive processing. In *How We Became Posthuman: Virtual Bodies in Cybernetics*, Hayles (1999) tackles how information lost its body as a result of an seeing the human being as a set of informational processes. She remarks "Because information had lost its body, this construction implied that embodiment is not essential to human being" (Hayles 1999, 4).

The presence of the body was not only ignored in the humanities, but has been underestimated in many other disciplines. Gallagher notes that "[t]o the extent that some cognitive scientists persist in approaches that refuse to recognize the complications introduced by the various roles of the human body in cognition, they run the risk of creating abstract and disembodied paradigms" (Gallagher 1995, 240). Since the late 1990s, alteration of body ownership within the realm of virtual experimentation started to rapidly underline the importance of embodied paradigms in cognitive exploration.

These early experiments had already demonstrated that exchanging first-person perspectives could provide evidence for future VR applications, extending in-depth research not only for the fields of cognitive science and neuro-prosthetics, but also for different media theories that focus on embodiment theory. Metzinger (2018, 5) emphasizes "We are already beginning to use VR technology for re-embodiment in other human bodies and many of the more recent empirical results are highly interesting from a conceptual and metatheoretical perspective." He further underlines that in order to develop a more accurate analysis of body awareness, following researchers should prioritize to distinguish different levels of embodiment and carve a deeper understanding for the subjects to locate and identify their body in time and space.

2.5.2 Technical Details of 2000's Body Swap

Before introducing the significant theories related to the MTBA set up, it is important to revisit the practical aspects of the original body swap from Petkova and Ehrsson (2008). They developed a body swap between a human body and life-sized mannequin with the intention to bring forth the illusion of full-body ownership. A substitute for today's HMD was a specially designed helmet with a CCTV camera mounted in it to enable the viewpoint of the experimenter

(Petkova & Ehrsson, 2008). This very first attempt of a body-swap illusion was conducted with the following setup:

"Two CCTV cameras (Protos IV, Vista, Wokingham, Berkshire, UK) were positioned on a male mannequin such that each recorded events from the position corresponding to one of the mannequin's eyes. A set of head mounted displays (HMD: Cybermind Visette Pro PAL, Cybermind Inter-active, Maastricht, the Netherlands; Display Resolution=640×480; true stereoscopic vision) connected to the cameras was worn by the partici-pants, and connected in such a way that the images from the left and right video cameras were presented on the left and right eye displays, respectively, providing a true stereoscopic image. Participants were asked to tilt their heads downwards as if looking down at their bodies. Thus, the participants saw the mannequin's body where they expected to see their own" (Petkova & Ehrrson, 2008).

After participants look down at the mannequin's body, experimenters repeat-edly stroke the abdomen of the participant in sync with the mannequin's ab-domen, and this is observed by the participant in the HMD. After establish-ing this tactile stimulation and link with the mannequin's body, they intro-duce a threat by attacking the mannequin's abdomen with a knife, resulting, in most of the cases, a reflex defense of the participant. The reflex was backing away from a non-existent physical attack towards his/her own body. To gather physiological evidence for owning a body ownership illusion, the threat motive was initially introduced by Matthew Botvinick and Jonathan Cohen (1998) with visual-tactile synchrony in their famous 'Rubber Hand Illusion' (RHI) experi-ment. They used a prosthetic rubber hand to induce a feeling of body owner-ship by combining the visual stimulation with synchronous tactile stimulation on the participant's own hand.

In both cases of the RHI and Ehrrson's stabbed mannequin, threat effect demonstrates "the experience of body ownership is bound to the brain's ability to receive and regulate the signals from different senses in a probabilistic man-ner" (Limanovski & Blankenburg, 2013). The purpose of implementing such a threat pattern in body-swap is mainly to enhance a more clear sensation of body ownership, and to observe whether the user has embodied an external en-tity as his/her own. Following a body-swap attempt with a mannequin's body, the next step was for the experimenter to swap bodies with a participant.

2.6 Spinoza and Bodies in Motion

During the "Open-Self Conference" in 2018, Pawel Tacikowski, a researcher from Ehrsson's group, reflected on their body-swap experiment: "Merging of self-concept and friend-concept during illusory ownership of friend's body: Updating of beliefs during illusory ownership of friend's body." He raised the question "Does the bodily self update multiple beliefs that constitute the conscious self-concept, and if so, what cognitive mechanisms underlie this updating?" He emphasized that there is an underlying relationship between cognitive functions and a sense of bodily self. By manipulating the visual and tactile sensory modalities during a body-swap in VR, it could be possible to enhance the sense of self, in addition to the sense of body-ownership. He emphasized, "Unity and coherence are the main principles of the human self, that are important for the normal cognitive functioning." Experiencing conflicting (asynchronous) tactile and visual sensory feedback during a body-swap with a friend, influences one's sense of bodily self. This conflict brings a causal update of self-concept. Tacikowski (2018) indicated further, "Own body perception dynamically shapes multiple conscious beliefs about oneself and this shaping is related to resolution of a conceptual conflict." Update of bodily self through sensory conflict requires an encounter, as it is in the case of any communication device, there has to be a sender and a receiver.

When we dig the literature on sensing the body on motion, we can see Spinoza's approach to the importance of this sensory conflict and its effect on the bodily self. In *The Conatus of the Body in Spinoza's Physics*, Sean Winkler (2016, 95) looks into Spinoza's theory of the individuation of bodies. Winkler underlines that in Part 3 of *Ethics*, Spinoza describes the "conatus" (striving) of the mind as 'will' and of the mind and body together as apetite/desire, but he [Spinoza] does not identify the conatus of the body. Winkler points out that this omission is interesting since Spinoza (2002, 253) identifies the body as "an unvarying relation movement" and this identification seems to be in line with his law of motion in Part 2 of Ethics where he states "A body in motion will continue to move until it is determined to rest by another body, and a body at rest continues to be at rest until it is determined to move by another body" (Spinoza 2002, 253).

Spinoza explains that when a body interacts and clashes with another body, the vitality either increases or decreases.[9] Concerning the exploration of mutual constitution of bodies and the affective process within this clash, Robert Seyfert adopts Spinoza's understanding of the body and agrees

> "to conceptualize the receptivity and mutual constitution of bodies, to show how affects do not 'belong' to anybody; they are not solely attributable either to the human or to any kind of body alone, but emerge in situations of the encounter and interaction (between bodies)" (Seyfert 2012, 27).

We understand and sense that these affects do not belong to anybody else, especially when we can explore this in a reflexive attitude. What would be Spinoza's take on the term "autoaffection"? Would he say, "auto" is constituted of several smaller bodies, and these bodies affect each other continuously, which contributes in the feeling of autoaffection?

It is shared among human and non-human bodies, and it proliferates during the correspondence. The nature of the contact depends on the related positions of these two bodies (which signifies the perspectival givenness) and also the speed of movement of these constituent bodies. As Spinoza (2002, 286) states: "Bodies move, whether with the same degree or different degrees of speed so as to communicate their motions to each other in a certain fixed proportion." The significance of this perspectival givenness and the importance of speed while moving, remain central to the MTBA experience; it aims for an optimal synchronicity, for a better feeling of embodiment. In the MTBA set up, the users depend on each other for the experience of affect. Could we explore the notion of "embodiment" from Spinoza's understanding of the 'moving body'? If the body's motor capacity, spatiality and motility as necessary conditions for an affective coexistence, can technological practices assist us further to reconceptualize and internalize this affect?

---

9   In her book Vibrant Matter, Jane Bennett (2010) envelopes this Spinozist clash of bodies with Deleuze & Guattari's (1987) "assemblage" to explain her idea of "non-human agency." When bodies clash, they may unite and reform a larger form of existence, as in Deleuze/Guattari's (1987) corporate body. This larger form can include all material and non-material agencies.

2.7 Gender Swap in VR

The central motivation of the MTBA setup was to bring the users the experience of a gender-swap. In the original gender-swap, users swapped their bodies without their clothes on. It was considered an ideal case for both users to clearly perceive and visually embrace the sexual organs and body parts that they do not possess.

During a gender-swap in VR, in addition to the general idea of embodiment, the users are asked to explore the corporeal sensations of their non-existing/counter sexual organs. The setup aims a visual simulation of sexual organs and consequently deliver a momentary perception of carrying the 'other' gender, as explained by Bertnard (2016, 4), "the brain integrates different senses to create your experience of the world. In turn, the information from each of these senses influences how the other senses are processed." BeAnotherLab's intention was to investigate the notions of gender identity, queer theory and feminist techno-science. This practical installation can be considered as an abolition of binary categorizations by visual manipulation, an exercise format for raising the momentary sensation of owning-disowning, and leaving-returning to the biological givenness of one's own body. Having an encounter is a significant detail in this play, as it brings a multitude of new meanings to the transformative power, as Grosz (2001, 69) underlines, "An encounter between bodies, which releases something from each and, in the process, makes a real virtuality, a series of enabling and transforming possibilities."

Such practical exercise of a gender-swap in VR lays an appropriate and literal ground for the users to explore the "neighborhood sex" Grosz (1998, 43) writes about. In the introduction of *Places Through the Body*, Heidi J. Nast and Steve Pile reflect on Grosz's approach to the "neighboring sex" as a better substitute for the rigidness of the "opposite sex." Nast & Pile (1998, 4) comment further that Grosz wishes to argue that the medical science's need for a clean cut between the genders might have enabled a better treatment of diseases specific to women, but it also generated a distinct opposition between men and women. This opposition has perpetuated a solid understanding of men and women are mutually exclusive, at all times. Yet, men and women have more in common with each other than with any other "thing." There can be an alternative understanding of embodied difference. This can start with adopting a perception of a conurbation of sexes, rather than seeing two sexes opposing each other.

I interpret Grosz's idea of "neighborhood sex" as a suggestion to rethink about the ontology of entangled bodies and reemphasize their coexistence. This attitude also can be explored in the grounds of new technology. Braidotti's indication of how technology holds a powerful hand when we speak of entangled bodies, as it unites "monsters, insects and machines into a powerfully post-human approach to what we used to call the body. To say that identity, sexuality and the body are transformed by this is at best an understatement" (Braidotti 2012, 214). This neighborhood and unification call back Spinoza's idea of "bodies in motion," but additionally, theorists like Grosz and Braidotti challenge the rigidity of binary gender identity by highlighting the gender fluidity. Computer mediated technology amplifies gender differences but also provides a myriad of opportunities to allow users to explore beyond the expected parodies and banalities of sexual adventures. Hayles (1999, xii) asks, "What do gendered bodies have to do with the erasure of embodiment and the subsequent merging of machine and human intelligence in the figure of the cyborg?"

In *Is that your Boyfriend? An Experiential and Theoretical Approach to Understanding Gender-Bending in Virtual Worlds*, Ferdinand Francino and Jane Guiller (2011) explore the theoretical and the psychological concepts of gendered selves, and how these selves manifest certain differences between online and real-life identities. Francino & Guiller specifically examined gender-bending experiences in virtual worlds by using opposite/trans/gendered avatars in cyber worlds (i.e. Second Life). Their approach can also be traced in Sherry Turkle's (2011) *Life on the Screen: Identity in the Age of the Internet*, in which she underlines the technology's role in the process of reconstructing the sense of the self. Turkle (2011, 34) indicates that technology is a powerful tool for the self to be reconstructed in cyber worlds: identity is a malleable concept within cyberspace. Furthermore, Francino & Guiller (2011, 65) advise that avatar embodiment has a therapeutic effect for virtual players, and helps the user with getting rid of their daily stress. Although such cyber gender-swapping/gender-bending experience does not always align with the offline-self's choices, Francino & Guiller (2011, 65–66) highlight the importance of future work in gender-swapping activities in virtual worlds "as a vehicle about learning about the self and broader issues such as gender inequality stereotyping and bias in the offline world." They also recognize Mel Slater et al.'s research on *First Person Experience of Body Transfer in Virtual Reality*, in which they explore how a woman would feel in a man's body and how would a man think mediated through a virtual woman's body (Slater et al, 2010).

Although a body-swap installation brings the possibility of sharing bodies[10] and thus alters the visual recognition of the 'other body' problem in the embodiment process, it also highlights the 'other minds' problem, which is emphasized by Thomas Metzinger (2018). Regarding the issue of social VR and the role of body-swap in contributing the 'other minds' problem, he writes:

> "For computer scientists, the question arises of what the 'perfect' form of social VR would actually be. In social VR, what exactly is the relationship between the phenomenal content locally instantiated in the brains of multiple users and shared virtual content created by causal interact ions distributed over different machines and artificial media? Social VR is a field that needs a combination of new technological approaches and rigorous conceptual analysis, for instance with regard to the concept of tele-immersion" (Metzinger 2018, 5).

Together with the other-body problem in VR, the other-mind problem will have to be solved, especially in the domain of social VR. If we already reject a Cartesian thinking subject, philosophers and computer scientists will certainly have to cooperate to answer this problem with BCI-coupling (brain-computer interface). Only we, as subjects, have the access to our own mind (and to our own body, interoceptively). We, as communicators, rely on symbols, words and any other signifiers to transmit the data, but such transmission remains inadequate and leaves us in a cumulative dissatisfaction. Affect studies (which I will discuss further in the following chapter) have been investigating other means of relating and communicating (e.g. affection, attunement, atmospheric phenomena) before symbols and words are being encoded into these modes of transmission. Beyond the means of communication via words and symbols, if we can emerge in the mind of the other via BCI-coupling, how would we perceive the body of the other? "Could social VR create more direct forms of knowing another person's mind?" (Metzinger 2018, 5).

---

10   Pete Mandik comments on the inaccessibility of both the other minds and the other bodies as "I seem restricted to perceiving various physical bodies; I don't introspect or perceive any other mind" (Mandik, 2010, 8).

2.8 On the dangers of empathy

The MTBA has introduced body-swap to several disciplines as a broader investigation for improving empathy. On learning empathy through VR, Bertnard (2018, 3) explains, "Several disciplines have investigated the interconnected empathic abilities behind the proverb "to walk a mile in someone else's shoes" to determine how the presence, and absence, of empathy-related phenomena affect prosocial behavior and intergroup relations. Empathy enables us to learn from others' pain and to know when to offer support." Although one of the main forces of behind the MTBA is to enhance feelings of empathy by facilitating an exchange of bodily attributes, it is important to remain skeptical about promoting media technology for empathy enhancement, especially how the notion of 'empathy' is disturbingly blended in VR marketing strategies. Let's leave the technological aspect aside for a moment and evaluate the debates against enhancing empathy as a problem solving strategy. The discourse against empathy can, on the contrary, support the use of such technological setups in a more grounded attitude.

As neuro-imaging studies indicate, empathy is not localized in any special area of the brain. Empathy is now understood as a correlated activity, which spreads throughout several regions of the brain (Jankowiak and Siuda 2011, 56). This indicates that our feelings, emotions and actions are interlaced and they play their own roles during the process of empathy. Empathy calls for aid from many different areas of the brain in order to connect with the person who is in distress or in pleasure (with a yearning for a saintly recognition, it is common to define empathy as sharing the pain of others, but to empathize with someone's success or well-being in general can be considered a difficult, yet, a very rich form of empathy). This may come effortlessly since empathy is biologically engrained in us, strongly compounded by our survival instinct. But when we deliberately cultivate and bring a deep focus on developing empathy, we may embark on the morally ambiguous landscape of it. In *The Dark Sides of Empathy*, Fritz Breithaupt (2019, 17) writes that empathy can elevate polarization of emotions and increase dysfunctional coping mechanisms. This accounts for both the empathizer and the recipient of empathy, since both become preoccupied with the transference rather than the necessary objectivity they both need for analyzing the course of action. In this way, empathy can cause biased judgement that may cripple our strategies. We are interchangeably the empathizer and recipient throughout our lives, unless one is caught in what Breithaupt (2019, 18) calls "vampiristic empathy," which is a dangerous variant of empathy, that occurs when a person expands their own life experiences by over-identifying with another person's experiences. As a result of such aspects, empathic intention might distract both the empathizer's and the recipient's ability to practice conflict resolution.

In his controversial book *Against Empathy*, Paul Bloom (2017) categorizes empathy as "emotional empathy" and "cognitive empathy." The former signifies being occupied with someone else's emotional state and letting those feelings define one's own mood. The latter is related to social cognition; allowing the intellect to deal with the situation and not being carried away with the emotional turbulence. Bloom thinks that a "good moral life" (Bloom 2017, 239) initially depends on our ability to distinguish these empathy models and act upon the situation while maintaining both kindness and self-control.

Bloom's distinction between emotional empathy and cognitive empathy resembles Rafael A. Calvo's (2014, 35) categorization of "Empathy" and "Compassion." Calvo indicates that empathy mirrors the emotion of the other while compassion does not necessarily contain the same emotion. Compassion has a more outward approach, therefore generating a more solution-oriented behavior, while empathy has a more inward focus ("I'm feeling the pain of the other," indicating how 'I' feel the pain, rather than suggesting a functional strategy to deal with the core problem of the other).

Calvo and Peters's (2014) fMRI research depicts that empathy is correlated with negative affect patterns in the brain, while compassion demonstrated positive affect patterns. Additional physiological measurements show that empathy causes significantly higher heart rate compared to compassion. Bloom's (2017) "cognitive empathy" and Calvo & Peters's (2014) "compassion" theories suggest that as long as we do not dwell on the emotions of others, both the empathizer and the recipient would benefit from the process of empathy. If understanding the pain of others would stress bodily resources and damage the psyche, then we can no longer talk about a beneficial cooperation in problem solving. This form of empathy seems to be more related to a self-sacrifice pattern. This kind of empathy directly relates to one's own guilty consciousness that could be in need of self-punishment. There are many other feelings surrounding this downward spiral, which has nothing to do with the recipient of empathy in front of us. We remain in a loop of emotional turbulence, with a predictable loss of quality in communication.

Calvo and Peters (2014, 3) elaborate on the influence of technology on empathy and compassion by investigating the notion of "positive computing."While acknowledging the potential pitfalls of developing technology geared towards increasing empathy, they carefully explain how the digital experience can actually help us to develop compassion and a wider understanding of being there for others. Calvo and Peters' approach is a refreshing one and carefully tailored against cultural-pessimism, but at the same time, not exactly rooted in techno-utopian grounds. Calvo's positive computing could be an elemental step towards solving the other-minds problem with BCI. In future, other-minds problem and conflict resolution with compassion can have an interlaced recognition.

If we return to the case of the MTBA, we may be more careful before calling it an "empathy machine." While seeing the MTBA as an empathy generating setup can start a fruitful discussion on the issues of racism, exclusion, and body dysmorphia, it is crucial to keep in mind that empathy is an asset that we, as conscious beings, already possess. Introducing the technological artifacts as the end-products of certain emotional assets could be risky, because in the future, we could be perceived as 'less human' without their assistance. This approach can result in a deeper cultural-pessimism, which may be dangerous for the further developmental phases of new technology. So rather than seeing new technology as a complementary system, we could see it as one other end product of evolution of human intelligence, which enables a reflexive understanding of ourselves. As Braidotti (2002, 257) expresses, "Technology has become a challenge, it is the chance we have given ourselves, as a culture, to reinvent ourselves and display some creativity. Technology should assist human evolution." In line with this approach, a simulation in VR is not supposed to represent a substitution of a human essential. But it may reveal unexpected standpoints and multiply the horizons of our inner and outer worlds.

Media installations stimulate visual and auditory neurons (among other sensory spectrum) and consequently engages the spectator on a visceral level. In the case of a VR exposure, this effect is stronger and therefore the engagement becomes more demanding and encapsulating. Computer scientist Lanier emphasizes: "VR is not about simulating reality, really, but about stimulating neural expectations" (Lanier 2017, 51). In a body-swap setup, these stimulated neural expectations are mirrored between two people within the course of shared movements, through a visual exchange of skin color and sexual organs.

There exists a large debate about the isolating and castrating effects of a long-term engagement with different forms of digital setups, whereby such digital engagements will rip the natural reciprocity from human interaction. Concerning the socially alienating effects of digital media exposure,

Turkle (2015, 10) reflects "Real people, with their unpredictable ways, can seem difficult to contend with after one has spent a stretch in simulation."

Turkle previously indicated that in virtual worlds we are invited "to give up the body" (Turkle 2009, 7), and that forgetting the body would eventually lead to a crippled understanding of social interaction. Similarly, Ken Hillis (1998, 60) reflects on the discourse of disembodied VR and writes that in virtual environments the physical distance between the subject and the object grows wider, and thus enhances a form of alienation in the material world. This alienation, he asserts, is a result of spending increasing amounts of time in all forms of cyberspace and losing the ability to maintain embodied social relations.

If we consider the 17 years of difference in between Hillis' (1998) and Turkle's (2015) critical stand points, we may understand Hillis' concern with the impossibility of subject-object relation and the gap between visually perceived images and our inability to interact with them. But between the 1990s and 2020, there has been a myriad of technological developments which have amplified the fact that the sense of presence and interactive process can only begin after simulating several different sensory modalities. For example, these implementations have been progressively aimed for a better sense of gestures and for a more fluid sense of motion, by developing proprioceptive and motoric outputs. None of these implementations are even close to the desired effect yet, but what really matters in this process is to develop a better understanding of the mind-brain-body cooperation. All of these efforts in technological developments contribute to the understanding of how mind, brain and the body are, in fact inseparable. Therefore, technological artifacts call for a cooperation across seemingly irrelevant disciplines and for a rejection of cartesian dualism. Turkle's warning about bodiless existence in VR stands exactly opposite to Lanier's take on how VR is about stimulating neural expectations. When we stimulate neural expectations, would not we automatically get to learn (anatomically) and feel (interoceptively and exteroceptively) more about our bodies? Aren't we actually recognizing and reorganizing our sensual abilities in VR, therefore studying our own perception in-depth? We do not recognize the existence of a muscle until we get into a posture or position which reactivates the sensation of this specific muscle. If there are approximately 640 skeletal muscles in the human body (Scott et al. 2001), it would be illogical to claim that we can feel each and every one of them without first putting ourselves into probing exercises. Similarly, the more we attempt to stretch the borders of our neural cognition with virtual illusions, the more we may discover beyond our defined cognitive abilities. Distancing from the empathy-enhancing potential of digital media, both

Turkle and Hillis refer to the absence of the 'real' in simulations. They indicate how such absence would create a sense of alienation, rather than a mirrored sense of cooperation with another self. In the case of a body-swap, it is about having a real body with a real self as our encounter, exchanging and adopting the 'real' givenness of the body on a virtual plane.

In her essay "Empathy in the Time of Technology: How Storytelling is the Key to Empathy," Patricia J. Manney (2008, 51) explores the "empathy-improving potential of trans-human technologies" by highlighting the attempt to integrate digital tools for the improvement of autism spectrum conditions. "It has also been observed that children with autism have abnormally low activation in the inferior frontal gyrus pars opercularis, which contains the mirror neuron system, while imitating and observing emotions. The lower the activation, the more the social impairment. Autism is a condition often associated with a reduced ability to empathize with others" (Manney 2008, 51). In line with this idea, the MTBA was also suggested as a model for imitation control and perspective taking tasks. Since people with autism spectrum disorder learn through imitation, it has been suggested that some of the MTBA tasks could improve role modeling and imitation skills. Another way to gain a better understanding of how media technologies may influence empathy development through neural stimulation is to explore mirror neurons.

2.8.1 Mirror Neurons and Subjectivity

The breakthrough identification of mirror neurons by Vittorio Gallese and Alvin Goldman (1998) enabled new debates about the nature of empathy, mainly on what influences and alters the process of empathic relations. Pierre Jacob (2009, 34) writes, "Mirror neurons fire both when a primate executes a transitive action directed toward a target (e.g., grasping) and when he/she observes the same action performed by another." Similarly, V. S. Ramachandran (2012, 123) underlines the importance of mirror neurons in empathy, "It's as if anytime you want to make a judgement about someone else's movements, you have to run a virtual-reality simulation of the corresponding movement in your own brain."

In *Mirror Neuron Research: the Past and the Future*, Pier Francesco Ferrari and Giacomo Rizzolatti (2014, 33) explain why the recognition of mirror neurons has enabled a wider reconsideration in cognitive disciplines. First of all, the discovery of mirror neurons has made "the problem of how we understand others" a priority in neuroscience. Second, since mirror neurons are motor neurons, they emphasized the deeply intertwined connection between the motor system and the process of understanding the other. Ferrari & Rizzolatti (2014) further reflect on this discovery, with a combination of insights from analytical philosophy and phenomenology. While both of these disciplines have a long history of rejecting one another's fundamental cornerstones, the discovery of mirror neurons validates the phenomenological reflection on the experience of empathy. Traditional analytical philosophy similarly formulates the other-minds problem:

> "An alternative view, put forward by phenomenologists, is that we understand others by comparing an action done by others with our own behavior in a similar situation. The discovery of mirror neurons did not disprove the conventional analytical view, but demonstrated the validity of the phenomenological stance, at least in most everyday life conditions" (Ferrari & Rizzolatti 2014, 2).

Cognitive neuroscience's validation of other phenomenological insights arose some sixty years later and these cumulative validations eventually introduced a new branch of scientific approach called neurophenomenology. Neurophenomenology was initially suggested by Varela (1996, 330) with an aim to blend phenomenological methods with the experimental work of cognitive neuroscience, in order to pave new ways to answer the so called "hard problem of consciousness." David Chalmers (1995, 200) proposed that the hard problem concerns the inexplicable relationship between physical attributes (e.g. brain processes) and the experience (e.g. qualia), while the easy problems of consciousness are "those that seem directly susceptible to the standard methods of cognitive science, whereby a phenomenon is explained in terms of computational or neural mechanisms. The hard problems are those that seem to resist those methods. The really hard problem of consciousness is the problem of experience" (Chalmers 1995, 200). Therefore, the subjective quality of the experience has become a core value, not only for understanding the hard problem of consciousness, but also for rephrasing the unexplored issues of human cognition in general. Empirical evidence remains insufficient in explaining the phenomena of consciousness, because each and every manifestation of consciousness has a unique and subjective pattern, as Bergson previously investigated under certain notions, such as the intensity of sensations and consciousness of time, in his work *Matter and Memory* (1884).

One other neuroscientific finding about the subjective experience is related to Bergsonian theories on memory,[11] more specifically, how he [Bergson] "anticipated the modern selectionist theories of memory" (McNamara 1996, 215). This comes as no surprise, as Bergson's philosophical understanding was largely influenced by scientific methodology with an ontological emphasis, and as a result, fundamentally evolved around mind and matter. Bergson clearly emphasized that subjective experience is a main component of perceptual experience, and tightly harnessed within mind and body.

These recognitions are mainly about the significance of subjective experience in perceptual processes and how the analytical approach remains insufficient for exploring inner experience.

2.9 Virtual and Cognitive Architecture of the Body

"Wherever the human body has a sensor, like an eye or an ear, a VR system must present a stimulus to that body part to create an illusory world. The eye needs visual display, for instance, and the ear needs an audio speaker. But unlike prior media devices, every component of VR must function in tight reflection of the motion of the human body" (Lanier 2017, 47).

As Lanier writes, there is an inescapable need to understand the cognitive nature of human manual skills, in order to trace new technological possibilities for an extending presence in VR, for developing the cognitive architecture of the virtual body, and immersing sensory perceptions to simulate a reality.

2.9.1 Multi-sensory Integration in Media Technology

The first attempt of multi-sensory integration in media technology was developed by Morton L. Heilig in 1962, a simulator he called "Sensorama." This simulator encapsulated the head of the observer, a structure he called a 'hood', in which a visual image projection was installed. In addition to the projection, the simulation included a breeze in the hood (with "at least one odor-sense stimulating substance"), binaural sound installation, and low vibrations to simulate movements and haptic sensations. He managed to stimulate four out of five

---

11   See Mark Hansen's *New Philosophy for New Media* (2006) for a detailed argument on Bergson's notion of "affection and memory render perception impure." Hansen filters Bergson's idea of subjective quality of image selection in terms of the digital age.

senses within one illusion. He argued that extensive virtual presence can only be realized by stimulating the nervous system with a wide range of sensory stimuli (Heilig 1962, 43). Within the following years, Heilig focused mostly on developing haptic feedback.

Empirical research on the bodily self has shown that the body representation is malleable (Blanke et al., 2017, 2) and prone to manipulation when conflicting sensory stimuli are presented. One of the most efficient ways to investigate this phenomenon further in a VR setting, as Heilig foresaw almost 50 years ago, is to bring haptic stimulation into the course of multi-sensory stimulation, since the sense of touch is fundamental element for the body in the space it occupies.

Haptic stimuli can be broadly classified into tactile and kinesthetic. A tactile stimulus is felt by our skin like temperature and vibrations, while a kinesthetic stimulus is the sense of force and position of our body parts (Jadhav et al., 2017, 2). The use of haptic feedback is fundamental for increasing the quality of the user-virtual object interaction. The results of an early experiment at the end of 1990s (Dinh, et al., 1999), which was conducted with a large number of participants (322 subjects), indicated that increasing the modalities of sensory input in a virtual environment can increase both the sense of presence and memory for objects in the environment.

A significant amount of neural processing related to haptic feedback is perceived from our hands, therefore the exploration of full-immersion through data gloves is important for overall immersion. Since the 1980s, developers increasingly focused on upgrading the power gloves and datagloves (Thomas G. Zimmermann and Jaron Lanier can be listed as pioneers of this developmental phase), and following this, the first data-suit with full-body movement sensors was developed in 1989 (VPL Research). Since 2016, AxonVR (now HaptX) has been working on a new body suit, which potentially aims to provide thermal and tactile feedback.

There seems to be an extensive investment in sensory devices for users to feel integrated in VR. Lanier lists all of the already existing solutions for the problem of sensory stimulation "like goggles, gloves and floors that scroll, so you can feel like you are walking far in the VR even though you remain in the physical spot" and he expresses with confidence: "the list will never end" (Lanier, 2017, 48). All hardware is developed with ergonomic concerns (exoskeletons, fabric based haptics which can cover the hands and other body parts, e.g. full body VR suit), aiming to bring free physical movement akin to real body agility, so that the inhibited virtual body can adopt a sense of flow.

Concerning the financial investment in sensory devices, Hayles[12] writes that there is already an industry worth hundred of millions of dollars, which aims to put the user's sensory system into a direct feedback loop with a computer (Hayles 1999, 26). Hillis (1998, 61) criticizes the speed of this developmental phase and asserts that the rush to visualize data flows in virtual environments mainly stems from the rush to make money. Unfortunately, my personal experience with VR companies, aligns with Hillis' critical approach. The industry care a little about the consequences of skipping developmental phases. These are, of course, no surprising news, since rapid production of technology owes its speed to disregarding the potentially turbulent effects of their products on human sensory systems.

Hayles argues that VR devices provide a multi-sensory interaction, bringing the illusion of being inside the computer. She reflects on her experience in VR simulations:

> "...I can attest to the disorienting, exhilarating effect of the feeling that subjectivity is dispersed throughout the cybernetic circuit. In these systems, the user learns, kinesthetically and proprioceptively, that the relevant boundaries for interaction are defined less by the skin than by the feedback loops connecting body and simulation in a techno bio-integrated circuit" (Hayles 1999, 27).

Here she highlights that tactile relations are relevant for interaction and how the virtual interaction lacks such a relation. In terms of interaction and relation with the outer world, skin is akin to a fundamental bridge, which operates faster than our conscious evaluation of ongoing perceptual activity. Angerer reminds us of Massumi's assertation that

> "the skin is faster than the word" and implies "[...] that is how, in the mid 1990s, Massumi outlines affect as an intensity that belongs to a different order: 'intensity is embodied in purely autonomic reactions most directly manifested in the skin—at the surface of the body, at its interface with things'" (Angerer 2017, 30).

---

12   More on VR-tech skepticism, Hayles (1999, 26) recommends further reading: Howard Rheingold (1991) *Virtual Reality* and Benjamin Woolley (1992) *Virtual Worlds: A Journey in Hyped Hyperreality.*

These autonomic reactions of the skin seem to be disabled when they are covered, neglected and numbed by bulky VR devices, which could explain Hayles' notion of relevant boundaries for interaction are less defined by the skin.

2.9.2 Nonconscious Cognition and Boundaries of Skin

The perceptual quality of the skin, how it operates faster than conscious cognition (therefore it binds us to the world even without recognition), and its fundamental function within the embodiment process can also be investigated in nonconscious cognition research. Hayles (2018) explains that over the course of 15 years, empirical research has been providing support for the idea that nonconscious cognition is able to perform essential tasks for consciousness. She gives the example that when we are being touched on our head and feet at the same time, since the feet lay at a larger distance to the brain, we actually feel the head touch first. It is the task of nonconscious cognition to surpass this time difference in perception; "nonconscious cognition is the level of neuronal processing that makes those two things appear to be simultaneous."[13]

She introduces an analogy between nonconscious cognition of biological organisms and computational media, "In the machine sense, it operates quicker than we realize." In her book *Unthought: The Power of Cognitive Nonconscious*, she clarifies that biological life forms and computational media are not completely akin to one another, since they have completely different material and physical contexts, but they perform similar functions. She explains, "Nonconscious cognition is a level of neuronal processing inaccessible to consciousness and in that sense it differs from both the Freudian unconscious and the so called new unconscious which is a kind of broad environmental background scanning" (Hayles 2017, 13). She underlines that the nonconscious cognition cannot be accessed through symptoms.

Hayles establishes the levels of cognition as "The tripartite framework of (human) cognition is a pyramid, from bottom to up: Material Processes, Nonconscious cognition, Modes of awareness" (Hayles, 2017, 40). Referring to her choice of the word "*Unthought*" in the title: "*Unthought* may also be taken to refer to recent discoveries in neuroscience confirming the existence of nonconscious cognitive processes inaccessible to conscious introspection but nevertheless essential for consciousness to function" (Hayles 2017, 1). These un-

---

13   Retrieved from the lecture (2018) "1. ZeM-Spring Lecture with N. Katherine Hayles" |
      "Are Sensing Technologies Cognitive? Making the Case."

thought aspects of nonconscious cognition and its importance in consciousness is also considered by neuroscientist Antti Revonsuo (2005). Revonsuo's research is concerned with the hard problem of consciousness and its connection
with biological phenomena, with an emphasis on the science of subjectivity.
On the distinction of unconscious and nonconscious, he writes: "unconscious
and nonconscious information is processed or encoded in the brain without
any subjective experiences being associated with them. Unconscious information can, however, become conscious information, it is potentially conscious,
whereas nonconscious information is not even potentially conscious" (Revonsuo 2010, 97). Although we cannot literally trace Revonsuo's (2010) initial definition of nonconscious in Hayles' (2017) work, they both focus on the on the
inaccessible character of nonconscious cognition. As humans, we may detect
the unpredictable leakages of unconscious, however nonconscious is beyond
our reach or identification.

We can summarize Revonsuo's levels of cognition from bottom to up:
atomic level, molecular level, biological level (cells), psychological level (conscious and subconscious) and phenomenal level of cognition (phenomenal
level of experience, metacognition). Nonconscious cognition operates in the
level of the first three: atomic, molecular and cellular level. For example,
through the recognition of a past event, we can recall related feelings, images
and sensations from our memory, and this would be a task for unconscious
cognition. But there are several other codings which are implanted on the
cellular level, those we cannot recall from memory, but nevertheless they do
hold information and influence subjective experience. Just because it is not
recognized in conscious experience, it does not mean nonconscious cognition
is not influencing subjective experience.

Hayles notes that VR users develop a sensation of the virtual body by implementing kinesthetic and proprioceptive perception. If we think of the haptic sensation as stimulated on the skin, and the sensation on the skin (touch) is
perceived at the biological level, and the nonconscious cognition operates on
this biological level as well, could we tap into the nonconscious cognition via
tactile stimulation in VR? Could we increase the importance of skin as a relevant boundary?

2.9.3 Role of Proprioception

The term proprioception derives from the term 'proprio' from the Latin *propius*,
meaning 'one's own, combined with the word perception. Radák (2018, 2) de-

fines proprioception as "the unconscious perception of movement." It allows the body to control its position for optimal locomotion. It is carried out by internal sensors such as the muscle spindle stretch receptor and Golgi tendon organ (Radák 2018, 3). While most of the VR devices bring about a reassessment of proprioception, the internal complexity cannot yet be integrated into this process. Another definition of proprioception is "the conscious or unconscious awareness of joint position, whereas neuromuscular control is the efferent motor response to afferent (sensory) information" (Davies & Gould 1985, 22). In other words, it is how we sense the spatiality of our limbs. Unlike the reality in which we can see our own limbs, in VR simulations it is disturbing and disorienting not to be able to see our own body. That is because the lack of visual data on the body parts creates an issue in the proprioception of the user who does not completely feel integrated to the environment (Salamin, et al. 2006). But the recognition of proprioception is not merely bound to visual perception. It operates usually at a subconscious level, in the movements and position of the body, independent of vision; this sense comes primarily from input from sensory nerve terminals (Proske & Gandevia 2018). Ritchie and Carruthers (2015, 367) write about proprioception as "bodily self-awareness as a kind of non conceptual primitive self-consciousness." Proprioception is involved in every sensory modality, and directly relates to our sense of body ownership and agency (O'Dea 2011). Both notions are central to the process of decision on a series of consecutive actions.

Siewert (2015, 46) explains the connection between body schema (which will be discussed in-depth in the following chapter) and proprioception, using an example of reaching for the phone: when it rings, the choreography of body movement reaching the phone is flawless. We have no awareness of the selection of movements during the course of a habitual action, as the body performs its own choreography. These smooth movements Siewert calls "varying manifestations of a unified skill or bodily habit." He continues,

> "Generally, I may say I experience an indefinite range of my own movements as in this and similar ways functionally equivalent. Thus I have a 'body schema': a systematic but open-ended capacity for engaging in patterns of movement, experienced as functionally equivalent, such as my task and situation require" (Siewert 2015, 46).

For example, when we reach out to a cupboard to get a plate, our body automatically stops and positions itself at a certain distance to the cupboard, calculating the distance between itself and the cupboard, including the distance when the door of the cupboard is open. "Postures and movements which are habit memories become sedimented into bodily conformation" (Connerton, 1989, 94). We happen to display the same ability with the cupboards we are not familiar with, so the occurrence of proprioception is not related to a habitual usage; we perform the same precision when we open a first-seen cupboard at a friend's kitchen, as well. In addition to determine the position of ourselves in relation to our surroundings, we use proprioception to sense the coordination and positioning of the limbs to one another, e.g. the position of the arm to the torso.[14] We use this ability also to move the arm and place the finger on the skin where we need to scratch. This ability is not clustered within the five senses of the body (namely sight, hearing, taste, smell and touch), in fact it is referred to as the "sixth sense" (Gandevia & Proske, 2016). With its mechanical and structural components, which are relatively easier to regulate, proprioceptive perception is a less challenging (in comparison to simulation of tactile perception) theme to play around with in VR.

Thus, body tracking systems and motion sensors which are integrated in the bodysuits are developed based on proprioception. Even when there is no perceived image of the virtual body, the spatiality of the body can be perceived by a modified proprioception. On the issue of body without an image, Massumi (2002, 58) points out,

> "...The spatiality of the body without an image can be understood even more immediately as an effect of proprioception, defined as the sensibility proper to the muscles and ligaments as opposed to tactile sensibility (which is exteroceptive) and visceral sensibility (which is interoceptive)."

The lack of skin contact in virtual interaction, which Hayles alludes to, is due to this prioritization of proprioception and to the current absence of exteroceptive and interoceptive perception in VR. But if we can ever talk about the sense of presence in a virtual environment, the skin and skin's conductive nature through the insides of the body also needs to be established. As Grosz (2017, 43) implies, "Sense must link the inside of bodies—their nature, qualities, their inclinations all material. Sense resides on the surface of events and in the depths of bodies."

Hayles' multi-sensory experience during the "Human Interface Technology Conference" was focused on kinesthetic and proprioceptive interaction, which

---

14   For initial literature on this information, see *The Integrative Action of the Nervous System*, Charles S. Sherrington (1906).

included finger mounted haptic devices, glove-based exoskeletons and robotic arm solutions. These devices are functionally convenient, as they can replace controller-based interaction, but they have primarily focused on rendering single haptic simulations, such as weight distribution. These devices aim to create the sensation of weight via spatial motion. The sensation of weight on the hands applies a kinesthetic force on the shoulders, thus contributes in implementing a stronger proprioceptive awareness during an interaction with a virtual object. But, in physical reality, when we grab a glass from the cupboard, in addition to its weight, we feel the smooth surface of the glass, and we sense whether it is cold or warm in contrast to our body temperature. The qualia of the tactile experience is harnessed within the immediacy of the movement. According to Massumi,

> "Tactility is the sensibility of the skin as surface of contact between the perceiving subject and the perceived object. Proprioception folds tactility into the body, enveloping the skin's contact with the external world in a dimension of medium depth: between epidermis and viscera. The muscles and ligaments register as conditions of movement what the skin internalizes as qualities: the hardness of the floor underfoot as one looks into a mirror becomes a resistance enabling station and movement; the softness of a cat's fur becomes a lubricant for the motion of the hand" (Massumi 2002, 58–59).

On the connection between movement and haptic touch, O'Shaughnessy (2003, 629) highlight how we perceive the circularity of an object by feeling the circular motion of our hands around the object, which is executed through proprioception. In this case, can steady haptic touch (without motion; without a circular or vertical movement to intensify or influence it) be less related to proprioception? Can we say, touch minus movement leads to less proprioceptive signification in perception? Because if the body doesn't move, the sense of proprioception is not clearly recognized. The intensity of haptic experience is compromised, and as a result, the quality of experience decreases.

On this issue Massumi states: "The living body's ultimate innards are the proprioceptive habits on a level with muscle fiber" (Massumi 2002, 205), which indicates that proprioception contains both exteroceptive sensation and sense of touch that eventually leads down to interoceptive states. These muscle fibers form closely ingrained passageways to the inner parts of the body (through muscle fibers, from epidermis to viscera), like inseparable knots of flesh. For the architectural development of the virtual body, the kinesthetic and proprioceptive sensations have been progressively constructed via exoskeleton gloves, motion-tracking body suits and other kinds of active-motion extensions. Inevitably, the tactile stimulation and haptic sensation comes as the next step, since bodily emergence is not only a matter of active movement but is tactilely embedded in the motion's quality. Like in Massumi's example, the phenomenal experience of caressing a cat is relevant to the softness of the cat's fur, influencing both the speed of active movement and the qualia of haptic sensation. And if we were to switch to the cat's phenomenal character of sensory experience, the touching hand's textural quality and the speed of movement is presumably significant for the cat's experience of being touched, as well.

2.9.4 Interoception, Introspection and Haptic Sensation

Interoception refers to internal perception of the bodily senses, for example the way we sense hunger and body temperature. Jennifer Murphy et al. (2016) summarizes interoception as the perception of the physiological condition of the body, including hunger, temperature, and heart rate. Neurotransmitters are not only in the brain but in other organs as well (Colombetti 2018). Therefore, interoceptive stages play a crucial role in identifying one's own emotion and bodily awareness; they imply "there is a growing appreciation that interoception is integral to higher-order cognition" (Murphy et al, 2016).

The haptic devices with integrated sensory models aim to provide the user with the sensation of texture of virtual objects. This stimulation is usually transmitted electrically, similar to the sensation we feel when our telephones vibrate in our hands. There are other systems, such as micro-fluidic stimulation, which aims to provide a smooth, less-mechanic and more life-like sensation (e.g HaptX).

Confrontation with any medium is not solely about perceiving a visual representation. The media-logical principle of the exposure establishes a bodily sensation, an unavoidable incoming request for a corporeal engagement. Concerning the ignored aspects of corporeality while being confronted with representations, Angerer refers to Steven Shaviro's note "We neglect the basis tactility and viscerality of cinematic experience when we describe material processes and effects, such as the persistence of vision, merely as mental illusions" (Angerer 1999, 178). Angerer relates this to Massumi's 'mesoperception':

"It is the medium where input from all five senses meet, across sub-sensate excitation, and become flesh together, tense and quivering. Mesoperceptive flesh functions as a corporeal transformer where one sense shades into another over the failure of each, their input translated into movement and affect" (Angerer 1999, 198–199).

Underneath the skin, there is "a second dimension of the flesh", Massumi notes, which is "deeper than the stratum of proprioception" (Massumi 2002, 60). This second dimension has a cellular memory and plays a significant role in subject-object relation: viscerality. Massumi's approach to cellular memory of a second dimension can be rethought of as Hayles' and Revonsuo's understanding of nonconscious cognition, as both state that nonconscious cognition operates in the cellular level. If this second dimension of flesh has the cellular memory within it and is responsible for interoception, could we say, the relation between interoception and nonconscious cognition co-operate on the same (cellular) level? Massumi underlines that the interoceptive process registers the intensity of the action even before it is taken. "Movement-vision as proprioception subtracts qualified form from movement; viscerality subtracts quality as such from excitation. It registers intensity" (Massumi 2002, 60–61).

Once again, this signifies the perception problem in VR caused by the lack of skin contact Hayles writes about. The absence of skin contact wrenches the connection to visceral sensibility, resulting in a disconnection of the body from the simulation. However, Metzinger (2018, 4) comments on the ways to integrate visceral sensibility into the avatar's body and how the lack of interoceptive perception in the virtual body reduces the possibilities of a full immersion. "The user's interoceptive self-model is firmly locked in the biological body; it cannot be simulated in an avatar, yet." Metzinger's statement can be considered as an explanatory answer for two of the central questions Hayles raises (1999, 27): "What transformations govern the connections between the user and avatar?" and "What stimuli cannot be encoded within the system and therefore exist only as extraneous noise?"

To overcome this obstacle and simulate an accurate identification with the avatar, Metzinger suggests two precursory solutions: "Either the avatar has its own interoceptive self-model that can be synchronized with the biological counterpart in the user's brain, or interoceptive experience is selectively blocked and another artificial unit of identification is created and technologically exploited" (Metzinger 2018, 5). Metzinger's suggestion resembles Grosz's indication of "material transformations." She suggests,

"...whether this results in the 'cross breeding' of the body and machine – that is, whether the machine will take on the characteristics attributed to the human body ("artificial intelligence", automatons) or whether the body will take on the characteristics of the machine (cyborg, bionics, computer prosthesis) remains unclear" (Grosz 1998, 50).

The virtual body does not yet have the technical infrastructure to contain a biologically human-like integrity. Focusing on the modification of the limbs with a tedious attention on haptic sensors could be a starting point to establish a biologically human-like integrity. Skin contact on these virtual limbs with haptic sensors can be considered as an initial gateway, a small step to create a ripple effect on interoceptive states.

Interoception is not to be confused with introspection. Introspection can be defined as an internal monologue, an inner examination of one's own state of mind, sensations and emotions. Introspection is debated in different disciplines, most commonly in psychology, philosophy and phenomenology. While philosophers and cognitive scientists such as Chalmers, Revonsuo, and Nagel highlight the importance of introspection in understanding the hard problem of consciousness and phenomenal experience,[15] other theorists such as Daniel Dennett and Peter Hacker reject the hard problem in analyzing subjective experience. LeBuffe (2010, 531) interprets Spinoza's take on introspection and indicates that he [Spinoza] comments on introspection as an elusive and unreliable way of self-examination, as it is rapidly influenced by a series of instantaneous stimulations, thoughts and interpretations of the mind.[16]

Spinoza also wrote that affective states are hard to conceptualize, as "an affect or passion of the mind is a confused idea" (Spinoza 1677–2001, 158). This 'confused idea' is promptly produced within the process of introspection; we cannot rely on it to cluster and understand the subjective experience, because it may vanish or appear unpredictably. Because we are preoccupied with the experience itself, the introspective resolutions are bound to be delayed. We reflect on the memory of the happening, not the happening itself, because by its nature, phenomenal experience cascades. Introspection, in this sense, has a paralyzing effect, we cannot analyze and act simultaneously.

---

15   According to Thomas Nagel (1974), experience is the root constituent of consciousness problem.

16   Perhaps this may explain why Freud wrote in his letter of November 14th 1897, to Wilhelm Fliess,: "Self-analysis is impossible in fact. I can only analyze myself by means of what I learn from the outside (as if I were another)." Could we then say that an excessive introspection as a method for self-actualization and self-recognition is limited in itself and prone to illusion about one's own self?

Spinoza's doubt in the method of introspection and Hayles' indication of how nonconscious cognition cannot be accessed via introspection, can be rethought in parallel. Introspection remains both insufficient and unreliable to explain mental states. On consulting introspection when one is exposed to multi-sensory stimulation, Mohan Matthen (2015, 615) comments,

> "What kind of evidence might we appeal to when adjudicating this issue? Although it is tempting to appeal to introspection, it is unclear whether the temporal grain of introspection is precise enough to be able to provide us with reliable information concerning this issue. Although many people claim that they are simultaneously conscious of stimuli in various sensory modalities, it is possible that these claims rest on an illusion of sorts, and that perceptual consciousness actually rapidly switches between different modalities."

On the connection between nonconscious cognition and introspection Hayles writes: "Cognitive nonconscious operates at a lower level of neuronal organization not accessible to introspection (Hayles 2014, 201). Similar to Revonsuo's biological level and Massumi's second dimension of the flesh level and the information contained within, this lower level cannot be explored via introspection. We can explore and dig through the unconscious, reflect on our outcomes which may be the symptoms, but there are no gates to the nonconscious for us to force our way through. "Therefore all thinking is cognition but not all cognition is thinking" Hayles (2017, 42) writes. Introspection can be considered a valuable method to be used on the phenomenal level, although it remains not so efficient for the interrogation of other levels. These inaccessible levels carry what Hayles calls "intention toward" (Hayles 2014, 201). Similar notions related to pre-reflective intentionality are also underlined by Merleau-Ponty as "being-in-the-world"[17] and in Bergson's "attention to life."

---

17   Merleau-Ponty (2002, 35) examines the notion of "being-in-the-world" parallel to the phenomenon of phantom limb. He explains that when a spider loses a leg, the intention to survive springs-forth and the spider sets a new configuration of the remaining seven legs in order to keep going. On the other hand, human beings need a longer time to develop a substitutional component (both physical and psychical) for the sense of loss, since we are in an ongoing state of interpretation of life. Yet, the animal is not able to interpret the living world. We (human being & animal) both experience the phenomenon of phantom limb, but the animal replaces a leg, springs forth and carries himself towards the world. But my organic repression enables me to create phantoms, and thus I differ from the animal, through cogito.

2.9.5 Role of Interoception and Introspection in Affect

Both interoception and introspection can partially guide us through under-standing how bodily existence is central to emotional experience. Spinoza (1677, 1994, 21) defines affects as follows: "By affect I understand affections of the body by which the body's power of acting is increased or diminished, aided or restrained, and at the same time, the ideas of these affections." We can see that Spinoza systematically avoids the mind-body division (while it remained significant to Descartes' dualism and in Leibniz's pluralism), he articulates "the mind and body are ontologically the same thing, the same reality and substance." He continues: "The mind is united to the body because the body is the object of the mind." The mind acts accordingly to what happens to the body, as he clusters affects into passion and action. [18]

In *Looking for Spinoza*, Damasio (2004) writes about the distinction between emotions and feelings:

> "...emotions are actions or movements, many of them public, visible to the others as they occur in the face, in the voice in specific behaviors. To be sure, some components of the emotion process are not visible to the naked eye but can be made 'visible' with current scientific probes such as hormonal as-says and electrophysiological wave patterns. Feelings are on the other hand, are always hidden, like all mental images necessarily are, unseen to anyone other than their rightful owner, the most private property of organism in whose brain they occur" (Damasio 2004, 28).

We may feel one thing, but as we go through life, we become more successful at protecting or masking the privacy of such delicate feelings and convert it to different 'apparent' emotions. As Damasio (2004, 28) notes "Emotions play in the theater of the body. Feelings play out in the theater of the mind."

In her essay "Postmodernism and the Affective Turn," Rachel Greenwald-Smith (2011) emphasizes Patricia Clough's definition of the "affective turn" and how preconscious feelings and impulses are altered by smells, hormones, ges-tures and images, and that these affective incitements change depending upon the qualitative conditions of social relations. In the mid-1990s, scholars started

---

18   Spinozist body and his notion of "mind and body can interact with each other" appears not only when we dig deep through analytical philosophy but also in cognitive science's approach to mind-body problem.

to focus on pre-individual notion of the body,[19] linked to autonomic responses, underlining the body's capacity to act or engage with others. This "affective turn" and the new configurations of bodies, technology, and matter that it reveals, is the subject of this collection of essays (Clough 2007). Affective turn has reformed the investigation of subjective experience, centralizing the bodily experience and the limits of human sensibility (Seyfert 2012, 45). Being the first philosopher who emphasized the inseparable nature of mind and body, Spinoza's attempt at uniting ideas and the things themselves (ideatum), can be recognized in affective turn's leaning away from representations.

Massumi significantly weights in on the exploration of the limits of human sensibility within the affective turn. He underlines that bodily movements and sensations influence our interaction in real and virtual worlds. These movements and sensations, as they heavily influence our inner perception of bodily sensation (whether it is interoceptively perceived hunger, or the automatic introspection when exposed to a certain sensation, e.g. the experience of being touched), might play an important role in affect theory regarding perceptual processes. Sibylle Peterson et al. (2015, 4) notes "The perception of bodily sensations is a particularly interesting field to conceptualize affect as part of the perceptual process."

Barret & Russel (1999, 45) suggest the term "core affect" as one of the basic levels of the interoception. They imply that valence and arousal are important signifiers for the affective experience in general. Valence is considered both negative and positive; joy and sorrow, pleasure and displeasure. Carruthers (2015, 360) argues that it remains unknown whether valence is a product of interoception, but that characteristics of arousal are certainly related to interoception (e.g. fear). Furthermore, affective experience is a central element in the cognitive process in general, by continuously influencing the context of thoughts and actions. Carruthers (2015) reformulates James' (1884) and Lange's (1885) suggestion "the emotions are equivalent to feelings" to "emotions as the constitution of interoceptive feelings" (e.g. one's awareness of threat/danger causes a distinct physiological change in the body). This feeling of fear becomes an interoceptive experience, but it also has the potential to be an emotion (emotion as an affect that is "sociolinguistically fixated" in the sense of Massumi). This is in line with Damasio's (2008, 45) "somatic marker theory," which in my

---

19   For further information see Thomas P. Keating's article "Pre-individual affects: Gilbert Simondon and the individuation of relation" (2019).

interpretation may correspond to what is called a 'gut feeling'. Damasio explains that the decisions we make can be influenced by the somatic marker to turn the current situation into our advantage. For example, we chose to walk on one specific street at night because the other street with no lights gives us a queasy feeling. Carruthers (2015, 359) suggests that the formulation "emotions equal to feelings" is no longer applicable to current research.[20] He explains:

> "The current consensus in emotion theory is that our experience of emotion is constituted both by an affective component (partially reflecting interoceptive experience) and by a set of appraisal dimensions through which one conceptualizes and categorizes one's affective experience, which form a cognitive component of emotion."

The interrelation between affect and interoception is also highlighted by Bergson (1896) in *Matter and Memory*. He explains: "We do not know our body only 'from without' by perceptions, but also 'from within' by affections" (Bergson 2004, 1). He adds, "I look closer: I find movements begun, but not executed" (Bergson 2002, 103). We know how we are going to insert a gesture before it is executed, it exists before the execution. We are eternally trapped in this inner correspondence with our pre-reflective consciousness. We are like reserved observers of the internal states of body, in a continuous and unavoidable interrogation of the consciousness. Additionally Varela & Depraz (2000, 59) explore the embedded relation between affect and interoceptivity:

> "The affective force manifests as a rapid, dynamical transformation from tendency to salience, involving one's entire lived-body as a complex [...] the gamut of autonomic action such as respiratory, heart rate, endocrine secretion, etc. as well as the ancestral motor pattern involved in posture and movement [...] a feeling grounded in the body's responsive repertoire."

Depraz notes that the 'valence' is the appropriate term to describe such an 'immanent vital move', which is also called "a 'primordial fluctuation: the gradually emerging change is an affect-emotion in the self-movement of the flow, of the temporal stream of consciousness" (Depraz 2003, 60). This 'primordial fluctuation' and its relevancy to the temporal stream of consciousness, calls to mind Spinoza's (1994, 54) definition of affect and how it is to be felt only as "a decrease or increase in body's vital forces."

---

20   Similarly, Damasio's differentiation of emotion and feeling neatly invites us to understand that they have distinctive features.

2.9.6 Degrees of Immersion and Immanent Vital Move

As mentioned above, when we try to develop the sensory architecture of the virtual body, we face the problem of an absence of the biological body. Visual-only attempts to create a sense of self-identification with the avatar/virtual body remain insufficient and foster a degree of depersonalization, since a flesh-like visual representation of the self is still in its infant stage. For certain scholars the stand of affective turn signifies a disinterest in representations (such as for Massumi (2002) and Barad (2007) but not for e.g. Sara Ahmed (2004), as she mainly focuses on the political implications of emotion). Their primary focus on being the thing itself is in line with this attempt to craft a bigger, general sensory structure of the body; the sense of immersion and presence of a bodily feeling is not limited to a visual representation. In order to be immersed, the sensory architecture of the virtual body requires something beyond what it can visually grasp. We are able to see a representation of the body, but if our entire sensory mechanism is not potentiated for action, if the urge is not incarnated within the virtual body, then we will not be able to talk about a full immersive feeling. An 'immanent vital move' will not linger, the sense of flow for self-movement in virtual space will be non-existent. At this point, to create a sense of primordial potentiation in order to increase the sense of immersion in VR, we can consider Metzinger's suggestion in his recent article "Why Virtual Reality is interesting for Philosophers?":

> "Perhaps the most interesting contribution VR researchers could make is to develop a reliable "volume control for realness." Obviously, a clear conceptual taxonomy is needed as well, but the role of computer scientists in this type of cooperation would lie in developing a metric for immersion and self-identification—a quantifiable approach. The interesting point here is that human phenomenology varies along a spectrum from "realness" to "mind-dependence." This frequently overlooked phenomenological feature provides another conceptual bridge into the representational deep structure of VR-environments: there are degrees of immersion. VR environments can be more or less realistic, and this general property is itself directly and concretely reflected in the user's phenomenology" (Metzinger's 2018, 5).

For such attempt to set "degrees of immersion," Metzinger proposes a set of values: Ordinary waking states as 1, then possible levels would include values> 1, leading to "hyperreal" phenomenologies (as in certain drug-induced states of consciousness, during "ecstatic" epileptic seizures, or religious experiences), and values< 1, as in "unreal" experiences like depersonalization or derealization disorder. These degrees of immersion, Metzinger suggests, can set the 'level of realness' for the VR experience. Metzinger's suggestion of increasing and decreasing the level of realness in order to pinpoint the dimensions of possible conscious experience in VR, resembles Spinoza's (1677, 1994, 54) definition of affective state ("a sensed decrease and increase in body's vital force"). If we consider Metzinger's hyperreal state in euphoric experiences as Spinoza's joy, we may trace the signs of immersion through joy in VR, since the experience of joy might weaken our rootedness in reality as the joy happening in VR becomes more significant. Therefore it may infuse a more a steady immersion in VR. An increase in the body's vital force could amplify the sense of presence in VR. Likewise, a decrease in vitality of the body could be seen as an unreal experience in VR, since the decreased vitality could be perceived when cognitive abilities are not intact. As a result, the person would feel unrooted in the immersive environment, oblivious and restless, which could correspond to a lower degree in Metzinger's degrees of immersion. Could we then suggest, a high degree of immersion in VR is relevant to an increase of vitality in the virtual body?

Understandably, to set an analogy between the ontology of Spinoza about reality, joy, action and Metzinger's suggestion for degrees of immersion is a risky approach. Though, if we would begin to apply philosophical insights into VR research, I believe that the Spinozist body may aid and influence our understanding of the virtual body.

Metzinger offers this parameter as a method for understanding the conscious experience of VR, with an elaboration on the sense of presence-absence. But this measure can also be used in experimental designs to explore the affective states in VR. Interactive mediality of VR brings a reflexive and bountiful endorsement. Researchers are now able to shed a light on human cognition, and through their theoretical investigations, developers can continue to improve the sense of immersion in VR environments. My focus here is to arrive at the junction of philosophical and scientific inquiries from a contemporary point of view, as to broaden the practical applications developments of the virtual body.

Chapter 3. Exhibition Project: "sit behind my eyes"

"No one wants to imagine their presence/their existence [...] they are abjected"
(Massumi 1992, 70).

"*sit behind my eyes*" is a virtual reality environment project designed to mirror the process of visual perception. The installation was exhibited during Transmediale's CTM Vorspiel (2016) week, in Berlin.[1] As the founders of the research group "autoscopie", Filiz Avunduk, Mert Akbal and I have designed a virtual eye ball (with a software called "Blender", see figure 9) where visitors could sit as if they were temporarily inhabiting the space within someone's eye ball, facing the world outside through the person's retina. The owner of this virtual eyeball is traveling in a train, looking at the passing images from the window. We enlarged and projected the pre-recorded video images within the sphere of this eye ball, as the animated blood vessels and nerves moving as the person turns around to discover the inner structure of the eye (see figure 10). As a result, when people put the VR HMD on, they experienced the illusion of sitting in an eye and being exposed to the light, speed and texture of the information penetrating the iris. The installation provided a visual manipulation of body size (small enough to cozily sit in someone's eye ball) and provided the observer with the percept of riding from the point of view of someone else.

---

1   "sit behind my eyes" is a project by autoscopie and the sound installation was created by Rony Nehme. (https://www.ctm-festival.de/archive/festival-editions/ctm-2016 -new-geographies/specials/vorspiel-2016/) "autoscopie" is a VR research group, founded in 2015 by Filiz Avunduk and Zeynep Akbal, in Berlin. The focus of our research lies on alteration of mind states through the use of emerging virtual reality and HCI devices. We conceptualize and realize installations and devise hands-on workshops to gather qualitative data with an artistic and philosophical approach for our individual research purposes.

The motivation behind this exhibition was to observe what it could look like inside a body by starting this journey from inside an eye ball. The body is our ultimate 'home' (in german das Heim), but ironically a 'home' which is not visually experienced from an inner perspective. We are absorbed in it, but in another way we are ultimately estranged from it. If we visualize our flesh and organs without the cover of skin, we have an instant aversion to the image. In this sense, the body, that seems to be the most 'heimlich' vessel, could also be perceived as the most 'unheimlich' entity. Within this exhibition, I proposed using VR to convert this 'unheimlich' state (the vision of what the innards of an eyeball could look like) into a 'heimlich' one (that is, being comfortably sitting at the middle of this environment in the eye ball). As a continuation of this project, I'm working on constructing a virtual environment of an inner body; a journey through the VR landscape of an inner body. In this project, my next step is to animate a virtual environment in which the user gets captured in a tear and to streams down the throat ending up in the digestive system. Or the journey can start in the mouth; the user explores the inner walls of cheeks, the tongue, the inner perspective of teeth structure, and then the owner of the mouth swallows the user and the digestion system journey starts. Or the user enters the body from the nose and travels down the respiratory tract, or the user is injected into a vein and travels through circulatory system.

Figure 9: Eye ball structure in Blender

Figure 10: Animated nerve web inside the eye structure

3.1   Unheimlicher Körper

In his essay "Das Unheimliche", Freud (1919) explores the meaning of the word "heimlich" (canny/homey) and "unheimlich" (uncanny/un-homey). Prior to Freud's publication, German psychiatrist Ernst Jentsch (1906) has described the "unheimlich" as something significantly frightening, yielding primarily to the fear of the unknown, whereas Freud delved into the etymology of the term and suggested that the feeling of 'unheimlich' includes the familiar (Heim) with a tint of hidden feature. He indicated "uncanny proceeds from something familiar which has been repressed" (Freud 1919, 242). The connection between the repressed and the familiar has formed the idea of this project, since the aversion we feel towards the innards can point out to the 'repressed', which resides eventually in the feeling of familiarity. Additionally, this project idea was accumulated from the intersection of my interest in alien phenomenology (Waldenfels 2000), uncanniness and something becoming 'uncannily too familiar', which relates to the theory of abjection (Kristeva 1982), body innards exceeding Euclidean geometry (Massumi 2002), plasticity and autoaffection (Malabou 2008) and the exploration of felt presence between the visible and the invisible (Merleau-Ponty 1968). These conceptualizations and their connections to the notion of uncanny will be explored in the followings sections of this chapter.

In the previous chapters, I have considered the use of VR while studying exteroceptive (interaction with the external world) and interoceptive (awareness of body from within) perception and I have explored how these studies could inform us for the further development of a virtual body. Could we also suggest using VR as a magnifying glass to visually explore the inner structure of the body? If we could be more informed about the flesh, would we have a more clear perception of the core dynamics of both interoceptive and exteroceptive processes? Is it not utterly an ironic fact that we feel disgust when we even think of what our liver or our throat would look like without the protection of the skin? Why do we turn away from looking deeper when a part of our body is exposed? Why does the imagination of our innards always lead to disgust and raises the need of censoring? What lays under the skin? Why do we avoid seeing a hidden part of the body? We cannot say out loud "it is a part of me", if we would not have a throat. Nevertheless, we would avoid to look at the throat itself and dare to touch it without the cover of skin.[2] As Malabou (2013, 67) emphasizes, Damasio would have put it, "if we could have a look at our internal neural processes, it would always be from the third-person perspective."[3] First-person perspective or first-person sense of body ownership is what we commonly adopt, when we perceive of our body through proprioception and somatosensation (i.e., I can watch my legs walking from an ego-centric perspective and meanwhile I can feel if I am hungry or not). When I stop to see my reflection from a mirror or from the reflection of a window, or from the recorded images with cameras, I see my body from a third-person perspective, as I see an object. Could we apply this perspectival change not only to our body image and its reflections, but also to the inner layers of our object body?

Previously, I have underlined the role of the enactive view, perspectival givenness (that is, the revealed side of the object to the subject's eye) and the importance of horizon and context from a phenomenological understanding. These notions can be similarly applied to the perception of flesh, since the

---

2   "Centering our understanding of the body not on a substance or unitary organization but on non-coincidence prevents us from declaring one of those modes the original core and others as negligible or improper—but it doesn't absolve us from carefully investigating the different modes and their relations. The body is a field of different modes of experience that are related but not identical. The implicit, adverbial lived-body that merges into its relation to the world can be seen, touched, hurt, dissected, and resconstructed from a third-person perspective; it is one body but this is not one" (Grüny 2019, 131).

3   "The surgery provokes the dissociation of two strata of the subject that are usually unified: the protoself and the conscious self. The third person, involved in homeostatic processes, and the first person, involved in conscious procedures, are disconnected and can look at each other at a distance" (Malabou 2013, 67).

inner parts of our body cannot be excluded from the totality of our body. The totality of the body is composed of several epidermal layers, and this seems nauseating for us to count. As Massumi (2002, 202) describes it, "the body is composed of a branching network, decreasing in size right down to the level of molecular tubes at the mitochondrial scale. Geometrically, a body is a "space-filling fractal" of a "fourth" dimensionality, between a two-dimensional plane and a three-dimensional volume." Without the vibrant density of flesh which forms and electrifies the system, we would not be occupying a condensed form in space. In all organisms "essential materials are transported through space-filling fractal networks of branching tubes" (West et al. 1997, 122). When the horizon of the flesh changes, the context for our conscious thinking about the flesh itself can also change. But in order to arrive at that point, we first have to be able to see, tolerate, resist and transform the feelings of the abject, and perhaps eventually let it influence a higher-order thinking. If we can overcome this abject and visit our insides, our 'unheimliche Heim', could we become more perceptive of our bodily selves and more attuned to our interoceptive states?[4] E.g., if I could see my liver precisely where it lays in the abdominal area, in contrast to other neighboring organs, would I be interoceptively more aware of it in my daily life?[5] Would we be more insightful about our well being in general because we are more aligned with our inner sensations, moreover how would a new awareness of something we do not habitually recognize in our daily life (in this case, awareness of an organ) alter our perception of what an 'unheimlich' feeling is? Or would we feel paralyzed, as if we are facing a total alien form, ripped from the comfort of our fixated reference points? Upon the arrival of this alien form, we cannot feel safe, even though it is just our own vitality in its most raw form. Is it possible that we actually cannot be aware of

---

4   In Heidegerrian existential phenomenology of being-in-the-world (Dasein) is reduced by the feelings of anxiety, correspondingly, this feeling manifests as "not-being-at-home" (nicht zuhause sein) (Heidegger 1962, 233). If we think of the body as our ultimate home, not knowing the body from inside out may be contributing in anxiety. Could we actually feel more-at-home if we can be more in tune with the innards of our bodies? If "not-being-at-home" is a fundamental and primordial phenomenon to comprehend what 'dasein' means, can we be comfortable in our abjected body?

5   Can this precision of interoceptive awareness of organs perhaps make it easier for diagnosticians to understand and treat the relevant diseases? Think of when you have abdominal pain, you are never a hundred percent sure where it is exactly coming from. Our abdominal area is full of organs which remains unidentifiable to the subject, the borders of these organs cannot be sensed via interoceptive awareness.

this inner self and simultaneously invade it as a self-containing lived-body? This ambiguity calls to mind of Waldenfels' (2011, 49) indication of the chiasm moment within the act of "touching and being-touched," and how these modes can be experienced only interchangeably. He explains: "This noncoincidence should be viewed as a liability, for it characterizes the very being of our body, which refers (Selbstbezug) to itself and at the same time evades (Selbstentzug) itself" (Waldenfels 2011, 49–50).

Waldenfels' conception of body escapes itself while holding itself as a self-referential point of existence (similar to Merleau-Ponty's notion (2002, 72) "house being seen from nowhere and also from everywhere"). Along the same line, it seems difficult to tolerate our alien selves (or is the confrontation with this alien-self causing what Waldenfels calls "Selbstentzug"?)which lay under the skin. Perhaps it is difficult for us to accept the fact that we are made of this condensed form of flesh, and meanwhile continue to be our self-conscious, pragmatic and functioning selves.

3.2 Materiality of flesh-body and Euclidean spaces

Our flesh is consistently present but we live in an absence of it's visual recognition. Such recognition could in fact intensify its totality. Spatiality of flesh is nothing we experience, we just perceive the dimension of it under the cover of the skin. "Our skin obeys the laws of three dimensions…but our internal anatomy and physiology is living in a four-dimensional spatial world" (West 1999, 39). Massumi (2002, 202) explains that, "the three enveloping Euclidean space plus the fourth fractal dimension of internal branching. A body lives in three dimensions only at the envelope of the skin. The "Euclidean" space of the body is a membrane." He then gives the example of two bricks leaning on one another. When we put a brick against another, we are not literally rubbing matter against matter; where we see the two bricks touch each other is actually where the electrons, nuclear particles, sub-atoms form an intense and incorporeal stability. Similarly, Malabou implies that there is a discontinuity between neuronal tissues and the cerebral space is constituted "by cuts, by voids, by gaps, and this prevents our taking it to be an integrative totality" (Malabou 2008, 36). The relation between two bricks actually resembles these voids and gaps between two neuronal tissues. Likewise, Jean-Pierre Changeux (1997, 83) addresses that the "nerve circuits consist of neurons juxtaposed at the synapses. There is a 'break' between one neuron and the other." These synaptic gaps, similar to the subatomic interaction between two bricks, causes a decisive understanding. Deleuze (1989, 218) underlines: "Our lived relation with the brain becomes more and more fragile, less and less 'Euclidean', and goes through little cerebral deaths."

Similar to an atom's, the body's innards are as incorporeal and abstract. In this sense, Massumi (2002, 205) explains that the body's innards are not only our internal organs. The flesh contains more, each neuron carries micro-social skills. Our innards are "enculturated memories lying at the crossroads of sense channels coursing through the flesh" (Massumi 2002, 205). These assets of flesh are similar to Hayles' indication of how nonconscious cognition operates on the lower level of neuronal organization and also to what Revunsuo calls biological level. We may not access these corridors of flesh where nonconscious cognition, memories and affects are stored. How can we then access these corners to reach beyond our habitual cognition? Massumi deliberately underlines the irony, "They [body's innards] are the pattern of preferential headings hinging on all of the above, which we somewhat grandly call our 'personality'" (Massumi 2002, 205). From nonconscious cognition, to the biological level of cognition, to the traveling neurons that carries "microsocial skills," these levels all influence our subjective experience, contribute to our sense of self, and influence many decisions we make. If we cannot use introspection to access these levels, can we really say that this is our "personality"? What I cognize to be my personality is merely my conscious evaluation of the bits of what I can only reach. In this line, even I, do not know myself. Perhaps the informations that are stored in these unknown levels of are also contributing to our tacit knowledge, as Michael Polanyi suggested "we can know more than we can tell" (Polanyi 1967, 4).

Now, I do not necessarily suggest that a visual recognition of our body's innards in VR could possibly uncover what remains inaccessible to our conscious cognition. But, I do suggest that a simulation can mirror the implicit disassociation we have with the body's insides, and therefore provide a ground for further exploration. Due to such confrontation, we can deconstruct our understanding of both what it is to be a 'bodily self' and of what I cognize to be myself (and see that this is not merely a product of my brain). A visualization can contribute to broadening the subjective experience of body, not only from outside (as in the case of the "Ambiguity in Lived Body Experiences" intervention) but also from inside. A decision is not only a task for my active brain cells. Neurotransmitters are everywhere; they are in a perpetual cooperation which contributes in the process of decision making. Perhaps, the over-exhausted inner muscles of my mouth are signaling and contributing in the content of what I am about to say. Out environment rapidly influences all of our senses, therefore the lived-body never ceases to process this stream of fluctuating information. It is always filtering and processing; regeneration and reformation of the body is constant.[6] This ever-wondering and ever-perceiving inner space of the body can be, in a biological sense, called a "circus of the body" as Massumi (2002, 203) writes. We watch this circus come to happening. He states that the membrane is not closed; the entire bodily membrane has several in and output doors: mouth, ears, nostrils, vagina, urethra. What we eat merely touches the walls of the innards, like traveling through a giant tube, and absorbed on the way out. The body is a leaky box and similar to its leaky nature, self is also open and leaky. Both the body and the self are constantly leaking into each other, influencing one another's intentions and actions, consequently, they are non-separable. Grosz (2017, 25–40) evaluates this inseparable nature of body by emphasizing the Stoic way of mixing the bodies. For Stoics (contrary to Plato), bodies are not separated from the Ideas. "The world is composed not of Being (to on) but of something (to ti), which exists in two forms. Some things either exist, in which case they are material bodies (somata) that act (as does pneuma) or acted on (as in the case of inanimate objects). All being is corporeal. Every object, force, quality, and state is corporeal" (Grosz 2017, 25). Stoics distinguish three types for mixing material bodies: juxtaposition, fusion and total blending. Juxtaposition is when two bodies mix but their individual features still remain detectable, e.g. when salt and sugar can be mixed in a jar; we can still distinguish between both. Fusion is when two bodies mix to a point where characteristics are no longer perceivable, e.g. we cannot perceive the distinct features of flour and eggs in a cake. Cake is no longer decomposable. Total blending is when two material bodies mix into each other but are still discernible, e.g. when we pour a glass of wine into an ocean-they blend together but each body still can be extracted from the blend. In all these three types of mixing modes, we can trace the human body's inner components; I simply cannot maintain a functioning self after I dissect a muscle fiber from my eye and cut out my eustachian tube. All sensory organs, as well as all other parts of the body, function together and have a blended, elemental influence over one another. A tiny cut on the tip a finger has the power to disrupt the bodily coordination, the pain of

---

6   "The successive deaths of our epidermal layers, our shedded, shredded snake-skins, our constantly new selves, never entirely the same, never exactly, recognizably different" (Baker 2010, 15).

the cut can be felt simultaneously at the edge of the eyebrow. Flesh is vibrant and conductive.

We could also appropriate an understanding, e.g. how mind, brain and body resembles a fusion. Similar to the impossibility of pointing out the sugar in a cake, we cannot heterogeneously classify whether a feeling has risen from the mind's inquiries, or from the brain's 'tricks' or from the body's assertive signals. They are all fused in the emotion, then one gets to ask: Why do we continuously harbor the need to deconstruct this fusion? Is it even possible? Why are we so fixated on the possibility that we can understand this complexity only when we are able to decompose and analyze them as separate entities? Why do we need to obey the brain's default mode of function that categorizes and stores information? Is there any other way to experience a self, other than asserting this only formula of 'categorizing and storing'? Can we not unlearn these processes and use the plasticity of our brain in other ways? If plasticity, by its own nature, allows us to reverse many disabilities with training, why would we not begin to apply this plasticity in metacognition? What we would need then, is to understand and study our senses in-depth.

One of the main goals of my project of the inner body journey in VR is to implement a sense of touch as the user travels through the body, since the technology of tactile feedback is highly neglected in research. In his article "Why Is There So Much More Research on Vision Than on Any Other Sensory Modality?", Hutmacher (2019) implies that there is excessive research in visual cognition, significantly more than any other sensory modalities: "There is a lot of off-the-shelf technology available for studying vision, but this is not the case for the sensory modality of touch" (Hutmacher 2019, 6). Perception is a juxtaposition of all senses and just because it is challenging to study the sense of touch, we cannot deny the significant entanglement of it with the visual sense.

Lacy and Sathia (2020) underline that vision and touch have a lot in common in terms of information processing, which manifest in behavioral similarities in terms of "categorization, recognition, and individual differences" (Lacy and Sathia 2020, 157). Such behavioral similarities imply that there is also a shared neural basis for visuo-haptic object perception. Indeed, without an in-depth exploration of the sense of touch, we may not be capable of developing a full understanding of sight. Touching, with all of its complex multi-dimensional experience (texture, heat, weight) is intertwined with the visual sense, e.g. when we see a glass of cold water, we see the moist drooling down the side of the glass because of a contradiction in temperature, we know that the liquid inside is colder than the room temperature. We also know how this certain amount of water requires a precise muscle force to lift the glass up, and we anticipate the exact muscle tension when we lift it up. We pre-consciously calculate and act upon an object before we touch it and sense all the qualities of the full glass of water with the aid of sight. We know, by habitual practice, how a full glass of cold water would feel in our hands. We anticipate milligrams, celsius, taste. We are trained in our senses, much more than we assume or remember. We automatically inspect and anticipate these qualities before we go to hold the glass. Therefore touch perception is tightly confounded in the sense of sight. Materiality remains fundamental in bodily cognition, a reminiscent of the inseparable nature of our sensory modalities.

Materiality of the human body is even more complex than the simple mixing of ingredients. Massumi implies that this biological "circus of a body" is covered with skin, but even the skin is not three-dimensional, it just "acts as it were." Skin, covering the inner dimensions, regulates the movements and shape-shifts in between dimensions. "We do not live in Euclidean space. We live between dimensions" (Massumi 2002, 203). As mentioned before, Husserl indicated that it is not possible to apply Euclidean geometry on the perception of one's own body, because we cannot objectify the body and stand beside it as an object in space, like we do when we apply Euclidean geometry to other objects. But what Husserl might have meant (like Massumi) could be that the innards of the body do not align with Euclidean geometry.

Similar to the dynamic of two bricks supporting each other with their subatomic parts, Massumi mentions that a building under construction also resembles a 'technology of movement', with placing relation against relation. "We build in Euclidean space when we design the kind of aggregate hinge-effects between swarmings and smudgings of experience that shake out in favor of maximum stability of cognitive result" (Massumi 2002, 204). Our bodies are not obeying Euclidean space but the sense of stability is accumulated from a cognitive structure.[7] Likewise, Grosz emphasizes, "Outside architecture is always inside bodies" (Grosz 2001, 16). Grosz (1998) also noted that the body, with its organization of flesh and organs, is incomplete. The body is "a series of uncoordinated potentialities which require social triggering, ordering, and long-term administration" (Grosz 1998, 43). In addition to social triggering as a means to evoke these uncoordinated potentialities, I suggest 'visual triggering'

---

7   Finding a strong cognitive stability in structure somehow can signify how the body is
      the homeland. This understanding can be thought in parallel to Husserl's formulation
      of "Wir wollen auf die 'Sachen selbst' zurückgehen" (Husserl, 1984, 10).

as a means to understand the complexity of the body's innards, in order to enhance the experience of owning both our sensual and cognitive capacities. Such visualization is not only an uncomfortable experience, but it is also a difficult one to achieve. Visualization is limited by the body image and we are not entirely invited to see more of it. Rötzer (2000, 154) neatly summarizes that our perceptional horizon does not permit us to have an inner perspective, one is only allowed to see the body parts from a limited amount of perspectives. Yet, the habituation of whatever body image we possess is in fluctuating transformation; we coordinate our appearance in the images we see – with the body image we have in our minds. We censor certain parts which may cause self-doubt. Rötzer emphasizes the irritation people experience when the innards of the body are suddenly seen through transparent imaging, e.g. with x-rays, computer or magnetic resonance imaging. "What is depicted in these images are known as sensations, but not from visual a perception. Such images of one's own body remain (still?) foreign, cannot (still?) be integrated into one's own experience" (Rötzer 2000, 154).[8]

Indeed, the MRI images barely depict the real, they are the vague and blurred slices of innards, exhibiting three different axis points for identification, they never provide a visual of an organ in its voluptuous entirety. Rötzer further implies that while the computer technologies remain insufficient to transfer a sense of realism and perfected immersion to explore this foreignness, artists seem to benefit from such sense of imperfection in terms of allowing the strange experiences and creative exploration of virtual body ownership. I suggest that such exploration should exceed the enthusiasm of fearless artists and be applied to both scientific and philosophical methodologies. Furthermore, such exploration could create an impact on media

---

8   I translated the quote from the original: "Wahrnehmungshorizont scheint eine solche Innerlichkeit nicht zu besitzen. Sieht man auf sich, dann erscheinen die sichtbaren Körperteile wie aus einer äußeren, aus einer Beobachterperspektive […] Die Gewöhnung an das Bild des eigenen Körpers erfolgt freilich schnell, denn immer häufiger werden wir einer kohärenten Umformung, unsere Erscheinung auf den Bildern mit unserem mentalen Körperbild zu koordinieren, zensurieren wir die anfänglichen Inkohärenzen der Selbstverdoppelung. Ein wenig erahnen läßt sich die Irritation noch, wenn das Körper-innere mit Röntgenbildern, Computer- oder Kernspin-Tomographen transparent gemacht wird, wenn man sich dann plötzlich von innen, mithin einen Leib sieht, den man gewöhnlich nur als Empfindung, nicht aber aus der Anschauung kennt. Solche Bilder des eigenen Leibes bleiben (noch?) fremd, sind (noch?) nicht in die eigene Erfahrung zu integrieren" (Rötzer 2000, 154).

technology that would eventually elevate the sense of immersion, and could improve the virtual body's lack of biological integrity (as a potential answer to Metzinger's (2018) and Hayles' (2018) request to establish biological integrity in a virtual body). If skin is less relevant for interaction in virtual environments, seeing underneath the skin can deeply connect us with the virtual body. If the skin is deceiving[9] and if I never have the skin of what I am, it is a reasonable urge to look beyond it.

By performing a close investigation of the inner body, it might be possible to understand Metzinger's indication that the user's interoceptive self-model is firmly locked in the biological body, or perhaps therein lies a connection to Revonsuo's biological level. To reach these biological levels, to unlock the biological body and to traverse the boundaries of skin seem to be an over-the-top suggestion, a disturbingly provocative idea. The skin is a border, a genuine protection between the visible and the invisible. It is understandably human to avoid what kind of rawness lies beneath, though this avoidance itself tells us again much about our ways to deflect.

3.3 Abjection and Autoaffection

The term abjection refers to being outcasted and it is explored in different studies such as in literary critical theory, social critical theory and in psychotherapy. In relation to my exploration of bodily innards, here I focus on Julia Kristeva's interpretation of abject, which she connotes with a psychological defense mechanism as a kind of avoidance. In *Powers of Horror* (1982), she explicitly refers to this kind of avoidance as 'abject', a strong feeling of disgust which is connected in somatic and symbolic realms. In the section of "Something to be Scared Of" in *Powers of Horror*, Kristeva writes:

> "The body's inside shows up in order to compensate for the collapse of the border between inside and outside. It is as if the skin, a fragile container, no longer guaranteed the integrity of one's 'own and clean self' but, scraped or

---

9   "Skin is deceiving -in life, one only has one skin-there is a bad exchange in human relations because one never is what one has. I have the skin of an angel but I am a jackal, the skin of a crocodile but I am a poodle, the skin of a black person, but I am white, the skin of a woman, but I am a man, I never have the skin of what I am. There is no exception to this rule because I am never what I have" (Moss 1996, 67).

transparent, invisible or taut, gave way before the dejection of its contents" (Kristeva 1982, 53).

This fragility of the skin threatens us with its easily penetrable nature, waking us up to the mortality of the flesh on daily basis. Kristeva suggests that a primal repression of this recognition of mortality is also connected to the rise of feelings of abject.

We feel abjection when something too familiar becomes too close, and although the familiarity is allowing such closeness, it feels overwhelming and as a result we feel nausea, as a psychosomatic manifestation. Everybody feels the undefinable comfort of their mother's smell, but it could also create strong abjection later in life as we are primordially programmed to separate from her in order to survive. Abject sets the rules of survival, but it also provides one of the most unpleasant feelings one can ever experience. In an interview series called "Women Analyze Women" in 1980, Kristeva says: "it [abject] is an urge to separate and be independent as an individual, meanwhile desperately facing the impossibility to do so." Which is why abject is an experience that simultaneously broadens our sense of self by inducing an accelerating toleration but at the same time discourages us from going further to explore what remains beyond the border. "The abject exists on the border, but does not respect the border. It is 'ambiguous', 'in-between', 'composite'" (Kristeva 1982, 4). Abject, similar to Merleau-Ponty's (1962) notion of chiasm, Heidegger's (1968) anxiety-tolerant "Dasein" and Waldenfels' (2011) "Selbstentzug", is nothing to push aside as a source of discomfort, but perhaps something to put under the microscope of our meticulous perception to explore. Maybe it is not meant to be considered as a disturbing aspect of owning a lived-body. On the contrary, it has its well-deserved place in philosophical exercise, since it always invades the lived experience. We may find a sense of liberation on the flip side of this avoidance, if we can tolerate the initial irritation.

Autoaffection is another notion which I have considered during the exploration of bodily innards. The idea of autoaffection goes back to Plato, in *Theatetus*, as he defines thinking as interior monologue (Lawlow 2014, 130). Derrida has taken this grounding motive of autoaffection and used as an object of deconstruction. Influenced by Derrida, a similar mode of deconstruction can be seen in Malabou's research in autoaffection. Her way of blending neuroscientific research with philosophical approach to construct a new plastic subject makes her a central figure in this chapter.

Malabou defines autoaffection as "the original and paradoxical manner in which the subject feels itself to be identical to itself in addressing itself to itself as to another in the strange space of its inner depths" (Malabou 2013, 221). Malabou's approach to autoaffection with its 'perceiving yourself perceiving' pattern is somehow aligned with David Hume's reflexive cycle of perceiving self: "When I enter most intimately into what I call myself, I always stumble on some particular perception or other, of heat, or cold, light or shade, love or hatred, pain or pleasure. I never can catch myself at any time without a perception, and never can observe anything but the perception" (Hume 2000, 165). McLuhan (1964, 52) also defined auto-amputation as the withdrawal of the self, a curling up towards within, and as a result technological extensions are used as prostheses to reconnect with the world outside.

We feel a form of alienation as we hear ourselves talk, as we sense our mouths talking. We reflect on this process from a third person perspective and we experience the succession of states of consciousness. This pendulum process of self-mirroring or self looking at the self, enables the fundamentals of the identity. "Autoaffection is the original power of the subject to interpellate itself, to autosolicit itself and constitute itself as a subject in this double movement of identity and alterity to self" (Malabou 2013, 221). Sensory modalities (e.g. the way I hear myself speak, the way I feel my own touch on my forehead) may be playing a significant role in autoaffection, as these acts bind the body to the self, remind us that the sense of self is inseparably linked to bodily feelings. Inevitably, abjection may occur as a result of autoaffection, since it requires a close look on the ways we deal with ourselves. Autoaffection requires an attempt to shake the habitual ways of practicing ourselves, and to transverse the borders to 'perceiving myself as a perceiver'. Ironically there is our alien-self we are not used to seeing, "within frontiers, the alien is already there" (Bukatman 1993, 42). In congruence with this thought, when I invite people to sit in an eyeball in VR, they could watch the eye watching outside. When we hear ourselves talking, we do not get to hear the real sound of talking from outside, we hear it from within.[10] The impossibility of the inner experience of sensory modalities is also articulated by Merleau-Ponty as he explains,

> "Like crystal, like metal and many other substances, I am a sonorous being, but I hear my own vibration from within; as Malraux (1951, 1978) said, I hear myself with my throat. In this, as he also has said, I am incomparable; my voice is bound to the mass of my own life as is the voice of no one else" (Merleau-Ponty 1968, 144).

Merleau-Ponty's example seems to point out to autoaffection, hearing ourselves from within and to previously emphasized as the act of touching our 'touching selves'. This corresponds to chiasm, or toleration of ambiguity, a paradoxical approval of bodily existence which contributes to the sense of identity.

The collection of VR designs I have detailed in the previous pages cultivates he experience of chiasm, as "Ambiguity in Lived Body Experiences" provides the user with the act of seeing oneself from outside (in reality we cannot take out our eyeballs and attach them to somewhere else to observe ourselves observing). In the "Machine To Be Another" (MTBA), in addition to the visual experience of the other's body, it urges the user to explore the connection between vision and touch (e.g the "synchronous stroking" exercise). In "sit be-

---

10   In "Speech Perception" O'Callaghan underlines the difference between linguistic and non-linguistic audition and implies "It is natural to think that the perceptual experience of listening to spoken language differs phenomenologically from the perceptual experience of listening to non-linguistic sounds, simply because speech sounds and non-linguistic sounds differ acoustically. Hearing the sound of a drop of water differs phenomenologically from hearing the sound of the spoken word 'drop' beause the sounds differ in their basic audible qualities" (O'Callaghan 2014, 477). What about perception of our own voice both from within and hearing it from voice recorders? Both sounds different due to the inner acoustic and outer acoustic perception. The reason why we feel estranged while listening to our own voice from a recorder could be related to this central acoustic difference. Additionally, our multi-linguistic selves have different acoustics in each language we speak as well. As an example: I have recorded my voice as I read out loud a passage from Kafka's Das Schloß, in three languages (translation of the exact paragraph in turkish, english and in the original language of the work, in german). In all three languages I have heard myself differently, from both within and from the recorded sound. To my understanding, this change of voice is due to the changing confidence one has in between different languages, as we speak one better than the others. Presumably, there is an altered self-perception of one's own voice while speaking different languages.

hind my eyes" the user is invited to explore the inner structure of an eyeball and observe the outside world while the eye muscles and tissues make up the environment. Technological developments, as peculiar and slow as they are, may boost the possibilities of autoaffection by providing malleable sensory experiences. These perspectival alterations can also influence and redefine our understanding of abjection. On the observation of 'a thing', Appelbaum describes that before we look at a wall, it already has had us in its gaze – this inverted intentionality overwhelms us while encountering both animate and inanimate things. "It [the thing] unsettles us as its awareness takes us in. The two gazes never intersect. Its looking fascinates us and we don't know how to take it—as a friend, a belligerent, a pervert, a nothing" (Appelbaum 2015, 3). If a wall's inanimate presence reflects this intentionality and frustrates us,[11] encountering one's own body image and innards and reflecting on such beyond our perspectival givenness could be challenging but also transforming and liberating.[12] If the body, as an object being, is something to avoid looking at, an understanding of the phenomenal character of subjective experience can be compromised. As Merleau-Ponty points out throughout *The Visible and the Invisible*, subject and object are ontologically juxtaposed, they are not separable – "they are the same thing: flesh" (Merleau-Ponty 1968, 137).

3.4 Body Image and Body Schema

Body image was first defined by Paul Schilder: "Body image is understood as the figuration of our body formed in our minds; i.e., the way the body is presented to us" (Schilder 1935, 11). He amplifies that the body image has a dynamic and tridimensional structure. Aside from Schilder's initial definition in neurology and psychoanalysis, body image is conceptualized in a range of different disciplines such as psychology, philosophy and cultural studies. Francoise Dolto articulates that body image holds the emotional aspects of lived experience, as if these subjective experiences are imprinted in the body image (Dolto

---

11   I relate to this frustration also with the over-repetition of certain words, how they lose their meaning due to repetition. Or if I look at my thigh persistently, I start to see it not as a part of my body, I feel depersonalized-as if my leg does not belong to me.

12   My suggestion of visiting bodily innards may sound like initiating a horror film production, since such images cannot be for the faint-hearted and can only be digested by people with a high toleration. Yet, abandoning comfort zones and exploring the rawness of nature can lead to a more universal understanding of the physical body.

1984, 22). On the other hand, she describes the body schema as an experience that is shared among all humans and it is felt unconsciously, pre-consciously, and consciously (Dolto 1984, 22–23).

The distinction between body image and body schema was a frequent theme in the VR experiments I have presented in this dissertation. Every subjective report I have gathered from the participants who spent a significant amount of time observing their own bodies in VR implicitly points out to the differences between body image and body schema (e.g. in "Ambiguity in Lived Body Experiences," a participant facing family conflicts after seeing himself from a top-down angle, another participant having seen her hair cut from behind and reconsidering her emotional distance towards her partner, another person reported feeling more grounded in his body after the exposure as he saw that "his back is not opening up to an endless space"). An extensive research on body image and body schema in neuroscience can be reframed within VR experiences. Perceived body image has a lot to do with the perception of object body, and the felt body schema pointed out to the plasticity of senses and to an increased sense of embodiment.

Although the differences between body image and body schema are articulated in different disciplines such as philosophy, phenomenology and neuroscience (Ritchie and Carruthers 2015, Noë 2009, Gallagher & Zahavi 2008, Holmes & Spence 2004), all eventually underline that body image reflects the subject's emotional approach to the body, whereas body schema is an assemblage of the felt body and may be seen as a neural representation of the body which is tightly connected to interoceptive perception.

Gallagher and Zahavi write that body image is composed of a system of experience and the intentional states of one's own body. These include three intentional elements: a subject's perceptual experience of their own body, a subject's conceptual understanding (including folk and/or scientific knowledge) of the body in general, and a subject's emotional attitude toward his or her body (Gallagher and Zahavi 2008, 146). These three elements indeed merge together on one gaze we direct toward our body image and then we evaluate what is seen. We intend to align with the desired image, which is shaped by cultural and individual experiences. Though, the limited perspectives from which we perceive the body image are also contributing to this paradox, since with these limited perspectives the total visibility remains inaccessible.

The perceived body image has corners we are not used to seeing. We are familiar with a limited number of angles of our body image; we know ourselves from those angles. We modify and align with this perceived image, which lays completely different in the eyes of the others. Our own image in the mirror is also not an original one, since it is a 'reversed' image of our features, which underlines the deceptiveness of the mirror image; our faces in reality are less symmetrical than we perceive them to be in the mirror image. Eventually, the body image we think we have is neither the one in the eyes of others, nor is the one in the mirror. Therefore the body image has a cumulation of emotional markers, assumptions and memories, all converted into an idea of the self we try to achieve while we gaze upon our own body. This corresponds to Lacanian body image, which I have discussed in detail in Chapter 1.

Some of the body images we perceive from photos or video images carry a strangely unknown perspective, perhaps from the profile, or from a top-down-angle from the right side or from the left side. We do not practice seeing these angles regularly. We may have a negative reaction to these specific attributes manifested in the image, and we weren't aware of how we appear to other people from this specific angle. We may have associated that image with someone we know or used to know, who we do not necessarily like and associate certain negative characteristics to that image. It evokes frustration. Obsessed with the 'seen'[13], we modify our hairdo, our clothes, our posture accordingly, as to not look like that unwanted image. This modification delivers yet another deceptive attempt; the perceived image of ourselves from a photo is not exactly the same in the eyes of the 'other,' either. The one in the photo has vanished and so did the image in the eyes of our perceivers. The body image updates itself rapidly according to our emotional associations. The significant twists and turns of our introspection on the self-image is ever changing, ever escaping our gaze and shamelessly reinventing itself without our consideration. On the notion of emotional tags Hayles writes: "In the grounded cognition view, the brain leverages body states to add emotional and affective 'tags' to experiences, storing them in memory and then reactivating them as simulations when similar experiences arise" (Hayles 2017, 49). We might consider that these tags are also applied on the body image. The same tags, with an intensive sense of abject, can be recognized when we think of the innards of the body. The sight of

---

13   Jean-Louis Comolli underlines: "The second half of the nineteenth century lives in a sort of frenzy of the visible...(This is) the effect of the social multiplication of images...(It is) the effect also, however, of something of a geographical extension of the field of the visible and the representable: by journies, explorations, colonisations, the whole world becomes visible at the same time that it becomes appropriatable" (Comolli 1980, 122–23).

an internal organ or an open wound which exposes the blood, fat and muscle tissues similarly evoke former associations and feelings of disgust. For some people, even the transparent imagery (such as x-rays and magnetic resonance imaging) of the body is intolerable. Just as with the first VR intervention 'Ambiguity in Lived-Body Experiences' I aimed to reform the self-perception of body image, the third experimental VR design 'sit-behind-my-eyes' is an attempt to normalize what 'unwanted imagery' is, as we direct our gaze within the body. Perhaps through such exercise, it is possible to understand that the body image is not limited only to what is seen outside of the skin, but it also can include what lies underneath the skin. What lies under the skin should not be excluded from what body image is.

No matter how strict our conscious effort is for distancing ourselves from our habitual associations with the body image, it is easy to fall back into the same pattern of perception. What is imprinted in a body image is rooted down at a very deep level, perhaps before our conscious recollection. It requires some sort of an extraordinary effort to peel the layers off of the body image. What if we were able to do this by using new media technologies to manipulate these aspects to improve our biased opinions of ourselves?[14] The camera eye, similar to the deceptive nature of mirrors, still stands as a proof of physical existence. As Jean-Louis Comolli notes: "The mechanical eye, the photographic lens[...]functions[...]as a guarantor of the identity of the visible with the normality of vision[...]with the norm of visual perception" (Comolli 1980, 123–24). Visual perception has influenced the use of the camera, and what the camera eye captures has defined the way we look around. Maybe it is possible to redefine our ways of looking and using technical artifacts to reverse these ingrained effects. If these apparatuses are invented by us, why can't we engineer their functionality in the way that we want?[15] If we can be courageous about extending the borders of self-knowledge, by not being afraid of knowing our own body image and not accepting what is imprinted on it, this might be possible.

---

14 This can be thought along the issue of filters that are used in Facebook and Instagram, and on other social media platforms. The ideal body image craves for add-ons. My suggestion here is to use media technologies, as opposed to this idea of add-on, to strip down the image until we reach what we could not see before. This motivation does not necessarily consider a purist view which tends to outcast software developments, but to deconstruct the ideal image, in order to redefine and personalize what the body image means.

15 For technology to assist us to what we want to see, and also enabling us a comfortable space within the exposure of the "truth."

Like the body itself, self is plastic. It is organically changing, leaving layers of characteristics over the course of a month, in the same way that our skin and hair is in constant renewal. Self and body co-evolve in this metamorphosis, experiencing transformation simultaneously, but without a conscious effort, it is not completely possible to become aware of their mutual and synchronous evolvement. If we want to redefine the functionality of the camera eye in order to achieve more information about the body image, VR could be a tool to begin with.

On the other hand, Hayles (1999) and Stone (1995) tackle the question of whether we really need VR to encounter the problem of the body. As indicated before, Hayles highlights that the virtual body lacks the relevant boundaries that are less defined by the skin and therefore bodily subjectivity is dispersed due to the lack of biological integration. Nevertheless, she frequently implies that simulations are necessary in order to grasp abstract concepts since thinking is entwined with the reenactment of bodily states and actions (Hayles 2014, 199–220). Stone (1995, 67) raises similar questions and says that if the written forms of communication (emails or a text-based MUD/multi-user dungeon) already challenge the sense of body in telecommunication, and we are nowhere close to deconstructing it, why would we let virtual technologies rupture our sense of reality and body? But the lack of polymodality of physical contact in current telecommunication (e.g. we combine the words we hear with the facial gestures of our encounter) could be further improved in virtual environments and telecommunication models (Braidotti 2002, 84). Of course, the interventions and collective subjective experiences I mentioned in this dissertation cannot fully provide enough evidence for this argument, but perhaps by studying the nature of perception with the use of VR can lead us to the fundamental understanding of our own body and sensory modalities, in order to elevate sensorial telecommunication with the others. Additionally, self-perception and body image can heavily benefit from developing telecommunication systems.

As mentioned in Chapter 2, the MTBA setup provided an interaction during which two people reflexively explored the nature of their body schema. The plasticity of the senses was explored by manipulating visual and tactile sensory contingencies. Altering simple inputs in our sensory modalities created the feeling of inhabiting another body. Gallagher & Zahavi (2008, 146) propose that the body schema contains two main attributes, "1) the close-to-automatic system of processes that constantly regulate posture and movement to serve intentional action; and 2) our pre-reflective and non-objectifying body-awareness" (Gallagher & Zahavi 2008, 146). Posture and movement regulation were fundamental during the MTBA sessions, as the synchronicity of movement and visual perception of the encountered body vastly influenced the body schema and consequently the sense of embodiment. In addition to posture, the intended synchronicity was actualized by both participants only when it was performed slowly and synchronously. The speed of movement influences the boundaries of body schema when exploring both a living encounter and/or with an object, as the speed of movement defines the quality of tactility, as well.

Bodily awareness and pre-reflective intentionality are elemental for the sense of body schema, as emphasized by Merleau-Ponty. Pre-reflectivity is a condition for 'being-in-the-world', as it is for Bergson's 'attention to life'. Movement and action influence and enhance the sense of body schema. As Noë (2009, 77) notes, my arms can be present to me without moving them (just by recognizing their existence internally), but for the act of reaching to the coffee mug on the table, I need a healthy and functional sense of body schema. This signifies that for establishing body schema, one needs to have developed habits of bodily activity along with proprioception. "This unarticulated and perhaps inarticulable knowledge of the body's readiness and availability with its natural degrees of freedom of movement supplies the foundation of everything we do" (Noë 2009, 78).

With a well-coordinated proprioception, tactility and sight, body schema seems to be an objective experience of body. This experience is common to all of us and reminds us that the body in its entirety is "the global awareness of my posture in the intersensory world" (Merleau-Ponty 2002, 102). Impaired visual cognition effects proprioception, and as a result we might accidentally hit the mug and spill the coffee, or we would not be able to grab it with precision. In contrast, body image is highly influenced by personal experiences and what contributes to this mental picture of ourselves that cannot be deconstructed as precisely as deconstructing body schema via sensory modalities. Noë highlights the example of how an anorexic teenager's 'damaged body image' leads to dysmorphia, but the body schema remains intact (Noë 2009, 78). In this line, the sense of body schema and body image are not necessarily interlaced. The body schema is a long-term, invading awareness which updates itself regularly and "relies on the proprioceptive, visual, haptic, vestibular, and motoric outputs" (Noë 2009, 79–80). On the other hand, the perception of body image includes a set of conscious and unconscious states and processes, "including our intermittent awareness of the body, our concepts and beliefs about the body, and our emotional responses to the body, and is sometimes claimed to be largely visual in nature....body image is much less closely related to proprioception" (Ritchie & Carruthers 2015, 365–366).

The adoption of objects into the body schema, phenomenologically speaking, points to the plasticity of sensory experience, and this remains a diverse theme in lived-body experiences. Body schema "accounts for the body's capacity to be open to, and intertwined with the world, enabling the integration or incorporation of seemingly 'external' objects into our corporeal activities" (Grosz 1995, 84). From Merleau-Ponty's (1962, 143) example of the blind man's cane and how it no longer feels like an object, but an extension of the hand which is holding it to guide to body, to McLuhan's (1964) technological apparatuses as embodied objects, it has been repeatedly argued that the body welcomes external entities to be a part of it after a persistent usage. The tip of the cane becomes a sensitive zone, as if the skin is stretched around it, and likewise, the recognized absence of our smart phones brings an alarming sense of incompleteness. Smart phones and laptop computers have unsurprisingly become a regular extension of our bodies. It is quite common to hear people articulating their sense of restlessness when they are distanced from their devices. We feel disconnected. A disconnection that includes a disconnection from the world wide web and also a disconnection from the physical sensation we feel towards the materiality of the devices. When people drop their devices or accidentally smash them, they tend to put their hand on the spot where the device is hit, in the similar fashion we do when we hit a part of our body. The things we habitually use, interact with, and/or simply keep close to our body, become extensions of us.

This steady feeling of connectedness can be understood through the theory of body map (Bonnier, 1905) which sets connections between body schema and a spatial configuration of the sensory system. As De Vignemont & Massin (2015, 304–305) explain, the body map plays a crucial role in spatially shaping tactile sensations with visual inputs. The body map can be thought of as a flexible (or plastic) web of structure which can quickly adjust to changes during interactions with external objects. When we wash dishes with a sponge, the felt size of our hand temporarily includes the size and texture of the sponge. When it is dropped, "the body map readjusts to the normal size of the body" (De Vignemont & Massin, 305).

Adopting Ihde's (1993) micro-perceptions (sensory perception) and macro-perceptions (interpreted perception), Sobchack reflects on automobiles and emphasizes it as "a technological artifact (whose technological function is not representation but transportation) has profoundly changed the temporal and spatial shape and meaning of our life-world and our own bodily and symbolic sense of ourselves" Sobchack (1994, 84). She adds that automotive transportation has not only changed our lived sense of distance and space, but it also altered the sense of our bodies by being incorporated into the body schema (the wheels resemble an extension of our legs which are capable of 'running' long distances without a break).[16] When we think of the moments of parking our car with an explicit consideration of centimeters, we surely demonstrate a well-functioning sense of proprioception by measuring the felt corners of the car as we put subtle pressures on the gas pedal. The car can be parked appropriately only with my precise consideration and calculation of the distance, and this precision represents the incorporated togetherness of me and the car. If I happen to get close to accidentally hitting the wall or other car, I perform a reflex similar to one my own body would use if it were about to hit something.

> "When our body schema is in this way transformed, our sense of what is near to us also changes. We can map space independently of ourselves, but we can also map it in relation to ourselves. Some regions of space are near us or within reach. Psychologists call this peripersonal space. Other regions are beyond reach. This is extrapersonal space. Transformations of the body schema can bring about extensions of peripersonal into what was merely extrapersonal space" (Noë 2009, 79–80).

If the external object we embodied were a living entity, things would become reciprocal, and therefore even more complex. For example, when we ride a horse, there are several aspects to consider about the nature of embodied cognition. Since I cannot communicate with the horse on a verbal level, and the horse does not have buttons for me to push to execute an order, my other sensory modalities actively search for ways to transmit my intention to the horse and vice versa. I should inhabit the ability to sense the horse's intention, whether it is obedient to my commands or not. The sense of touch and audition become means of communication. The sense of touch and haptic communication (directing the horse with the inner part of the thighs, tapping the horse's torso with the heels, pulling the ropes which are connected to the horse's mouth, or simply caressing its head and body with our hands to strengthen our bond) become fundamental in the communication and we

---

16   "The vernacular expression of regret at "being without wheels" is profound, and ontologically speaks to our very real incorporation of the automobile as well as its incorporation of us" (Sobchack 1994, 86).

start to communicate with the body.[17] Like all animals, the horse is a very perceptive and sensitive animal, one that can develop a sense for even the smallest
intentions. When we are in this ongoing haptic communication with a horse,
it is accepted into the body schema. My body schema extends to include the
dynamic relationship with the horse, and possibly the other way around, the
horse attunes to my body's posture and movements. I intuitively know this,
and have to retain a flexible posture which would move fluently accordingly to
the horse's movement, so as to avoid injury. Meanwhile, the horse is trying to
determine the exact speed of movement I want to attain. We are incorporated
in each others' intentions and give feedback to each other on a corporeal level,
which can exceed the limitations of verbal communication and constructed
moral restrictions. If a car or another non-living object becomes a part of my
body, this could be considered as a static embodiment, whereas embodiment
with another living thing can be felt even stronger due to the dynamic relationship between our body schemas. Haptic communication contributes to
intentionality when two living things interact, and this synchronous link of
mirror neurons lead to a common purpose.

Similarly, with the experience of owning a virtual body, these habitual extensions can be constructed by haptic communication and incorporated into
body schema. Once again, the critical point for extending the borders of the
virtual body is to simulate the neural expectations, by exploring one's expectations of the lived-body. But this remains to be a thing to look forward to in
the future, since haptic stimulation requires very precise implementation patterns in VR. A full transformation of the 'normal' environment and its interactive models into a VR environment is not possible, yet. As Braidotti states,

> "The VR scenario we have conjured is not one in which we see and feel and
> act just as we normally do; rather, it is a scenario in which it misleadingly
> seems to us as if that were the case. VR gives us as, at best, virtual experience
> and virtual minds" (Braidotti 2002, 176).

---

17   This detail of haptic communication I underline is similar to the importance of haptic
communication between dance partners: "[...] humans dance by mind-reading through
touch, they inconspicuously and swiftly understand their partner's control, this communication is modulated by the interaction mechanics. Haptic communication requires simultaneous information exchange, unlike serial verbal communication. Partners
do not have to trust the partner as they check directly. Scalable: The more the better"
(Takagi et al. 2017, 4).

Likewise, even the most well-known VR fanatic Lanier warns,

> "There will always be circumstances in which an illusion rendered by a layer
> of media technology, no matter how refined, will be revealed to be a lit-
> tle clumsy in comparison to unmediated reality. The forgery will be a little
> coarser and slower; a trace less graceful. Remember, we can't outrun the in-
> teractivity of reality" (Lanier 2017, 49).

Nevertheless, the attempts continue, and a virtual body schema is best
achieved by simulating proprioceptive perception. As Ritchie and Carruthers
underline: "Holistic perception and representation of our bodies has been
associated with the notion of body schema. Thus we now turn to the question
of the relationship between proprioception and this construct" (Ritchie and
Carruthers 2015, 365). Simulations which highlight virtual body ownership
could be eligible ground for tackling the relationship between proprioception
and body schema. For example, in a VR game, although I do not see my hand
I can interact and change things in the virtual environment with a controller.
Through this interactivity, I know the ratio between my head and my hand.
This sense of being in control of my movements and actions already evokes
incorporeality, and I seem to have the reflex to jump away when a sudden
threat occurs. "The effects of technology do not occur at the level of opinions or
concepts, but alter sense ratios or patterns of perception steadily and without
any resistance" (McLuhan 1994, 9).

Another frame for exploring the plasticity of perception and body is the
phenomenon of phantom limb, as it allows a reevaluation of body schema and
helps us to tackle issues such as: absence and presence, visible and invisible,
reality and virtuality, presentation and representation, felt presence and appearances, and prosthesis as technologically embodied objects. This also explains why one of the earliest rehabilitative uses of VR was about providing
different exercise methods for amputees, by altering visual simulations of the
absent limb and stimulating the nerve endings to evoke the movement (Dunn
2017, 4). These exercises in VR can be approached as extended versions of Ramachandran's mirror box therapy (more information in the upcoming section),
in which the image of the lost limb is simulated in the mirror image of the intact limb. In the case of VR, images of the lost limb that are virtually generated
can be manipulated, displaying different movements in different directions.
As presented in the rubber hand illusion experiment, the body schema is able
to integrate an external object into itself. In the same way, a loss of a limb does
not necessarily damage its felt-presence.

"Merely losing a limb in an accident doesn't alter the body schema; thats why the phantom lives on. And merely being a detached bit of plastic or rubber is not enough to prevent something from getting incorporated into the body schema" (Noë 2009, 78).

3.5 The phenomenon of phantom limb

The phenomenon of the phantom limb occurs when the subject experiences the sensation of a limb even though it has been amputated from the body. The sensation of the phantom limb suggests that the subject is continuously recognizing memories and emotions related to the amputated limb, which can also lead to a physical sensation from the non-existent limb. The phenomenon remains a fundamentally obscure one, yet we can still use this phenomenon to explore how psychical determinants and physical conditions are interlaced with each other.

Phantom limb has been investigated by numerous scientists, physicians, perception theorists and other philosophers throughout the years. Its initial description 'post-amputation sensation' was described by Ambroise Paré in his book *Treatise on Surgery* (1564) reporting that several amputees have complained about a distinctive pain where the amputated limb should be. Following the studies by Charles Bell (1830), Magendie (1833), Rhone (1842) Guéniot (1861), S. Weir Mitchell in 1871 coined the term 'phantom limb'. According to the recent research of Kassondra et al. (2018, 6), "Almost all (amputees) will experience the feeling of the amputated limb as still present, termed phantom limb sensation (PLS). Over 85% will also experience excruciatingly painful sensations known as phantom limb pain (PLP)." The amputee still feels a lingering sensation of an absent limb because

"the somatosensory cortex still contains a representation of the it (amputated limb), and immediately after the amputations begins to receive input from another part of the body that it interprets as coming from the missing limb" (Ramachandran 1992, 583).

In 1994, Ramachandran suggested the mirror box therapy for amputees who underwent upper body amputations. The visual therapy had a simple mechanism: a box with a mirror at the middle of it. When the amputee places the existing hand next to the mirror, it created the illusion that the missing hand was laying next to the other, through the mirrored image. When amputees opened and closed the existing hands, the visual and proprioceptive feedback within the mirrored image caused a decrease in the phantom pain. The missing visual trigger of a desired action and the attached memory of owning the limb were considered the main causes of phantom pain. This experimental design allows us to explore the connection between bodily practices, habitual movements and memory within the phantom limb phenomenon. The presence of a surrogate limb brings forth its felt presence, and releases its persistent phantom sensation.

We are not always aware of the ownership of our body parts as we use them in a fluent series of intention-action patterns. Each limb functions with an established sense of flow due to the habitual configurations we have assigned to them over time. The body habitually exhibits its own choreographed order of movements and we no longer consciously engage with this order, as Hayles (1999, 204) implies "by their nature, habits do not occupy conscious thought." There is a continuous circuit of neural processing throughout the body regardless of our conscious attention on it. The recognition of owning a limb remains vaguely veiled by its functionality. However, we seem to drastically recognize its existence, ironically, when we lose it. There is a tight connection between the habitual use and felt absence, as habitual use frequently bypasses conscious decisions. Presence melts away during habitual use and lingers as absence. Noë comments on the phantom sensation from this habitual aspect:

> "[...] what makes a hand yours is its involvement with your habits and projects. I still imagine that I hear the rattle of my dog's collar in the night, even though he has been dead more than a year [...] the absence of your hand is not real until it fails to be at your disposal when you prepare to reach with it or stop your fall with it. A limb is quasi-present as a phantom limb when the behavioral, environment-involving attitudes and engagements outlive the loss of the limb. Only when you fully adapt to your new circumstances—only when you break the habit of acting with and on your hand—will your ghost hand finally be put to rest" (Noë 2009, 77).

Indeed, this adaptation to a series of new circumstances is also the time we unlearn/forget the defined habitual cycle. For a deeper understanding of this, we can consult a memory from our lived experiences, for example any physical injury we might have experienced. Any injury, even if it is a paper cut on the tip of a finger, causes fluctuating pain, disabling the whole flow of movement, as we try to avoid any contact with the wound. We grab things differently, which can alter the balance and posture of the body; a small fracture of pain has the power to disrupt the fluidity of habitual movement. Through this loss of balance, we lose the totality in sensual grabbing. We lose habitual configuration as we touch, grab, hold, press, and squeeze objects and other external things around us. This reminds us of how we used to practice these acts without even realizing how naturally fluent were before the injury. But through this disruption, we face the fundamentals of mastering everyday skillful action and how this skillful coping requires innate skills which unknowingly allow us to find the optimal situation.

It is as if we suddenly become aware of the presence of a functioning limb, through the experience of the damage. This might be the point where habitual use cracks with the experience of an injury and re-connects us back to conscious thought (in reverse to Hayles' above mentioned "by their nature, habits do not occupy conscious thought"). Thus the habitual is disrupted with the absence, and gives access to conscious thought on the limb, related to the limb—to the memory of the limb. In this sense, memory and habit meet in absence. Memory appears at the breaking point of the habitual. For example, in the experience of typing slowly because of an injured fingertip, the memory of typing (which is sedimented in the body) lingers more drastically and as a result we become more conscious of our normal speed of typing. The loss of ability, proliferates the significance of the habitual ability. We awake to what we have when we do not have it any longer. Therefore, presence amplifies itself within the absence. Agitation in the midst of felt absence and discomfort illuminates the innate normalcy of bodily integrity. As in Adorno's (1951, 30) aphorism (isolating its political thematization, I refer to the 'splinter' here literally) "The splinter in your eye is the best magnifying-glass."

If we think of the lived body as presence and the virtual body as absence, they are dependent on one another for evolution: not only does the cognitive architecture of the lived body rapidly influence the virtual body, but also the virtual body repeatedly reminds us of what we own, but seem to have forgotten. Through the absence in a virtual body, we re-experience our lived body. The recognition of what we do not have within the virtual body anchors vividly and rapidly—so much so that on the biological level it can cause motion sickness. This is also why phantom limb phenomenon was one of the first research areas in VR therapy, as it is also occupied with understanding absence and presence.

In VR, through the absence of a physical body there is clear recognition of the physical properties of the lived body, which might be occurring within the perceived absence of visual and tactile perception of the body. This perceived absence offers an opportunity for a rehabilitation of the lived-body and its configurations. Lanier offers different VR definitions and one of them suggests: "(Fifth VR Definition) A mirror image of a person's sensory and motor organs, or if you like, an inversion of person" (Lanier 2017, 48). Like the amputee's mirrored hand in Ramachandran's mirror box, the perceived virtual body can be constructed; a model of sensory and motor organs. Evidently, one of the pioneering rehabilitation models in VR was developed to prevent phantom limb pain, in a similar fashion to the mirror box. This VR therapy method reduced the phenomenon of phantom limb pain (Murray et al. 2006). The system provided a visual representation of the amputee's whole body and used electromagnetic tracking hardware to transpose the existent limb into movements of a virtual limb. As a result, the amputee gained control of his amputated arm in VR and experienced a significant loss of pain. The system provided the amputee with the illusion of owning and moving the non-existent limb, and the patient gained a sense of relief. Recent research "Immersive Low-Cost Virtual Reality Treatment for Phantom Limb Pain" by Elisabetta Ambron et al. (2018) also showed that these immersive systems are relatively cost efficient.

Murray & Sixsmith (2008) apply a phenomenological perspective to explore first person embodiment in different VR applications and raise the question about whether a visual representation of a virtual body plays a crucial role in different applications. They specifically focus on the cases of "disrupted" bodies, such as phantom limb, dissociation of the self from the body, paralysis, and objectified bodies. They provide a context specific understanding of embodiment in VR. They indicate that further investigations will need to be carried in order to understand the virtual body's sensorial architecture and its interwoven nature with the real body (Murray & Sixsmith 2008, 1).

Corporeality and the sense of bodily presence are particularly important for therapeutic designs in VR, since interaction is necessary for rehabilitation. Perceptual-motor disturbances, proprioceptive problems occur as a result of neglected visual representations of bodily self and such neglecting may limit the progression of treatments, specifically in psychotherapeutic usage of VR (Holmes & Spence 2006, 4).

The therapeutic application of VR, known as "Virtual Reality Therapy" (VRT) started during the 90s with Max North in his first publication on the topic titled "Virtual Environment and Psychological Disorders" (North 1997). VR has been extensively used as a therapeutic tool for treating depression, post- traumatic stress disorder (PTSD), eating disorders and body dysmorphia, autism and post-stroke symptoms (Oliver et. al. 2014). It has been determined from a media theoretical perspective that VR technologies are "purposefully attributed with their own therapeutic agency so to have an impact on users' feelings and change both their psychological condition and behaviour" (Friedrich 2016, 88).

3.6 Phenomenological Approach to Phantom Limb Phenomenon

Merleau-Ponty takes up Husserl's definition of the phenomenal body and bodily experience through the concept of embodiment, and emphasizes the lived body. He stresses the notions of body schema and motor intentionality, under which he also examines the case of PLP (Phenomenon of Phantom Limb). This is where Merleau-Ponty departs from Husserl's approach, by taking experimental and clinical studies under consideration (e.g. his application of Gestalt psychology), especially "ones having to do with psychological deficits and pathologies" (Siewert 2015, 143). By doing so, Merleau-Ponty seems to be rejecting the common dissociation made between phenomenology and science. Additionally, we could state that this reversal signifies Merleau-Ponty's nod toward Hegelian phenomenology and objective idealism.

Merleau-Ponty emphasizes the body primarily as 'lived-body'; our body is not only a vehicle under the domination of mind, it thrives in the external world and manifests our intentions beyond the defined order of the mind. In other words, the lived-body represents the unity of mind-body which interacts with the world. He claims, to the contrary of empirical statements, that it is important to pay attention to the lived body's pre-reflective engagement with its surroundings while we examine the lived body in terms of its spatiality (that is, the body's relation to other external objects). The lived body, by its nature, is ambiguous, since it is both physical and self-conscious (it is both physiological and psychological). There are underlying, interwoven sensations which bring an ambiguous quality to the experience of owning a lived-body. Any experience related to 'lived experience' and 'human phenomena' could be taken as an ambiguous experience. A significant example is the phenomenon of the phantom limb, with its obscure physical and psychical indications.

According to Merleau-Ponty, ambiguity shall be taken as a source of our new understanding of lived bodily experience and as a reminder of 'being-in-the-world'; therefore ambiguity is not a disturbing aspect of owning a lived body that is to be ignored, disregarded and dissolved in philosophical thought, "ambiguity is essential to human existence, and everything that we live or think always has several senses" (Landes 2013, 56). His [Merleau-Ponty] acceptance (and to a certain extent, appreciation) of ambiguity paves the way for his ap-

proach on ontology of flesh and chiasm. Chiasm, derives from greek word ‚chi'
which means crossing over relation or arrangement (Landes 2013, 37). In Merleau-Pontian terms, it's used to describe the rhetorical structure or crisscross-
ing structures of nerves in the brain, such as in the experience of touching and
being touched. Both acts cannot be experienced at the same time, thus the ambiguity proliferates in this chiasm.

Although Husserl was the first philosopher who put the body, and specifically the notion of lived-body at the center of his research, Merleau-Ponty has
largely focused on the ambiguous nature of the body. The examination of our
given ambiguity may be observed during interactions with the outside world
(which also gives way to Merleau-Ponty's primary focus on subject-object relations), since the lived body is always oriented towards the outside world, in a
cascading attitude. When we inhabit a virtual space, we have the ownership of
two different lived bodies; the one which is rooted in the physical world, and the
other which is felt as virtually present. The latter company is felt but not entirely
conquered, and therefore it is similar to the feeling of an anesthetized layer on
the body. The virtual body resembles a more mechanical and less-intentional
representation of the lived-body. This ground, where we have double ownership of both bodies, could bring a productive state, a method for exploring the
untackled dimensions (which are usually taken for granted and hard to wake
up to in daily life) of the lived body and its ambiguous nature. We can explore
what Merleau-Ponty (2002, 34) points out with "not with a detached awareness
of objects but with an active involvement of the body." The body continues to
exist in the physical world, but at the same time we are embodied in the virtual world. The embodied virtual body imitates (or springs forth?) our bodily
intentions and moves, interacts and manipulates within its perceived virtual
field. Such simultaneous ownership of body, which is rarely experienced (perhaps only in pathological cases of dissociative states), could enable us to revisit
the notion of chiasm.

In VR it might be possible to investigate the existing ontological ambiguity between lived-body and Körper. Such attempts can underline the need of
an interdisciplinary dialogue, and could amplify the importance of owning a
virtual body. As a response to the neglect of the body, Cathryn Vasseleu underlines, "The aims of many who are investigating virtual environments are being directed toward the legitimation of fantasies of disembodied mastery and
eradicated corporeal limits...But this fantasy is bound to the bodies it excludes"
(Vasseleu 1998, 82).

Could it be possible to use virtual reality technologies to re-organize and approach the intentions of the lived-body, in order to understand/observe the ontological ambiguities that exist between Leib and Körper? Haraway indicates "Communication technologies and biotechnologies are the crucial tools for re-crafting our bodies" (Haraway 1984, 13). In this line, how can we make use of virtual environments to deliberately identify the bifurcation of our bodily being? Could such intention of "re-crafting" the body finally be practiced in VR?

3.6.1 Anosognosia

Anosognosia can be another subcontext to discuss along the felt absence and felt presence of virtual limbs in VR. Anosognosia a condition in which the paralyzed patients deny their paralysis. The state of being in either acceptance or refusal of a physical condition signifies an obvious psychological state. When a part of the body, for example an arm, is paralyzed and the subject continues to sense the presence and the absence of the arm at the same time; the existence of the paralyzed arm resembles "a cold and long snake" (Merleau-Ponty 1945, 2002, 88), which the subject is not in control of. This 'snake' of an arm was taken under examination in a VR setup called "Extending Body Space in Immersive Virtual Reality: A Very Long Arm Illusion" (Kilteni et. al, 2012). Their findings enrich previous results that multi-sensory and sensorimotor information can reconstruct our perception of the body shape, size and symmetry even when this is not consistent with normal body proportions. In the case of anasognosia, the brain cannot connect to the paralyzed arm to raise it, but the arm somehow still feels like a part of the body, this is similar to the moments of bugs in VR immersion as we look down on the virtual body and we cannot move the integrated limbs.

Can we say that the unconscious memory tolerates this ambiguity and insists on the refusal of deficiency, since it is constantly bonding with the brain? The existence of the limb still lingers both when the sensory conductors are paralyzed or numbed with anesthesia[18] and also when the limb is amputated. Therefore, to explain the phenomenon of the phantom limb, and also the case of anasognosia, we need both psychological and physical inquiries. Merleau-

---

18   Similar to the sensation of the hand getting enormous after partial anesthesia or one can also feel this when the arm falls asleep. When we wake up and feel this strange presence of a snake like thing flopping around/out of control.

Ponty (2002, 89) suggests a mixed theory that constitutes the simple effect of an objective causality and 'cogitatio'; a common ground between physiological facts (which are in space) and psychological facts (which are nowhere). He brings an existential perspective to the ambiguous nature of the phenomenon; the habitual body cannot perceive the absence of the limb, so it cannot adjust itself to the new objective body.

Merleau-Ponty questions if "being in the world" is something like Bergson's "attention to life," which is the consciousness we gain from 'nascent movements' in our body. Reflex, as a nascent movement, is consciously observed as 'a happening coming into existence',[19] yet our consciousness is not engaged in the process (e.g. sneezing). Perhaps we can say that the reflexive movements are the acts of our habitual body, and our objective body becomes a spectator to them. Unlike the stimuli-receptor engagement, reflex movements do not need a stimulus to occur; they adjust to the environment and they do it without waiting for a stimulus. Evidently, 'being in the world' also includes experiences that do not require stimulation. Or actually, aren't we constantly interacting with our environment, stimulated at all times, with or without our conscious recognition? Merleau-Ponty suggests that we examine an inner mechanism which functions beyond the sensible contents of the brain, where one can explore the ambiguity of one's own body and develop deeper insight about the experience of being in the world, by waking up to the junction of the psychical and the physiological.

We can approach cases of both anosognosia and the phenomenon of phantom limb as the body's representations of presence and the absence. The feelings of ambiguity arise where these concepts interlace with one another (or separate from one another). We can interpret anosognosia as 'the absence of a fragment of the body's representation', meaning, the related limb is in fact present. The phantom limb is 'the presence of a part of the body's representation' which is in fact, absent. Aside from the physical experience of it, even the attempt to understand the ambiguous nature of this polarity is nauseating, yet this is exactly where the body parts establish themselves through their absence, with each part being equally constituent for the body's integrity. Thus the "ambiguity is essential to human existence and everything that we live or think always has several senses" (Merleau-Ponty 2002, 196). We can broaden

---

19   This thought can be traced in Bergson's statement: "I look closer: I find movements
      begun, but not executed" (Bergson 2002, 86).

our understanding of the human phenomena by experiencing different ambiguities, which will eventually shift our perception of the lived body from unfamiliar to "uncannily too familiar" (Kristeva 1982, 45).

The anosognosic patient finds his paralyzed arm unfamiliar to himself, but beneath his unfamiliarity, he figures out where exactly the paralyzed limb is, he knows where the deficiency lies, so that he can avoid it. Here again, the opposites substantiate each other; he would not define and feel the unfamiliar, if he hadn't experienced the familiarity. He avoids encountering his deficiency, just as a psychoanalytic subject attempts to move away from the conflict, as soon as he penetrates the borders of the main problem (in Freudian terms, deflecting). Denial calls forth the self-awareness, otherwise we wouldn't define 'the self' as an autonomous being who guide their own life by reason and sensuality, but also as a perplexed being, disintegrated by their own complexity. Therefore, for our pre-reflective consciousness, both the presence and absence are familiar and readily established in the mind, and are also carnally felt. Absence and presence coexist in our being simultaneously and continuously.

In the case of the phantom limb, the person is not aware of the absence of the limb and continues acting as if life still flows through it. Because he feels the limb's presence just as a subject who hasn't lost a limb would, he doesn't need direct consciousness of his body in order to start a movement. The body has an 'indivisible power' which tolerates the absence of the limb (phenomenal field is the zone, which can tolerate ambiguity); our habitual body acts in continuous adaptation. Can we therefore say that the phantom limb has a consciousness of its own? What we articulate (sense) as 'ambiguity' might actually be a complementary system, a collaboration of the habitual and objective body, as a resistance against the mutilated limb so as to protect the ontological integrity of the body. The amputee feels his leg, as I can feel the presence of a friend who is not in front of me. Merleau-Ponty exemplifies Proust's situation with his grandmother as an example: Proust can "certainly recognize the death of his grandmother without yet losing her to the extent that he keeps her on the horizon of his life" (Merleau-Ponty 1945, 122). As mentioned before, our receptors do not necessarily need an external-physical stimulation to experience an actual arousal, similarly, we can experience emotional reactions to an imagined event. Our transversal functions allow us to experience a percept that presents itself from a memory or from an anticipated possibility. Such thoughts can create psychophysiological reactions, such as laughter, crying, goose bumps, and sweating.

Likewise, the absence of the limb, the lack of an external stimulation or the person would not prevent me from sensing it/them as if they are there. The denial of the amputation or the deficiency of a limb is not a conscious decision made by the subject. He does not consider whether to continue feeling the presence of the limb or not, as the recognition of the phantom limb does not occur in the state of thetic consciousness. The desire to have a fully functional body cannot be articulated with the state of "I think/want that," therefore the phantom limb phenomenon reminds us of the body's attempt to carry itself forward as a whole, having its own consciousness that challenges the mind and eventually challenges us to understand how both physiological and psychological aspects clash within the experience of absence.

Paradoxically, the absence of a limb strikingly binds my body to the world. My hand is a vehicle to manifest my habitual intentions; I connect to the world of manipulable objects through the integrity of my limbs. My hand is undeniably the most reliable bridge that reminds me of my sensory and motor interactions with the world. If my hand unites me with the world, the absence of it reminds me even more of our strong bond. If I lose my ability to manipulate an object, I disconnect from the universe that I carry myself towards. My attempt to grasp the objects around me is also my attempt to remind myself of my body. If I cannot fulfill my practical intentions, my perceptual connection with the world becomes distorted.

Similarly, when we inhabit the virtual world without a body, or having a body with no arms or without a torso and having only hands, we experience this distortion drastically. We experience the lingering presence of the lived body more when we perceive the absence of it in virtuality. Similar to the rubber hand illusion, in which the visual and tactile sensations are interconnected, the absence of one modality can be simulated by bolstering another. Noë explains that the RHI allows us to rethink the unique relationship with our bodies:

"...it [rubber hand illusion] does not consist merely of the fact that my hands and arms, say, channel nerve tissue into me, or rather, into my brain. Connectedness, attachment, contiguity—these are important but mere connectedness or attachment yields only a superficial explanation of what the body is. What makes connection and contiguity important is that they themselves track coordination and common fate...Part of what makes it my hand is the fact that it is the one with which I grasp the cup...I feel with it (e.g. the cup is too hot!) and in it (I am being tapped and stoked!). Its 'mine'ness consists in the way it is actively, dynamically, visually involved in my living" Noë (2009, 74–75).

3.6.2 Organic repression

The nature of the phantom limb can also be explained through the concept of repression. Repression, in Freudian terms, is being stuck in an attempt which neither forces the person out of the struggle he faces, nor helps him to acknowledge the obstacle he has to deal with. Merleau-Ponty (2002, 90) describes repression as a pattern which disables us from being aware of our own place in the passage of time. Repression is revealed when we lose our ability to interpret the present with actual circumstances. In other words, our fixation on the past makes us resistant to develop new ways to deal with the obstacle, and we become unaware of the fact that we cannot apply an old solution, which we once produced in the past, to a new, unique and complex present. We remain partially open to a future with new possibilities, yet a part of us continues to be haunted by our past selves, who are trapped in the numbing comfort of familiar struggles, such as ones we encountered in 'adolescent love' or in a 'parental universe.' Our fear of discovering new worlds reveals our hesitation to explore, which could be perceived as 'traumatic'.

The repressed thing is something that is not only unhealed but also not understood, and what is not understood is something to repress, since we have not provided a space or time to experience the unique representations. What is intended to be repressed resembles an experience I have encountered before, but that experience has also been repressed and hides itself behind another moment; thus I continue to repress, repressing also the memory in question. Therefore, repression has a scholastic quality of existence, since our concept of 'now' becomes a perpetual ring of past events, a continuous absence of present perception.

As long as I place myself within the physical world, I continue to be in the multitude of causalities, which constantly remind me of my being in the world as a subject-object. The rhythm of my life is therefore not something I always have power over; I'm placed in the stream of happenings and, as a being in the world, the rhythm happens to me as a result of the milieu I conquer. This almost 'impersonal' fashion of existing is an inner sphere of my personal existence, in which I do not recognize myself and take it for granted.

Beneath my personal view and everything I maintain in it, I am primordially aware of the fact that I first have to belong to a general world. My body as an organism has this 'pre-personal adhesion' to the world and it flows in the stream of impersonal existence with the other beings. Beneath my personal life, there is an 'innate complex.' Contrary to my personal intolerance of mortality, there I accept my own finitude as well. The impersonal fashion of existing brings me an initial knowledge that my own finitude is a unique way of 'being there' (Dasein) and '[being] for itself'. Therefore, as an organism, I am pre-conscious about life and its rhythm. What is aimed to be repressed remains undeniably harnessed in our volitional being. But our personal existence represses the organism. For the personal existence, the trauma's autonomous existence is too painful to accept and it is repressed without transcending or even being identified as happening. My gaze escapes to wander to other objects in the natural and cultural milieu, just to avoid recognizing what is about to be repressed.

Our past distinctively feeds our present by our constant re-evaluation of the experiences we have had. We approve of our totality by making sense of our intentional acts in the past. We claim to understand our past 'better than it understood itself'. Therefore my present becomes a reconsideration of previous presents I have experienced and gathered; my concept of time repeats itself in this cycle and never actually seals itself off. My consciousness in any given instant is over-occupied with figuring out the ambiguity of being in the world and the ambiguity of time. Merleau-Ponty (1945, 22) explains that the amputee's non-existent limb represents a repressed experience: "a previous present that cannot commit to becoming past." If the limb is felt through an emotional print rather than a physical appearance, then the memory of the limb lingers as an emotion, which becomes the origin of the phantom limb, a carnal memory. The state of carnal emotion is a refusal to deal with the problem but also not a complete abandonment of the present condition. As in the case of repression, instead of analyzing the causes and revolting against the burden of the trauma, within the passage time the amputee seeks relief in the memory of the limb, in the memory of a world where he is complete and the limb is present. He stays in that world so strongly that the collaboration of his mind and body enables him to sense the non-existent limb through afferent conductors; they keep the amputated arm within the circuit of existence, they let him feel the phantom. Therefore, through the phenomenon of phantom limb we understand how the refusal of deficiency can be so powerful that it can even interfere with and manipulate our sensorimotor circuit. Also, the other way around, my body can reverse what I reflect upon the world and upon my subjective world. I am not just a psyche or just an organism; my intentionality and personal acts occur from my ability to switch in between these states, as a way to tolerate the ambiguity. Yet, what is already tolerated by our organism cannot be articulated easily, physically or psychically.

When we explain the phantom limb phenomenon as an organic suppression, we can't determine whether this repression has psychical or physiological roots. Therefore we have to develop a deeper understanding of the concepts of substitution, instinctual awareness and objective consciousness. The phenomenon of substitution includes both psychical and physiological aspects, unfurling in the perception of those who have lost limbs. An insect substitutes a healthy leg to perform the function of a removed leg. And if the leg is not removed but only trapped, the substitution does not occur, because the impulse to perform the action continues to circuit through the trapped limb; the world still passes through that limb. But when the leg is removed/amputated, the insect instinctually sets a new configuration of the legs, so as to keep functioning in the same world. This reconfiguration can be emphasized in Malabou's (2008, 27–28) "Reparative Plasticity: the brain and its regeneration" approach. Cellular renewal, synaptic plasticity and the brain's ability to build natural prostheses all represent forms of plasticity. The re-organization of motor function (according to Malabou, testifies to the plasticity of brain mechanisms) is both a topic in phantom limb phenomenon and the virtual body, since in both cases there is a preoccupation with felt presence through the absence of a limb/body. In both cases, the absence of visual perception does not disable the sensation, a visual absence/or a distorted visual does not fully blur the body schema's intention to incorporate the felt representation.

3.6.3 Onticity or Intention Toward: Biology of Instinct

Figure 11: A moment of synchronicity: A tiny spider's leg on the word "phantom" as I was reflecting on the topic of leg substitution in insects.

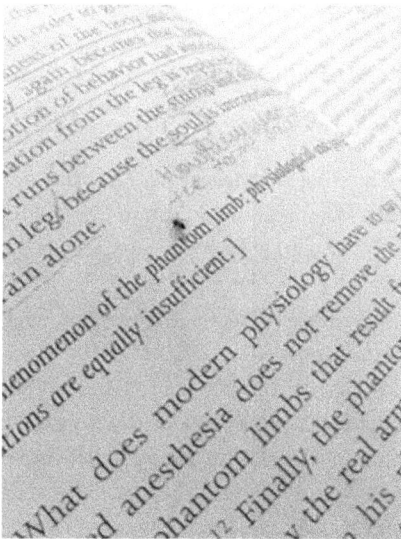

Hayles compares the subjective experience of humans and non-human organisms and comments that we (humans and other organisms) both lack an ultimate reason to carry on, but nevertheless we pursue our "onticitiy in the world" (Hayles 2017, 16). She compares a bacterium to human beings, and underline our mutual will to pursue our destination. Similarly, Kovac writes that the bacterium "is already a subject, facing the world as an object. At all levels, from the simplest to the most complex, the overall construction of the subject, the embodiment of the achieved knowledge, represents its epistemic complexity" (Kovac 2000, 59). Likewise, Damasio (2004, 41) writes that even a simple organism like a paramecium has emotions. Both Hayles' bacterium and Merleau-Ponty's insects with absent legs could be clustered with Damasio's paramecium, in terms of the will to live without having a concrete reason for why and how. Damasio (2004, 41) writes that the instinctual responsiveness to life belongs to every living thing. Even a unicellular organism is capable of detecting danger and can move away from a threat to protect the wholeness of its membrane. "A brainless creature already contains the essence of the process of emotion that we humans have—detection of the presence of an object or event that recommends avoidance and evasion or endorsement and approach" (Damasio 2004, 41). Living things are able to preserve life and bypass the dangerous moments, not because of well-regulated intentional thought patterns, but because of an automatically driven instinct to do so.[20] But of course, as Damasio explains, having a more challenging environment than a paramecium's, human brain has developed to overcome more complicated obstacles in our environments. Clearly, as Malabou (2013, 36) implies, for Damasio, 'ontological' is another name for 'biological'.

Whether we call it instinct, somatic marker (Damasio 2008, 165) or gut feeling, it is mutual among human and nonhuman living things. With or without a brain, we all share the urge to keep going and surviving (what Hayles (2014, 45) calls "intention toward"). The phenomenon of phantom limb highlights this connection between absence and the felt presence of 'being in the world', and this connection is further apparent in virtual worlds, as we are consciously experiencing an ongoing absence of limbs and related abilities.

We all intend to carry ourselves towards the world in all of our power. For this purpose, substitution occurs almost automatically. We know that a substitution does not occur when a limb is trapped (i.e not amputated but tied up), although its function is disabled by being caught. We can say that the phenomenon of substitution is not entirely related to functionality or a lack of functionality. Substitution occurs when the insect loses the ontological status of the removed limb. 'Being in the world' is more crucial than focusing on the functionality. We can't claim that the insect makes conscious decisions; rather we can say that the insect's bodily recognition is triggered by its survival instinct. Substitution comes as a reflex. We substitute unintentionally, maybe somewhere along the nonconscious levels, but nevertheless it somehow fulfills exactly what needs to be substituted.

In his book *Out of Our Heads, Why you are not your brain and other lessons from the biology of consciousness*, Alva Noë (2009, 55) examines the phenomenon of phantom limb and underlines the importance of the primary somatosensory cortex in animals and humans. When an amputee is touched on the face, she

---

20   Can sensation be considered as the basic material of subjectivity, rather than cognition?

may also feel a touch on her missing hand. Noë explains that this is due to the close intersection of hand and face areas in the cortex. Because of the amputation, the hand area receives less input and the neighboring face area seems to get entangled with the hand area.[21] Therefore the feeling of being touched on the face now evokes two different sensations. A similar indication comes from Ramachandran:

> "[…] sensory processing involves a one-way cascade of information sensory receptors on the skin and other sense organs to higher brain centers. But my experiments with (my) patients have taught me that this is not how the brain works. Its connections are extraordinarily labile and dynamic. Perceptions emerge as a result of reverberations of signals between different levels of the sensory hierarchy indeed across different senses. This account of neural plasticity helps us to understand that emotional and affective mechanisms are not predetermined" (Ramachandran 1999, 56).

Ramachandran warns us to be careful about the 'brain as a computer' analogy, similar to Changeux's indication, "The human brain makes one think of a gigantic assembly of tens of billions of interlacing neuronal 'spider's webs' in which myriads of electrical impulses flash by, relayed from time to time by a rich array of chemical signals" (Changeux 1985, 126). Neural plasticity of the brain may be less predictable and reliable than computers (as previously underlined, Hayles also warns that biological life forms and computational media are *not* akin to each other, but rather they perform similar functions).

Noë claims that the phenomena of feeling touch on a phantom limb after stimulation of the cheek seems to contradict with Mriganka Sur's (1992) ferret experiment, where ferrets see with their auditory senses, rather than with their eyes. "Sur's ferrets don't hear with their eyes, they see with their auditory brains: the auditory cortex changes its function for consciousness as a result of receiving stimulation from the eyes. But in the case of 'referred sensation' to a phantom limb, things are just the other way around. The phantom limb, crazy as this may sound, feels on his hand with his face" (Noë 2009, 55–56).

---

21   Jaak Panksepp, who has coined the term "affective neuroscience" explains: "There are no unambiguous 'centers' or loci for discrete emotions in the brain that do not massively interdigitate with other functions, even though certain key cirucits are essential for certain emotions to be elaborated. Everything ultimately emerges from the interactions of many systems. For this reason, modern neuroscientists talk about interacting 'circuits', 'networks' and 'cell assemblies' rahter than 'centers'" (Panksepp 1998, 177).

In this context, sensory substitution seems to play a crucial biological role in the instinctual way of being-in-the-world. When a fundamental link is ripped from us, we quickly and compulsively seek for another way to re-engage with the world, and this attitude bypasses conscious thinking, similar to habits. If, by their nature, habits do not occupy conscious thought, can we suggest that substitution is a deeply biological and fundamental habit? Does the absence of a limb bind us through a myriad of complicated neural pathways back to a sense of presence? Then, is that yet again another indication of how absence strengthens the feeling of presence? With or without a brain, subjective experience of survival and being in the-world has much to do with perception. Maybe, it is really about sensation, rather than cognition.

Because my main motive is to simulate neural expectations of a lived body in VR, I find it crucial to explore sensory substitution, as we frequently deal with the absence of sensory modalities in a virtual body. Vision, obviously, is central for VR experience. As Lanier (2017, 53) puts it, vision functions by pursuing and detecting changes instead of constancies, therefore a neural expectation exists. In between anticipated changes and expected results, in VR it could be possible to explore the holistic nature of the nervous system via sensory substitution. Then the question remains: "How do my other senses give me access to the world?"

3.6.4 Sensory Substitution

In the late 1960s, Paul Bach-y-Rita came up with a visuo-tactile experiment to explore the plasticity of perception. With the help of a camera and array of vibrators, he enabled a substitution of visual sense with tactile sense. In his article "Tactile Vision Substitution: Past and Future" Bach-y-Rita (2009, 29–32) explains that he placed the vibrators on the thigh or abdomen of blind subjects. These vibrators transmitted tactile stimuli on the subject's skin, correlating to certain visual aspects of the object that the camera recorded. Through tactile stimulation, the blind subject could perceive the content of the objects, such as the shape and the size of the objects placed on the table.[22] As a result of this visuo-tactile substitution system, the blind person could guess what was placed

---

22   To have a better understanding how this setup functions, we can imagine the game in which a friend writes a letter or number on our back with their fingertip and we try to guess which number or letter is written as we focus on the movement and touch of their finger.

on a table and they could even throw a ball precisely to the desired target. This setup has established a different way of connecting individuals to the environment, even if they lack a fundamental sensory modality (visual).

Similar to the importance of movement in vision, active movement is also a central issue in sensory substitution. The speed of movement in tactile stimulation can alter the perception of what the feedback could represent. For example, in Bach-y-Rita's experiment, a fast stimulated letter 'A' could be perceived as a triangle. The process of tactile stimuli being translated into visual information involved a very complex network of events in the brain, so much that we may even consider nothing remains tactile about this perceiving. As Noë comments, "In touch, we find out about things around us by coming into contact with them, but tactile-visual sensory substitution enables us to tell how things stand around us and at a distance, in precisely the way vision does" (Noë 2009, 62).

Sensory substitution and the sensorial structure of the body influence both the way we perceive external coordinates and the conscious experience of the body. Perceptual consciousness is crucial for the body's everyday interaction and coping with the environment. Of course, we would not be able to see, touch and hear if we didn't have a brain (although, what about the bacterium?). It is established that the brain magnificently marshals the body's integrity, but equally, we would not be able to see, touch and hear without a body, either. This inseparable embeddedness between mind, brain and body, continues to disprove cartesian dualism. Furthermore, there are many more juxtaposed compounds which contribute in this unification of the psychical and the physical. Dewey's (1884, 278) foresight points out to the same direction:

> "...we see that man is somewhat more than a neatly dovetailed psychical machine who may be taken as an isolated individual, laid on the dissecting table of analysis and duly anatomized. We know that his life is bound up with the life of society, of the nation in the ethos and nomos; we know that he is closely connected with all the past by the lines of education, tradition, and heredity; we know that man is indeed the microcosm who has gathered into himself the riches of the world, both of space and of time, the world physical and the world psychical."

Although all the neural pathways lead to the brain and the complexity of sensory perception is widely explored in neuroscience, as Noë (2009, 63) indicates, the brain does not generate perceptual consciousness the way a stove generates heat. He refers to the functional nature of musical instruments and how they do not generate sound and compose music on their own. Without the influence of human capacity to make use of it, a musical instrument remains as a dysfunctional tool, deprived of its elemental qualities. Through this analogy, Noë (2009, 64) opposes Francis Crick's (1994) idea of "You are your brain" and underlines the importance of body while exploring the phenomenon of consciousness. Digestion is not only about the phenomenon of stomach, a laughter is released from the mouth after a complex informational process, and a self-playing orchestra is definitely an absurd idea to consult. Similarly, Damasio highlights the role of bodily perception, "The mind exists because there is a body to furnish it with contents" (Damasio 2004, 206).

3.6.5 Why phantom limb phenomenon is relevant to VR investigation?

The phenomenon of phantom limb is particularly relevant to the investigation of the virtual body, because both the virtual limb and the phantom limb are about representation. In fact, the entire virtual body resembles a phantom body, not entirely seen but felt through presence. Phantom limb lingers as a habitual memory which is sedimented in the body's ligaments. The visual absence of the limb does not affect the sensation of it. The representation of the absent limb continues to be felt and the visual absence does not entirely blur the body schema's intention to incorporate the representation of the limb. A virtual limb, although it may not be in our visual field, can be felt and manipulated through proprioceptive perception (remembering Massumi's (2002, 58) "The spatiality of the body without an image can be understood even more immediately as an effect of proprioception"). Telepresence and VR creates a unique sense of presence, a sense of 'being there' in the remote or virtual environment (Murray & Sixsmith 1999, 324). Although the surroundings and necessary modalities seem to be physically absent, it is possible to create the sense of presence within these inaccessible environments. What seems to be absent, can be felt even more drastically, such as the violated expectation from an invisible touch. Lanier gives the example of theremins, to explain the effect of invisible touch. A theremin is an instrument with metal antennas where the user is able to create sound by controlling oscillators for frequency and volume. The user controls the sound with certain hand gestures in the air close to the antennas, without actually touching them: "[...] nothing is touched, and playing gives you the feeling of contact with a virtual world" (Lanier 2017, 19). Similarly, in a virtual environment we can interact with the surrounding objects and we can still direct the course of events, even without a visual representation of hands and other limbs. We can manipulate visuals, bend the forms and influence the narration of a story in VR. Interaction with a 'non-existent' materiality can still transmit a feeling of interaction. How would an interaction without materiality effect our sensory modalities? A theremin could be also thought in terms of mid-air haptics technology. Mid-air haptics use ultrasound to project tactile sensation on the user's hand, a recent example is produced by the company Ultrahaptics in 2019.[23] Obrist et al. (2015) used Ultrahaptics to detect "Emotions Mediated Through Mid-Air Haptics", which opens up new opportunities for interaction.

Lanier (2017, 53) proposes that with the progress of VR, human perception will be nurtured and we will be able to have a more extensive experience with physical reality. Could this be a result of a continuous experience of both absence and presence during an interaction with new technology? Could we grow a more nurtured understanding of our cognitive and perceptual capacities, by repeatedly facing the absence of these attributes in virtuality? Are we simultaneously registering the presence of these through their absence? For example, I hold a bottle in VR without having a visualization of my hand, and I manipulate the controllers in the physical realm which implicitly indicate the borders of my hand. Therefore, I am at some level aware of the boundaries of the object I am about to interact with, thanks to my body schema, which is still functioning in the virtual realm. I can grasp and hold the bottle in the air, throw it away and manipulate the materialistic nature of it, indicative of the control I have of the object and its position in the environment. But I fail to sense its weight, texture and temperature. The best I can do at that moment is to recall from my bodily memory how that specific object would weigh and feel in my hand, since weight, texture and temperature are explanatory components for feeling an object. Furthermore, I become aware of owning a hand, my own hand, and its receptivity. As Braidotti explains: "The body is not only multi-functional but also in some ways multilingual: it speaks through temperature, motion, speed, emotions, excitement that affect cardiac rhythm and the like" (Braidotti 2002, 230).

Owning a multilingual body and limbs, is indeed something we neglect and take for granted. Phenomenological meditations precisely suggest that this wakeful recognition of the body and its parts is fundamental for constructing a sense of being-in-the-world. Experiencing the absence of limbs in VR and waking up to their presence, or their innate givenness in reality,

---

23   https://www.ultrahaptics.com/about/, 2019

resembles a phenomenological exercise to try to let go of the attitude of taking the body for granted. Therefore, VR can be seen as a tool to incorporate in the phenomenological exercise, which could amplify the suggestion of post-phenomenology, as it aims to include technological developments into the philosophy of perception.

One of the main intentions of this dissertation is to suggest that the experience of VR will strengthen subjective experience of body ownership and will retrospectively deepen the phenomenological understanding of this experience. VR will not necessarily reform traditional phenomenology, but it may re-emphasize the common theories which overlap with technological borders. Because both the technology and phenomenology inherently and persistently incorporate the study of the body, perceptual experience, cognition and perceptual consciousness, together they can open new gates for a deeper understanding of these concepts. VR could be seen as a tool which demands scientific, philosophical and technological attention. As Lanier puts it, virtual body can be deprived of human traits, yet, it is also the "farthest-reaching apparatus for researching what a human being is in the terms of cognition and perception" (Lanier 2017, 1).

In *The End of Phenomenology*, Tom Sparrow (2014) reevaluates the phenomenological tradition and, contrary to the title of the book, he delivers a fair account of the work of Merleau-Ponty and Emmanuel Levinas. He draws fundamental insights from both, while preserving his distance from the "frustrating methodology" of phenomenology and it's "tiring antirealism" (Sparrow 2014, 5). Agreeing with Graham Harman's (2018, 189) "speculative realism", he [Sparrow] suggests a 'new realism' as a way to reconnect phenomenological insights back to this century. Both speculative realism and new realism highlight the importance of an "Object Oriented Ontology" (OOO). OOO criticizes radical philosophy's stand against objects and suggests that everything we encounter can be counted as an object. By asserting the importance of objecthood, a reflexive relationship between object and subject can be determined and this can be highly important for further understanding of subjective experience. Commenting on Harman's work on real and sensual objects, Sparrow compares this to Heidegger's philosophy of 'Zuhandenheit' (readiness to hand), or 'tool-being'."Tool-being unlocks Heidegger's familiar theory of equipment just as much as it explains the concept of "withdrawal" that permeates Harman's speculative realism. A brief exposition of Zuhandenheit and its dueling partner Vorhandenheit (presence-at-hand) will enable us to get to the bottom of tool-being and, by consequence, the with-drawn status of real objects" (Sparrow 2014, 124). In this way, by subtracting the real object status from the 'presence-at-hand', Harman's speculative realism tends to explore the hidden nature of objects, as opposed[24] to Heidegger's neglect of the invisible life of things. Graham and Sparrow's intention to explore beyond appearances can be seen akin with Massumi's (2011, 42) question "[...]what exactly does the inconvenient reality that we see things we don't actually see say about the nature of perception?"

Sparrow considers OOO through Nagel's (1974, 435) "objective phenomenology", which requires the understanding of "what-it's-like"ness as the core dynamic of phenomenal character of subjective experience. A bat relies on auditive stimuli to survive in the dark more than it's visual perception. This perceptual experience is, however, inaccessible through empathy or imagination. In this case, as Sparrow points out with the alien phenomenology's (Waldenfels 2011) opposition to the objective phenomenology. The only way to access the what-it's-like "is through metaphor or analogy, that is aesthetic devices crafted to allow sensual objects to interact in the sensual ether. Metaphor, of course, does not literally bring two objects together (which would entail reductionism). It does, however, enable us to characterize object perception, which withdraws from experience no less than the real object itself. Metaphor is what we use to understand what camera sees. The so-called New Aesthetic tries to do the same thing by other means" (Sparrow 2014, 173).

In the online interview "The New Aesthetic Needs to Get Weirder" (2012), Ian Bogost defines the New Aesthetic as a technologically governed form of artistic impression, which aims to explore everyday life and technology from the use of computers.[25] VR is able to expose these metaphors, simulate sensual objects, and expand analogies by exploiting sensual experience and manipulating the perceptual quality of telepresence; it will certainly widen a recognition

---

24   Also partially opposed to Husserl, as Sparrow astutely raises the point: "If Husserl claims that the invisible side of the object is still real,then the real is never detached from human consciousness, even if we do not see it" (Sparrow 2014, 125).

25   In this interview Ian Bogost (2012) further speculates: "Why stop at the unfathomability of the computer's experience when there are airports, sandstone, koalas, climate, toaster pastries, kudzu, the International 505 racing dinghy, and the Boeing 787 Dreamliner to contemplate?" Apparently, Bogost sides with the importance of object theory and reminds us of the danger which may come with an intense focus on 'technology-only' attitude, which can in fact distort the main intention to explore this kind of what-it-is-like-ness.

in New Aesthetic. Furthermore, it could be possible to swap first person perspective, in this sense, MTBA experiments could be seen as a humble beginning for it. Could we then suggest that Nagel's objective phenomenology has a chance with the use of VR through swapping first person perspective? Could we swap bodies or perspectives with a bat through the use of BCI (Brain Computer Interface) and VR? Or start with a flight navigator in VR to simulate the flight experience of a bat? Can technology answer the questions philosophy of perception has raised since years? If technology is the answer,[26] then we have to formulate the question carefully.

Harman (2011, 25–26) reformulates Husserl's 'intentional objects' as 'sensual objects'. Sensual objects can offer us (subjects) the experience of recognizing the nature of objects beyond their contingent features. Sparrow further comments on this: "[...]what Harman takes away from Husserl's sensual object is the concept of 'allusion'. This is how sensual objects, to the phenomenologically sensitive observer, indirectly refer to their real, hidden features" (Sparrow, 2014, 121). When we explore a sensual object, we let go of the object's ordinary traits and meet its onticity, regardless of our subjective and pre-defined gaze upon it. This sensitive attitude towards the object, which bypasses its appearance, is in Harman's definition (2007, 171), the "allure effect", or a "bewitching emotional effect" (Harman 2007, 171).[27]

The difference between the phenomenal quality and essential givenness of an object could be observed during an interaction with virtual objects. Virtual objects, similar to the sensual objects, can represent beyond their physical attributes. Because of the virtual object's non-materialistic existence, when we encounter them, we automatically switch to see what is beyond its appearance. We cannot grab or touch it. But, just seeing it already composes a sensation how it would feel if we were to reach out and grab it, and we experience the feeling of touch by anticipation. The anticipation accumulates a wider range of emotions to reflect on compared to the habitual interactions we have with objects in daily life. As Noë puts it, "Technology increases the scope of our access, and so it increases the extent of what is or can be present for us" (Noë 2009, 83).

Furthermore, as I previously implied, the possibility of controlling a virtual object with a virtual hand could evoke the subjective quality of owning a hand.

---

26   Cedric Price, Technology Is the Answer, But What Was the Question?, London from 1960.

27   Could this "bewitching emotional effect" be also considered as affect?

A chiasm, or a double sensation within the virtual mode, can occur. How would this object feel if I were to touch it? How would my hand feel if I were to touch this object in its real form? Or if we think back Bach-y-Rita's visuo-tactile substitution for the blind, wouldn't the tactile stimuli on its own be considered as a great example for encountering a sensual object?[28] Could we harness the substituted sensation more vividly when we are deprived of another sensation, as it is the case with the phantom limb phenomenon? How would this particular deprivation alter our perception for objects and thus influence our subjective experience of the body, since the subjective body is in an ongoing interaction with the objects? Does the technological development consider the position of the disabled and direct its attention accordingly? Perhaps, not enough, not yet.

3.7 Biotechnology and Disability

In *Carnal Thoughts: Embodiment and Moving Image Culture* Vivian Sobchack describes that the phenomenological approach to film experience highlights the importance of spatial consciousness and the sense of existential presence of in the body (Sobchack 2006, 328). For her theoretical approach, both subjective sense and material presence are drawn out by human beings' interaction with cinematic and electronic media devices. The phenomenological approach generally supports the explanatory nature of subject-object relationships, but when engaging with media technologies as objects, their materiality invites us to explore a very particular and multi-layered subjective experience. Each technology offers our lived-bodies radically different ways of "being-in-the-world" (Sobchack 2016, 45). Technological artifacts are not neutral entities, they are not merely instrumental. They are historically informed capsules, constituting cultural and social fluctuations in time. Furthermore the materiality of technology is experienced when it is in contact with human beings, when it is incorporated and sedimented into lived-experiences (here, Sobchack's approach aligns with Noë's idea that 'a self-playing orchestra is not possible'). As a result of this incorporative process, subject-object relations become "cooperative, co-constitutive, dynamic, and reversible" (Sobchack 2006, 84). In this understanding of reversibility and dynamic cooperation, the plasticity of our relationship with media mirrors the plasticity of our perceptual processes, as

---

28   Seeing is feeling, feeling is seeing.

both the body and the brain do not have a rigid structure. "On the contrary, it is open to external influences and affects" (Malabou 2013, 28).

Hayles criticizes Malabou's focus on plasticity, and instead suggests the term 'flexibility,' as "the context of human neurology is too narrow to express adequately how flexibility occurs in biological and technical media" (Hayles, 2017, 215). In my experience, the interoceptive perception in VR (how we feel our body from within when we are exposed to VR), elevates our awareness of both the plasticity and flexibility of our sensory modalities. Why would Hayles prefer the term flexibility instead of plasticity, when flexible is a very explanatory adjective to plasticity? From my own experiences in VR, I can attest to certain awarenesses of the plasticity in sensory spectrum, which have accompanied me even after leaving the VR environment. For example, in our most recent research "Multi-sensory integration and the role of tactile stimulation in VR",[29] together with my colleagues Sebastian Schäf and Benjamin Dupré, we had several problems while calibrating the datagloves with the actual movement of the hands. After several months and countless attempts, the alignment with the virtual hand movement was still not as stable as we desired it to be.[30] Virtual hands are supposed to synchronize with the real hand movement through motion tracking (a combination of integrated motion trackers in the fabric of the datagloves, and the LeapMotion[31] which was attached on the VR HMD). Due to several reasons, we could not solve this calibration issue. After experiencing over twenty minutes of a visual delay between the movement of my real hands and my virtual hands I see in VR (see figure 12), I was convinced that this delay existed even after leaving the VR environment.

---

29   "Multi-sensory integration and the role of tactile stimulation in VR" (Akbal, Gaebler, Trump, Dupré, Villringer 2019–2020) is the research project, in which we have been exploring the role of tactile stimulation with a pair of datagloves in VR. The project is financially supported by Max Planck Institute for Human Cognitive and Brain Sciences and Max Planck Institute for Human Development.

30   "Der Trick, eine solche Immersion hervorzurufen besteht darin, die dabei auftretenden Inkohärenzen zu zensieren, also das Wissen und das Gefühl, gleichzeitig an zwei oder drei Orten zu sein, auszuschalten und die Situation durch Projektion bzw. Identifikation eindeutig zu machen [...] Er funktioniert freilich nur, wenn die VR-Welt sich synchron zu den Körperbewegungen und kognitiven Erwartungen verhält, also wenn beispielsweise nicht Unvereinbarkeiten oder zu lange Verzögerungen zwischen Kopfbewegungen und daran gekoppelten Bildveränderungen bestehen [...]" (Rötzer 2000, 156).

31   https://www.ultraleap.com, 2019.

When I placed the HMD aside and walked to the bathroom, I started to feel that I was moving in a slower pace, compared to what I would consider my normal speed of movement. Additionally, when I looked down on my body, I saw my feet were stepping forward with a visual delay. As I put my hand towards the door knob to open it, it arrived with a delay, much longer than how I would normally orient my hand and arm to complete the act of opening the door. This was most likely due to my time spent adjusting the delay in VR. I moved slower in the VE in order to cope with the miscalibrated virtual limbs. Due to this adaptation to a miscalibration of movement, I realized that even a twenty-minute exposure was long enough to influence my habitual gaze and proprioceptive perception in a non-VR environment. It was not easy to leave my modified perception behind, I needed time to come back to my senses to recognize that in the real environment there is no delay between the executed movement and the visual percept of that specific movement. The immediacy between an intended action and the visual demonstration of it was much more apparent in conscious effort, due to the practiced delay of it in VR. This experience supports Lanier's explanation: "Your center of experience persists even after the body changes and the rest of the world changes. VR peels away phenomena and reveals that consciousness remains and is real. VR is the technology that exposes you to yourself" (Lanier 2017, 55). One sense can regulate other senses and beyond. In the case of the delay confusion in my post-VR experience, it was visual perception altering proprioceptive perception. Even though I intellectually knew and acknowledged that this virtual delay was due to an underdeveloped setup, my visuospatial processing was manipulated to a point of misalignment even when I switched back to the physical reality. Our senses are indeed like the plastic. Within the first few seconds after burning the plastic, it twirls and shapes itself in various directions.[32] Human perception grabs all visual, tactile, auditory data and skillfully process them into a meaningful message. This is what Noë (2004, 2) precisely means by an "enactive view," we do not turn off one sense to attune to the other, they are complementary and always active. Unlike a computer that records and processes data (this interchangeability of human and computer 'mind' can be seen in concepts outside of traditional computational models), we can respond while recording. Instead of being static and passively enduring, we react from the juxtaposition of our senses. Thus, the brain is fragile, because, as Malabou says, "...it depends on us

---

32   "The arrow touches a thing in the night that becomes its target. We are a sense, hungry for signs" (Deguy 1990, 44).

as much as we depend on it—the dizzying reciprocity of reception, donation, and suspension of form that outlines the new structure of consciousness" (Malabou 2008, 8). The MTBA setup provided several lived experiences (both for me and for the over 40 people I worked with) which have highlighted the richness of sensory experience which comes with reciprocality.

When we think of our interactive process with an object, e.g with a table, even there is an ongoing perceptual experience as we walk around it, feel the quality of the material, sit on it to test its resistance, lift it to feel its weight or sit by it to study on it. On the other hand, our interactive processes with any 'material' within a virtual environment occurs on a different level. We inscribe a visual story by altering our angle with bodily movements (motion parallax in VR), additionally we may have the ability to manipulate the shape and consistency of objects around us (I cannot manipulate the size of a real wooden table with my two fingers, but I can divide the virtual table into two with a subtle touch). Consequently, we experience a drastic perceptual manipulation and as a result we may recognize the plasticity of our own senses in a non-habitual way.

I always find it fascinating when researchers' lived-experience, somewhere along their lives, aligns with the main focus of their own research.[33] Influenced by the amputation of her own left leg, Sobchack explains how she becomes her own subject, using her body as an 'intimate laboratory', reflecting from her lived-experience on the analogies between absence-presence and phantom-real (Sobchack 2010, 51). Beyond the explanatory powers of neuroscience and medicine, she explains, the experience of phantom sensation is understood more on a level of subjective consciousness (Sobchack 2010, 51–52). Phantom sensation has experiential effects which are immediately perceived. The experience of absence (and consequently dealing with the memory of presence) and its immediate access to conscious experience is indeed something phenomenological, as much as 'first philosophy' is occupied with. The contemporary understanding of embodiment, neuro- and cognitive sciences has been influenced by the reformulations of phenomenological methods (e.g. Gallagher, Thompson, Zahavi). Embodied consciousness first requires a clear

---

33   Another intriguing example of this can be phenomenologist Kevin Aho's heart attack experience. He reflected on his lived-experience in his article "Notes from a Heart Attack: A Phenomenology of an Altered Body" (2019). He explains the limitations he experienced after the heart attack and how this sense of precarity has enabled him to develop a stronger bodily awareness.

recognition of subjective reflection, a reflection upon what first is lived. For Sobchack, phantom limb phenomenon can gather the disciplines around itself, like an inexplicable box of wonder, forcing each to exchange information to articulate material causes and processes; and beyond, the subjective awareness of absence and presence (Sobchack 2010, 55).

Within the experience of having phantoms and adjusting to a prosthetic leg, Sobchack hints at the similarity between the disabled and the experience of becoming a cyborg. She warns us about the consequence of the deprivation of flesh:

"What many surgeries and my prosthetic experience have really taught me is that, if we are to survive into the next century, we must counter the millennial discourses that would decontextualize our flesh into insensate sign or digitize it into cyberspace...Prosthetically enabled I am, nonetheless, not a cyborg. Unlike Baudrillard, I have not forgotten finitude and naked capacities of my flesh nor, more importantly, do I desire to escape them" (Sobchack 1995, 209).

Subjective understanding of bodily sense should be considered as a priority as we develop our techno-culture. The case of disability could be a central starting point, since the experience of absence within a disability points to the gap between the needs of disabled and the biotechnological developments. It also points to the similarities between human beings and cyborgs.[34]

In "The Travel Narratives of a Cripple", Michael Leverett (1998, 184) criticizes Donna Haraway, Elizabeth Grosz, and Rosi Braidotti[35] for their distanced attitude towards the 'messiness' of disability. He suggests that they indulge in 'myth and metaphor' in their approach to the cyborg. I find Leverett's critique not necessarily useful or true: Haraway's cyborg often considers both non-binary assets, and shifting percepts of the gendered and disabled body. Grosz often amplifies the importance of the body in the junction of critical analysis of post-human and disability, and Braidotti is considerate of the symbiotic relationship between human and machine—all attempts to grow beyond what a 'myth' signifies and such attitudes require quite messy roads to travel. Nevertheless, he does thoughtfully argue why disabled people's experience should be considered more in technological developments, as they "often strive to rework

---

34   "You are the cyborg, cyborg is you" (Hayles 1999, xii).

35   Leverett calls these writers "the literary figures of three poststructuralist feminists" (Leverett 1998, 184).

the biotechnological revolution to their advantage" (Leverett 1998, 139). By constructing a virtual body via neural expectations, it could be possible to convert digital limb movements into new forms of prosthetic extensions. As Braidotti underlines: "Far from abolishing or replacing the body, the new technologies strengthen the corporeal structure of both humans and machines" (Braidotti 2002, 244).

Conclusion

"No matter how virtual the subject may become, there is still a body attached. It may be off somewhere else...but consciousness remains firmly rooted in the physical. Historically, body, technology and community constitute each other" (Allucquere Rosanne Stone 1992, 81).

In the light of Stone's warnings of a non-critical acknowledgement of Cartesian dualism, it becomes more crucial to understand the inseparable connections between the mind and the body, especially now that there are a myriad ways to acknowledge it, as we move towards the so-called 'Information Age' of technology.

The conventional debates about VR and cyber-spaces deny the importance of corporeality and bodily perception, defining them as media technologies of distortion (to an extent of sensual mutilation) and disembodiment. These debates can be summarized in certain insights such as: "in the end, a smile is not important because it's a mouth. It's important because it transmits data" (Goldin-Meadows 2017, 27), "in cyberspace minds are connected to minds, existing in perfect concord without the limitations or necessities of the physical body" (Heim 1993, 34), "it's like having had your everything amputated" (Barlow 1990, 33). In this dissertation I aimed to represent the opposite stand to such debates, defending a consideration of the body not only as a necessary, but also as a fundamental condition for improving the sense of presence within 'inaccessible' remote environments. Why do we need a body in a virtual environment? Our biological embeddedness requires to reign the physical space in order to achieve a sense of presence. As Noë emphasizes, we need the polymodal affection of physicality: "We hear the words and see the facial expressions and feel the heat of each other's breath and jointly attend to what is going on around us" (Noë 2009, 84). Presence is established with the perceiving brain, which receives constant information from the ever-perceiving body, which is busy with converting environmental and internal signals. In virtual worlds, all these modalities are underdeveloped and as a result, the need to establish a totality of bodily perception arises for the virtual body to continue processing information.

The notion of the lived-body has influenced my approach to the virtual body. In a phenomenological sense, the body is the baseline of all perceptional experience. In order to immerse and live in a virtual world, we have to reach the conformity of a virtual body, by placing the body again at the center of all perception. With this niche in mind, I traced the formative and sensitive formulations of the lived-body within my practical approach of constructing and evaluating a virtual body. The experience of inhabiting a virtual body, or the attempt to exist in one, also enabled another understanding for the notion of 'being-in-the-world'. As long as I place myself in the physical world, I continue to be entangled in the multitude of causalities, which constantly reminds me of my being in the world as a subject-object. Likewise, in the virtual world, the integrity of my subject-object being is clearly recognized, perhaps with a more drastic impact due to the excessive perception of the absence of my sensory modalities. As a consequence, with this dissertation I can affirm that there are noteworthy parallels between a lived body and virtual body, and between the sense of 'being-in-the-world' and 'being-in-the-*virtual-world*'. Both the virtual body and the lived-body are placed in the stream of happenings and the rhythm happens to them within the milieu they conquer. Both the virtual world and the living world are there as a milieu for us to observe and reflect upon; it is the background of all our happenings. I have taken the basic description of the phenomenological approach as "the study of things that appear" and applied this to the virtual world from the perception of a virtual body. The realization was there: the virtual body strictly demands a sort of curiosity about one's own subjective experience, akin to the one we need to practice in reality, in order to discover the depths of being-in-the-world. In this line, the products of new technology, in my case VR technologies, have helped me to clarify, validate and amplify the role of subjective experience of the body.

In my opinion, which has been influenced and shaped not only by the literature I have introduced in this dissertation, but also by my practical work in VR, bodies can directly contribute to knowledge production. This was very clear to me, as the body, when it is exposed to VR, continuously collected and absorbed information, and reacted accordingly. For instance, we know for a fact that the sense of touch is intermingled with the sense of sight. But e.g. due to the virtual body's lack of sense of touch, which results in the absence of an optimal grip, we understand that for an intact body to have a lived-experience, we need to consider the proximity of all senses. A cat's fur may look smooth because it looks shiny and flat, but we cannot attest to its softness unless we slide our palm on its back at least once. Knowledge is already there: multi-sensory integration enriches the sensory experience itself. But the reproduction of knowledge may be possible when we centralize the body in practical exercises. It is possible, only after putting the body through these probing acts in VR that we can trace the fundamentals of multi-sensory experience within the perceived absence of these modalities. Reproduction continues as we apply this incarnated knowledge into the developmental phase (both in software and hardware applications). For example, if we were to touch a virtual flower, we would expect it to feel different in contrast to the haptic feedback we expect to receive from touching a virtual table. The organic texture of a flower is carved in our haptic memory; it is soft, furry, bumpy like a succulent, or spiky, whatever our visual connotation of the flower is, we anticipate to achieve that specific sensation through a very specific haptic feedback. The sensational quality of this haptic feedback is still not distinguishable in virtual objects because thus far, the existing vibro-tactile devices and textile-based wearable electronic interfaces still cannot provide specific contents (as I have discussed in Chapter 3). Still, with the existing technology, it is possible to address and optimize the intensity of vibromotor configurations to at least transmit the difference between fine touch and coarse touch. Additionally, in my recent work in which I tackle the role of haptic feedback in multi-sensory integration in VR with a pair of datagloves, I have tried to simulate the illusion of grabbing an object by modifying electrovibration feedback which is released at the tip of each finger and in the palms of gloves. Consult your memory of the moment when you grab an object, lets say a wine glass. In this moment, not every finger applies the same amount of pressure in order to stabilize and hold it. Mainly, the thumb and the joints of the index and the middle finger supports the hold, remaining fingers supports the object as well, but only to attain the ideal balance (though such fine touches are not to be underestimated, since a fine attunement is also very crucial in terms of achieving the desired posture and intended stability). When we grab a virtual wine glass, we can simulate these pressure points by modifying the haptic feedback, in this case: the intensity of vibration is 80% in the thumb, in the index finger tip, and in the sensors which are close to these two fingers on the palm. Remaining fingers receive fewer vibrational feedback, so they feel less in contact with the virtual object. We can create the illusion of tension we feel as we grab an object, but not the surface tension. Still, even to simulate the pressure points and the sense of weight accounts for a positive beginning, perhaps one day we can simulate the surface tension to distinguish the sensation of a flower pedal from the wooden surface of a table.

I give this example to underline the reciprocal relationship between the experiencing and reporting subject in VR and the developer and/or theorist who applies these feedbacks back into the development. When the user of the datagloves (e.g. in the case of grabbing a virtual wine glass) – communicates to the programmer about which intensity of vibrational feedback feels more natural and more realistic, they automatically start to work together to achieve the ultimate realistic feeling. Body is central to all this process and a phenomenological investigation into one's own subjective experience of the body therefore remains as the milestone of this development.

Thus, we embark on the reflexive cycle between the body and the technology: the information is absorbed by the body, which evaluates and embodies the effect, purges out the consequences which signifies the phenomenal experience of the subjective body, and continues to influence the development itself. Through the VR experiments and interactive installations I have presented in this dissertation, I can advocate that the responsivity of the body enabled me to reproduce the theories and knowledge behind the VR applications. As chronologically presented in 3 chapters, each experiment represents a layer, unfolding deeper into the body. The first layer, "Ambiguity of Lived-Body Experiences" focused on the outer layer, body image. I used a product of new technology as an extendable and manipulable mirror to investigate the common notion of phenomenology I mentioned above: to study the things that appear. In this context, I actively studied the perception of one's own body image. With this intervention, it was highlighted that the body image contains subjective experiences and that there are significant shifts in our understanding of these imprinted subjective experiences. As a result of this intervention, further research can look into whether it is possible for humans to disconnect from a predefined habitual gaze upon their body image, and to switch to a series of new subjective connotations surrounding their body image.

Chapter 2 introduced the MTBA experiments, which signifies the attendance of a second person into the virtual environment. This represents the second layer towards within, because the process of embodiment pointed out to the presence of felt-body, which is experienced within the body schema. The moments of embodiment through bodily practices in MTBA thus have raised the importance of the plasticity of sensory spectrum, which pushed me to investigate how body schema is prone to sensual manipulation, when multi-sensory (in the case of MTBA, the visual and tactile sensory modalities) integration occurs. The moment of embodiment lingers as a gateway to internal states, as the embodied self explores the sensation almost on a visceral level. In the specific case of MTBA trials, we (me, as a frequent visitor of the system and many other participants) often had the need to ground the body in the body itself, since what we saw (e.g. mirrored image of someone else when I look down on my body) did not match with what we felt (as we saw this mirrored image of someone else was being stroked on the hand-and we did not feel it on our hands). The perplexity that arose within the perception of a visuo-haptic mismatch proliferated the sense of body ownership, once again highlighting the interconnectivity of sight and touch. These tackled perspectives are felt on a deeper level, deeper than what the body image represents. Consequently, this has underlined how the feeling of body schema is mutual and shared among all of us, unlike the personally modified nature of one's perception of body image. The complex and manipulable structures of VR has provided us a ground to carnally distinguish the difference between body image and body schema. I suggest that in the future such differences will be more apparent when reinterpreted on the basis of owning a virtual body.

In comparison to the first 2 chapters, Chapter 3 has a more personal and demanding intensity, as it is the core dynamic of this dissertation. This chapter has shown (to me and hopefully to the reader) that when the subject and object of the research become the same thing, self-alienation is an expected result. This kind of alienation appears due to a constant attitude of distancing oneself (subject) from the main theme (object) in order to analyze it. To analyze, we need distance, the kind of distance we put in between us and the painting we see on the wall, in order to perceive the depth and nuances in it. So when we constantly remain objective to our own becoming self, we become increasingly distanced from ourselves. This distance is aligned with the core dynamic of the last chapter (or paradoxically, the distance provided the context), as it dealt with the notions of "Unheimlicher Körper", the phenomenology of the alien and the urge to convert the meaning of uncanny into something familiar. In Chapter 3, I presented the exhibition project 'sit behind my eyes', which highlighted the inner experience of the body and how we, as the owners of our bodies, remain strangers to the inner parts of our bodies. If we can effort to integrate the innards of the body into the idea of the body image, I suggested, we can have a more concrete and wider understanding of what the body image really should and could mean for us. We tend to think that the innards are

excluded because they are abjected, but I carved a point of view that it is abjected because perhaps they have been excluded from our visual perception.
When something is out of our view and out of our reach, it becomes fundamentally hidden, reserved and not acknowledged. As a result, we look away
and feel disgust as soon as it is exposed. It is uncanny and we are not ready
to explore it, because it reminds us of the alien in ourselves, a part that we do
not dare to inquire (imagine the exposed flesh from a fresh wound, or the moment when a syringe pierces the skin). I questioned, whether this abject we
feel towards the innards (or towards any idea of an access to the innards) has
something to do with a more complex rejection of the totality of our body. The
abjection, according to Kristeva (1982, 53), happens when something/someone
gets too close, asserts and imposes a threatening familiarity. The flesh we live
in (or the flesh we are constituted of) can symbolically and literally (since abject connects symbolic and somatic) stand for the complexity of this issue; it is
too close to us, we are surrounded and contained by it, but we cannot dare to
look inside, explore and acknowledge its raw nature. It is an ironic fact, since
the very compound of our physical existence is the flesh itself, what keeps everything in a condensed and livable form. Yet, it remains hidden, out of reach
and disgusted when it is visually exposed. Of course, the coverage of the skin is
necessary in terms of protection since it covers and protects the most vulnerable parts of our body. What I suggest should not be understood as a delirious
motivation to dismember and dissect the body in order to acknowledge it fully,
but what I predominantly underline here is to unlearn these constructed associations we have with our bodies. If we cannot effort to meet and confide in the
reality and in the totality of our bodies, how can we speak about a revolution
of the body? How is it possible to be authorized by the body's knowledge, if we
prefer to look away from it in disgust and reject its totality which includes the
vibrant flesh? This idea was persistent as I delved into Merleau-Ponty's ontology of the flesh, as the flesh signified the border between the visible and the
invisible, as the "absolute untouchable void which rises upright before vertical
being" (Merleau-Ponty 1968, 148). The flesh is elemental, it captures the lines of
the world and modulates the visible, as Massumi emphasizes the second dimension of the flesh which lays underneath the skin and the body is trapped
in the illusion of three dimensions because of the skin. "The Euclidean space of
the body is a membrane" (Massumi 2002, 203). The flesh constitutes the body
and electrifies the body schema.

The ontology of skin has to be reemphasized within its clash with the technology, and this clash requires a new understanding and a new approach for

the technicity of the human body, which recalls Virilio's (1994, 53) prediction of "living in the body itself". Virilio distinguishes the life as; "the life in the living room' (20. century), 'the life on oneself' (21. century), as we wear the desired apparatuses on ourselves." Also indicated by Angerer, "In the early 21. century, the relations between bodies and external and internal environments are rewired by information technologies[...]" (Angerer 2017, 41). According to Virilio, "the life inside oneself" will be the state in the future; the life will soon take place inside oneself (Virilio, 1994, 54). Though, Virilio has a skeptical and a rather pessimistic understanding of this 'living inside oneself', I suggest that this form of existing in oneself will bring a more refined knowledge, as we will inescapably turn towards our bodily existence and consequently face what is hidden. This discovery can be vertically and horizontally broadened (both in visual and metaphoric sense) with the usage of technologically governed apparatuses since they can provide a meticulous access to inaccessible environments. In Chapter 3, these environments are considered as the bodily innards; if we can effort to visually grasp and acknowledge the existence of our innards, due to the reversal of an uncanny environment into a familiar one, we may feel a decrease in abjection and therefore have the audacity to acknowledge what we are made of. This would eventually alter the way we think about body image, body schema and beyond, the inexplicable discomfort we lament in existential crisis. We are in this body and we need to know every corner of it, instead of looking away from it or dismiss it in disgust.

In "Corporeal Virtuality: The Impossibility of a Fleshless Ontology", Richardson & Harper underline the dominant goal of VR as creating "a unified field of awareness similar to our lived phenomenological experience" and they reveal the necessity of phenomenological approach, since it offers "a useful foundation for developing a model of embodiment relations in which the virtual is both a technological ensemble and always-already a corporeal condition" (Richardson & Harper 2002, 6). Likewise, Riemer suggests that VR finally brings the long debated abstract concept of embodiment into our direct experience and thus shifts the function of phenomenology into the broad research of techno-science. He indicates, "Merleau-Ponty's insights about the embodied mind are a bold and refreshing challenge to the new era of virtual reality and artificial intelligence, as scientists and psychologists discover the centrality of the body to mind and intelligence" (Riemer 2013, 42).

In line with these indications, I have discussed why combining media theory with a phenomenological approach is necessary while exploring the bodily self in VR environments. The outcomes of this research are continuing to assist and influence my current work "Behavioral Changes Induced by Heartbeat-linked Tactile Stimulation in VR." Furthermore I continue implementing ways to travel in the digestive system in a virtual body.

In my dissertation I underline the importance of bodily representation in VR through a phenomenological approach. I have addressed the connections between my prior VR experiences and corresponding theories. In this way, I provided a contribution to post-phenomenology, as I highlighted the short-comings in traditional phenomenology and I aimed to re-contextualize these neglected parts within new techno-scientific horizons. Based on these con-clusions, practitioners should consider relevant media theories and insights from phenomenological philosophy as they improve the usage and availability of technological assets. Hereby, as I conclude, I would also like to raise an im-portant point which has been ghosting me pages after pages. When I underline and excessively remark the importance of 'sense of presence', 'immersive envi-ronment' and 'improving the sense of immersion', I did not necessarily mean to pave the ways for the consumerism's 'faster, stronger, better' attitude. On the contrary, my intention with improving the sense of presence relates to the at-titude of providing an open source, which contains clear and factual informa-tion, reproducibility and easy access of technology. Products of new technology should be available for everyone who wants to look into their own experience, not only for an isolated group of privileged consumers. During the production of each VR intervention and implementation, I have worked towards this aim and provided resources for anyone who was interested in investing their time and effort to duplicate my methods.

In order to understand the implications of this dissertation, future studies can address how subjective experience, physiology and behavior unfold in nat-uralistic contexts when one is exposed to VR. Additionally, future directions for media studies can consider how VR can be used as a philosophical tool to see how bodily perception operates, facilitates new borders and can grow beyond it's existing capacity (as it is clear by the example of the plasticity of our sensory modalities when they are exposed to different stimuli in VR). While to some readers, the overall intention of this work may seem like a radical and provoca-tive way of coexisting with the virtual, one should have the courage to navigate through the unknown, into the virtual. This work aims to suggest a reforma-tion of technology in order to understand the nature of perception, beyond the conventional methods practiced to this date. In order to deal with the concep-tual complexities in a virtual world, we ought to dig deeper into the subjective experience of the real world.

Bibliography

Ahmed, Sara. 2004. *The Cultural Politics of Emotion*. Edinburgh: Edinburgh University Press.

Aho, Kevin. 2019. "Notes from a Heart Attack: A Phenomenology of an Altered Body." In *Phenomenology of the Broken Body*, edited by Espen Dahl, Cassandra Falke and Thor Eirik Eriksen, 188–201. London: Routledge.

Althusser, Louis. (1970) 2014. *On the Reproduction of Capitalism: Ideology and Ideological State Apparatuses*. London: Verso.

Ambron, Elisabetta et al. 2018. "Immersive Low-Cost Virtual Reality Treatment for Phantom Limb Pain: Evidence from Two Cases." *Frontiers in Neurology* 9, no. 67. doi: https://doi.org/10.3389/fneur.2018.00067.

Angerer, Marie-Luise. 1995. *The Body of Gender: Körper. Geschlechter. Identitäten*. Vienna: Passagen Verlag.

Angerer, Marie-Luise. 1999. *body options: körper. spuren. medien. bilder*. Vienna: Turia + Kant.

Angerer, Marie-Luise. 2017. *Ecology of the Affect*. Lüneburg: Meson Press.

Appelbaum, David. 2015. "'What Is a Thing?' At the Discretion of the (a-) Thing: Derrida and German Thought." *Konturen* 8: 62–70.

Aristotle. 2016. *On the Soul, De Anima*. Translated by J. A. Smith. The Internet Classics Archive. http://classics.mit.edu/Aristotle/soul.html.

Aron, Raymond. 1969. Progress and Disillusion: The Dialectics of Modern Society. London: Pall Mall Press.

Bach-y-Rita, P. 1983. "Tactile Vision Substitution: Past and Future." *Int J Neurosci*, 1–4: 29–36. doi: https://doi.org/10.3109/00207458309148643.

Baker, Adrian. 2010. *Shape of Snakes*. Leipzig: Averse Publications and Berlin: Broken Spine Productions.

Barad, Karen. 2007. *Meeting the Universe Halfway: Quantum Physics and the Entanglement of Matter and Meaning*. Durham, NC: Duke University Press.

Barglow, Raymond. 1994. *The Crisis of the Self in the Age of Information: Computers, Dolphins, and Dreams*. London: Routledge.

Barlow, John Perry. 1990. *Being in Nothingness. Mondo 2000*, no. 2: 34–33.

Barsalou, L. W. 1999. "Perceptual Symbol Systems." In *Behavioral and Brain Sciences* 22, no. 4: 577–660. http://dx.doi.org/10.1017/S0140525X99002149

Barsalou, Lawrence. 2008. "Grounded Cognition." In *Annual Review of Psychology* 59: 617–645.

Barzilai Shuli. 1995. "Models of Reflexive Recognition: Wallon's *Origines du caractère* and Lacan's 'Mirror stage.'" *Psychoanal Study Child* 50: 368–382.

Bennett, Jane. 2010. *Vibrant Matter: A Political Ecology of Things*. Duke University Press.

Bergson, Henri. 2002. *Key Writings*. London: Bloomsbury.

Bergson, Henri. (1886) 2004. *Matter and Memory*. Translated by Nancy M. Paul and W. Scott Palmer, London: Allen & Unwin.

Bertnard, Philipp, et al. 2016. "Virtual Body Swap: A New Feasible Tool to be Explored in Health and Education." 2016 XVIII Symposium on Virtual and Augmented Reality (SVR): 81–89.

Bertrand, Philippe, et al. 2018. "Learning Empathy through Virtual Reality: Multiple Strategies for Training Empathy-Related Abilities Using Body Ownership Illusions in Embodied Virtual Reality." Frontiers Robotics AI, 5. https://doi.org/10.3389/frobt.2018.00026.

Biocca, Frank. 1997. "The Cyborg's dilemma: Progressive Embodiment in Virtual Environments." Journal of Computer-Mediated Communication 3: 2–26. https://doi.org/10.1111/j.1083-6101.1997.tb00070.x.

Blanke, Olaf, Theodor Landis, Laurent Spinelli, and Margitta Seeck. 2004. "Out-of-Body Experience and Autos Copy of Neurological Origin." *Brain* 127 (part 2): 243–258. https://doi.org/10.1093/brain/awh040.

Blanke, Olaf, H.G. Debarba, S. Bovet, S., and R. Salomon. 2017. "Characterizing First and Third Person Viewpoints and Their Alternation for Embodied Interaction in Virtual Reality." *PLOS One*. https://doi.org/10.1371/journal.pone.0190109.

Bloom, Paul. 2017. *Against Empathy: The Case for Rational Compassion*. London: Bodley Head.

Bonnier, P. 1905. "L'Aschematie." In *Revue Neurologique* 13: 606–609.

Bordwell D. 1977. "Camera Movement and Cinematic Space." In *Ciné-Tracts* 2: 19–26.

Botvinick, Matthew and Jonathan Cohen. 1998. "Rubber Hands 'Feel' Touch That Eyes See." In *Nature* 391: 756. https://doi.org/10.1038/35784.

Braidotti, Rosi. 2002. *Metamorphoses: Towards a Materialist Theory of Becoming*. Cambridge: Polity.

Breithaupt, Felix. 2019. *The Dark Sides of Empathy*. Ithaca: Cornell University Press.

Bukatman, Scott. 1993. *Terminal Identity: The Virtual Subject in Postmodern Science Fiction*. Stanford: Stanford University Press.

Carruthers, Ritchie. 2015. "The Bodily Senses" In *The Oxford Handbook of Philosophy of Perception*, edited by Mohan Matthen, 360–372. Toronto. Oxford University Press.

Chalmers, David J. 1995. "Facing Up to the Problem of Consciousness." In Journal of Consciousness Studies 2, no. 3: 200–219.

Changeux, Jean-Pierre. 1997. *Neuronal Man: The Biology of Mind*. Princeton. Princeton University Press.

Clough, Patricia. 2007. *The Affective Turn, Theorizing The Social*. New York: Duke University Press.

Collins J., Jervis J. 2008. "'On the Psychology of the Uncanny' (1906): Ernst Jentsch." In J. Collins and J. Jervis, eds., *Uncanny Modernity*, 216–228. London: Palgrave Macmillan.

Comolli, J. L. 1980. "Machines of the Visible." In T. de Lauretis and S. Heath, eds., *The Cinematic Apparatus*. London: Palgrave Macmillan.

Connerton, Paul. 1989. *How Societies Remember*. Cambridge: Cambridge University Press.

Crary, Jonathan. 1992. *Techniques of the Observer: On Vision and Modernity in the Nineteenth Century*. London: MIT Press.

Crick, F. 1994. *The Astonishing Hypothesis*. New York: Simon & Schuster, 1994.

Culkin, S. J. and M. John M. 1967. "A Schoolman's Guide to Marshall McLuhan." In *The Saturday Review*, March 18, 1967, 51–53.

Curley, Edwin M. 1985. *The Collected Works of Spinoza*. Princeton: Princeton University Press.

Damasio, Antonio. 2004. *Looking for Spinoza*. London: Vintage Books.

Damasio, Antonio. (1994) 2008. *Descartes' Error: Emotion, Reason and the Human Brain*. New York: Random House.

Davies, G. J. and J.A. Gould. 1985. *Orthopaedic and Sports Physical Therapy*. St. Louis: Mosby Press.

De Beauvoir, Simone. 1945. *La Phénoménologie de la perception*. TM-Les Temps Modernes (Zeitschrift) 1945: 363.

De Boer, Theo. 1989. *Hermeneutiek*. 1989. Amsterdam: Boom uitgevers.

Deguy, Michel. 1990. *Arrêts fréquents*. Paris: A.M. Métailié.

De Lauretis, Teresa. 1998. "Perverse Desire: The Lure of the Mannish Lesbian" In *Places through the Body, Bodies-Cities*, ed. Heidi J. Nast and Steve Pile, 171–182. London: Routledge.

Deleuze, Gilles. 1968.1994. *Difference and Repetition.* Presses Universitaires de France, Columbia University Press.

Deleuze, Gilles. 1988. *Spinoza: Practical Philosophy.* Translated by Robert Hurley. San Francisco: City Lights Books.

Deleuze, Gilles. 1989. *Cinema 2 The Time-Image.* Translated by Hugh Tomlinson and Robert Caleta. Minneapolis: University of Minnesota Press.

Deleuze, Gilles. Guattari, Felix. 1987. *A Thousand Plateaus: Capitalism and Schizophrenia.* Minnesota: University of Minnesota Press.

Depraz, Nathalie. 2005. "Radical Embodiment," in Body Image and Body Schema: Interdisciplinary Perspectives on the Body, edited by Helena De Preester and Veroniek Knockaert, 173–186. Amsterdam: John Benjamins Publishing Company.

Deranty, Jean-Philippe, et al. 2021. "Bremen and Freiburg Lectures: Insight Into That Which Is and Basic Principles of Thinking (Studies in Continental Thought)." In *For Work / Against Work*, 2021, https://onwork.edu.au/bibi tem/2012-Heidegger,Martin-Mitchell,Andrew+J+J-Bremen+and+Freibur g+Lectures+Insight+Into+That+Which+Is+and+Basic+Principles+of+Thi nking+(Studies+in+Continental+Thought)-excerpt+p.25/.

Dewey, J. (1922) Human Nature and Conduct: An Introduction to Social Psychology. Henry Holt, New York.

Dewey, J. 1884. "The New Psychology." In *Andover Review* 2: 278–289.

Dinh, Huong. et al. 1999. "Evaluating the Importance of Multi-sensory Input on Memory and the Sense of Presence in Virtual Environments." From *Virtual Reality Conference, IEEE* (1999). http:/ doi.ieeecomputersociety.org/10.1109/ VR. 1999.756955, 1999.

Diodato, Roberto. 2018. *Phenomenology of the Virtual Body: An Introduction.* In: *Eco-Phenomenology: Life, Human Life, Post-Human Life in the Harmony of the Cosmos.* Smith W., Smith J., Verducci D. (eds) Analecta Husserliana (The Yearbook of Phenomenological Research), vol CXXI. Springer, Cham. https://d oi.org/10.1007/978-3-319-77516-6_46

Dolezal, Luna. 2009. "The Remote Body. The Phenomenology of Telepresence and Re-embodiment." In *Human Technology, An Interdisciplinary Journal on Humans in ICT Environments* 5, no. 2 (November): 208–226.

Dolezal, Luna. 2015. *The Body and Shame: Phenomenology, Feminism, and the Socially Shaped Body.* Washington: Lexington Books.

Dolto, Francoise. 1984. *L'image in-consciente du corps*. Paris: SEUIL Press.

Dreyfus, Hubert. 2001. *On the Internet*. London: Routledge.

Dunn J., et al. 2017. "Virtual and Augmented Reality in the Treatment of Phantom Limb Pain: A Literature Review." *NeuroRehabilitation* 40, no. 4: 595–601. doi: https://doi.org/10.3233/NRE-171447.

Eriksen, Thor Eirik. 2019. "Brokenness, Uncanniness, Affectedness." In *Phenomenology of the Broken Body*, edited by Espen Dahl, Cassandra Falke and Thor Eirik Eriksen, 101–120. London: Routledge.

Eyers, Tom. 2012. *Lacan and the Concept of the Real*. UK: Palgrave Macmillan Press.

Ferrari, Pier Francesco and Giacomo Rizzolatti. 2014. "Mirror Neuron Research: The Past and the Future." In *Philos Trans R Soc Lond B Biol Sci* (Jun 5): 369.

Flaubert, Gustav. (1869) 2004. *Sentimental Education*. London: Penguin Classics.

Flusser, Vilém. 1996. "Gedächtnisse." In *Philosophien der neuen Technologien*, ed.ARS ELECTRONICA, 41–57. Berlin: Merve Verlag.

Foucault, Michel. 1979. *Discipline and Punish: The Birth of the Prison*. Translated by Alan Sheridan. New York: Vintage.

Francino, Ferdinand & Guiller, Jane. 2011. "Is That Your Boyfriend?" An Experiential and Theoretical Approach to Understanding Gender-Bending in Virtual Worlds. In *Reinventing Ourselves: Contemporary Concepts of Identity in Virtual Worlds*. 153–175. Ed. Anna Peachey, Mark Childs. London: Springer.

Freud, Sigmund. 1919. "Das Unheimliche." In *Gesammelte Werke*, Band 2. Berlin: Anaconda Verlag.

Friedrich, Kathrin. 2016. "Therapeutic Media: Treating PTSD with Virtual Reality Exposure Therapy." In *Media Tropes* 6, no. 1: 86–113.

Gallagher, Shaun. 1995. "Body Schema and Intentionality." In *The Body and the Self*, edited by Jose Luis Bermudez, Anthony Marcel, and Naomi Eilan, 240–320. Cambridge: MIT Press.

Gallagher, Shaun. 2000. "Philosophical Conceptions of the Self: Implications for Cognitive Science." In *Trends in Cognitive Sciences* 4, no. 1: 15.

Gallagher, Shaun and Dan Zahavi. 2008. *The Phenomenological Mind: An Introduction to Philosophy of Mind and Cognitive Science*. UK: Routledge.

Gallese, Vittorio. 2014. "Bodily Selves in Relation: Embodied Simulation as Second-Person Perspective on iIntersubjectivity." In Philosophical transactions of the Royal Society of London. In *Biological sciences*, Series B 369(1644), 20130177. https://doi.org/10.1098/rstb.2013.0177

Gallese, Vittorio and Alvin Goldman. 1998. "Mirror Neurons and the Simulation Theory of Mind-Reading." In *Trends Cogn Sci*. 1998 Dec 1;2(12):493-501. doi: https://doi.org/10.1016 s1364-6613(98)01262-5. PMID: 21227300.

Goldin-Meadow, Susan. 2017. "Gesture, Sign, and Language: The Coming of Age of Sign Language and Gesture Studies." In *Behavioral and Brain Sciences*, 40, E46. doi: https://doi.org/10.1017/S0140525X15001247.

Greenwald-Smith, Rachel. 2011. "Postmodernism and the Affective Turn." Special issue, in *Postmodernism, Then, Twentieth Century Literature* 57, no. 3/4 (Fall/Winter 2011): 423–446.

Gregory, Dominic. 2013. "Showing, Sensing, and Seeming, Distinctively Sensory Representations and their Contents." UK: Oxford University Press.

Grosz, Elizabeth. 1994. *Volatile Bodies: Toward a Corporeal Feminism (Theories of Representation and Difference)*. Bloomington, Indiana. Indiana University Press.

Grosz, Elizabeth. 1995. *Space, Time and Perversion: The Politics of Bodies*. Sydney: Allen & Unwin.

Grosz, Elizabeth. 1998. "Bodies-Cities." In *Places through the Body, Bodies-Cities*, ed. Heidi J. Nast and Steve Pile, 31–39. London: Routledge.

Grosz, Elizabeth. 2001. *Architecture from the Outside: Essays on Virtual and Real Space*. Cambridge: The MIT Press.

Grosz, Elizabeth. 2014. "Bodies of Philosophy: An Interview with Elizabeth Grosz" In *Stance: An International Undergraduate Philosophy Journal* 7 (April 2014): 115–126. https://doi.org/10.5840/stance2014712.

Grosz, Elizabeth. 2017. *The Incorporeal, Ontology, Ethics and the Limits of Materialism*. New York: Columbia University Press.

Grüny, Christian. 2019. "No Way Out" In *Phenomenology of the Broken Body*, edited by Espen Dahl, Cassandra Falke and Thor Eirik Eriksen, 119–136. London: Routledge.

Gualeni, Stefano. 2015. *Virtual Worlds as Philosophical Tools: How to Philosophize with a Digital Hammer*. UK: Palgrave Macmillan.

Hadjioannou, Christos. 2016. "Heidegger's Critique of Techno-science as a Critique of Husserl's Reductive Method." In *Heidegger on Technology*. Ed. Aaron James Wendland, Christopher Merwin, and Christos Hadjioannou. 57–73. London: Routledge.

Hansen, Mark. 2006. *New Philosophy for New Media*. Cambridge: The MIT Press.

Haraway, Donna J. (1984). 2018. *Donna Haraway's a Cyborg Manifesto: Science, Technology, and Socialist-feminism in the Late Twentieth Century*. London: Macat International Press.

Harman, Graham, 2007. "On Vicarious Causation." Collapse:171-205. PhilPapers. https://philpapers.org/rec/HAROVC.

Harman, Graham. 2011. *The Quadruple Object*. London: John Hunt Publishing.

Harman, Graham. 2018. *Speculative Realism: An Introduction*. Cambridge: Polity Press.

Harrison, Jesse Smith and Michael Neff. 2018. "Communication Behavior in Embodied Virtual Reality." In *Communication Behavior in Embodied Virtual Reality Journal*, 1–12. doi: https://doi.org/10.1145/3173574.3173863.

Hayles, Katherine. 1999. *How We Became Posthuman: Virtual Bodies in Cybernetics, Literature, and Informatics*. Chicago: University of Chicago Press.

Hayles, Katherine. 2005. *My Mother Is a Computer*. Chicago: University of Chicago Press.

Hayles, Katherine. 2014. "Cognition Everywhere: The Rise of the Cognitive Nonconscious and the Costs of Consciousness." *New Literary History* 45: 199–220.

Hayles, Katherine 2017. *Unthought: The Power of the Cognitive Nonconscious*. University of Chicago Press.

Heidegger, Martin. 1977. *The Question Concerning Technology and Other Essays*. Translated and with an introduction by Willia Lovitt. New York: Garland Publishing, Inc.

Heilig, M. L. 1962. Sensorama simulator. US Patent 3,050,870, filed January 10, 1961, and issued August 28, 1962.

Heim, Michael. 1993. The Metaphysics of Virtual Reality. Oxford University Press, 1993

Held, Klaus. 1986. "Einleitung." In *Edmund Husserl, Phänomenologie der Lebenswelt*, edited by Klaus Held, 5–53. Stuttgart: Reclam.

Hillis, Ken. 1998. "Human.language.machine." In *Places through the Body, Bodies-Cities*, ed. Heidi J. Nast and Steve Pile, 39–54. London: Routledge.

Hobson, Peter. 1990. "Concerning Knowledge of Mental States." In *British Journal of Medical Psychology*. Volume 63, Issue 3, September 1990, 199–213. https://doi.org/10.1111/j.2044-8341.1990.tb01613.x.

Holmes, Nicholas, P. 2004. "The Body Schema and the Multisensory Representation(s) of Peripersonal Space." *Cognitive processing*, 5(2), 94–105. https://doi.org/10.1007/s10339-004-0013-3; https://www.ncbi.nlm.nih.gov/pmc/articles/PMC1350799/.

Hume, David. (1973) 2000. *A Treatise of Human Nature*. Ed. David Fate Norton, Mary J. Norton New York: Oxford University Press.

Husserl, Edmund. 1977. *Cartesian Meditations: An Introduction to Phenomenology.* Translated by Dorion Cairns. Dordrecht: Springer Netherlands.

Husserl, Edmund. 1983. *Studien zur Arithmetik und Geometrie (1886–1901).* Husserliana XXI. The Hague: M. Nijhoff.

Husserl, Edmund. 1984. *Logische Untersuchungen, 2. Band, 1. Teil.* Edited by U. Panzer. Husserliana XIX/1. The Hague: M. Nijhoff.

Husserl, Edmund. 1992. *Gesammelte Schriften.* Edited by Elisabeth Ströker. Hamburg: Meiner.

Hutmacher, Fabian. 2019. "Why Is There So Much More Research on Vision Than on Any Other Sensory Modality?" In *Frontiers Publication.* Department of Psychology, University of Regensburg, Regensburg, Germany. https://www.frontiersin.org/articles/10.3389/fpsyg.2019.02246/full.

Ihde, Don, 1993. *Postphenomenology: Essays in the Postmodern Context.* Evanston, IL: Northwestern University Press.

Ihde, Don. 2016. *Husserl's Missing Technologies.* New York: Fordham University Press.

Ilharco, Fernando. 2015. "Screens of Fire: Surviving the End of the World." In *Hazardous Future: Disaster, Representation and the Assessment of Risk*, edited by Isabel Capeloa Gil and Christoph Wulf. Berlin, München, Boston: De Gruyter, 2015, pp. 195–204. https://doi.org/10.1515/9783110406610-015.

Introna, Lucas D. et al. 2000. "The Screen and the World: A Phenomenological Investigation into Screens and Our Engagement in the World." In *Organizational and Social Perspectives on Information Technology*, 295–318. Editors: Baskerville, Richard, Stage, Jan, DeGross, Janice London: Routledge.

Introna, Lucas D., Ilharco, Fernando M. 2004. "On the Meaning of Screens: Towards a Phenomenological Account of Screenness." *European Journal of Information Systems* 13, no. 3 (September): p. 57–76.

Izard, Carroll E. 2007. "Basic Emotions, Natural Kinds, Emotion Schemas, and a New Paradigm." In *Perspectives on Psychological Science* 2, no.: 3: 260–280.

Jacob, Pierre. 2009. "A Philosopher's Reflections on the Discovery of Mirror Neurons." In *Topics in Cognitive Science* 1, no. 3: 570–595.

Jacob, Pierre. 2015. "Action-Based Accounts of Perception." In *The Oxford Handbook of Philosophy of Perception*, edited by Mohan Matthen, 220–242. Oxford: Oxford University Press.

Jadhav, S. et al. 2017. "Soft Robotic Glove for Kinesthetic Haptic Feedback in Virtual Reality Environments: The Engineering Reality of Virtual Reality." In *Electronic Imaging* 6: 19–24.

Jameson, Frederic. 1992. *Postmodernism, Or, the Cultural Logic of Late Capitalism*. Durham, NC: Duke University Press.

Jankowiak-Siuda, Kamila., Krystyna Rymarczyk, and Anna Grabowska. 2011. "How We Empathize with Others: A Neurobiological Perspective." In *Med Sci Monit*. 17, no. 1: RA18–RA24. doi: https://doi.org/10.12659/MSM.881324.

Jaspers, Karl. 1973. *Allgemeine Psychopathologie*. Berlin: Springer.

Kassondra L. Collins, et al. 2018. "A Survey of Frozen Phantom Limb Experiences: Are Experiences Compatible with Current Theories." In *Front. Neurol.* Vol. 9, July 2018: 599–567. https://doi.org/10.3389/fneur.2018.00599.

Keating, Thomas P. 2019."Pre-individual affects: Gilbert Simondon and the individuation of relation." In *Cultural Geographies*, volume: 26 issue: 2, page(s): 211–226. doi: https://doi.org/10.1177/1474474018824090.

Kelly, Michael. 2005. "Making a Case for Husserl in The Philosophy of Technology." In *Philosophy Today_* 49 (3):225-235. doi: https://doi.org/10.5840/philt oday200549341.

Kierkegaard, S. 2014. *The Concept of Anxiety*. New York: Liverlight.

Kilteni, K, et al. 2012. "Extending Body Space in Immersive Virtual Reality: A Very Long Arm Illusion." In *PLoS ONE 7L* 7: e40867. https://doi.org/10.1371/journal.pone.0040867.

Kittler, Friedrich. 2012. "Of States and Their Terrorists." In *Cultural Politics* 8, no. 3: 385–397.

Kovac, L. 2000. "FP-Fundamental Principles of Cognitive Biology, Evolution and Cognition." (2000) In *Evolution and Cognition* 6, 51–69.

Krekhov, Andrey, Sebastian Cmentowski, and Jens Krüger. 2019. "The Illusion of Animal Body Ownership and Its Potential for Virtual Reality Games." Ithaca, NY: Cornell University Press. https://arxiv.org/abs/1907.05220.

Kristeva, Julia. 1982. *The Powers of Horror: An Essay on Abjection*. Translated by Leon S. Roudiez. New York: Columbia University Press.

Lacan, Jacques. 1960. "The Subversion of the subject and the Dialectic of Desire in the Freudian Unconscious." In the conference *La Dialectique*, (p. 19–23). September, 1960.

Lacan, Jacques. 1997. *Écrits: A Selection*. London: Routledge.

Lacey, Simon and Lawson, Rebecca. 2013. *Multisensory Imagery*. Switzerland: Springer Nature Press.

Landes, Donald A. 2013. *The Merleau-Ponty Dictionary*, London: A&C Black.

Lanier, Jaron. 2017. *Dawn of the New Everything: Encounters with Reality and Virtual Reality*. New York: Henry Holt and Co.

Laplanche, Jean and Pontails, Jean-Bertnard. 1988. "Narcissism." In *The Language of Psychoanalysis*, 240–262. New York: W. W. Norton.

Latour, Bruno. 1988. *Science in Action*. Cambridge: Harvard University Press

Lawlor, Leonard. 2014. *Jacques Derrida: Key Concepts*. Edited By Claire Colebrook. London: Routledge.

Lay, Stephanie, Nicola Brace, and Graham Pike. 2016. "Circling Around the Uncanny Valley: Design Principles for Research into the Relation Between Human Likeness and Eeriness." In *Sage Journal* 7, no. 6: 1–11. doi: https://doi.org/10.1177/2041669516681309.

LeBuffe, Michael. 2010. "Theories About Consciousness in Spinoza's Ethics." In *The Philosophical Review*, 119, no. 4: 531–563.

Leder, Drew. 1990. *The Absent Body*. Chicago: University of Chicago Press.

Lenggenhager, Bigna. 2007. "Video Ergo Sum: Manipulating Bodily Self-Consciousness." In *Science* 317: 1096–1099.

Leverett Dorn, Michael. 1998. "Beyond nomadism: the travel narratives of a 'cripple'." In *Places through the Body*, edited by Heidi J. Nast and Steve Pile, 136–153. London: Routledge.

Levinas, Emmanuel. (1961) 1991. *Totality and Infinity: An Essay on Exteriority*. Amsterdam: Springer.

Lewin, Roger. 1999. "Ruling Passions." In *New Scientist* 3 (April)nr. 2199: p. 39–45.

Limanovski, Jacob and Blankenburg Felix. 2013. Minimal Self-Models and the Free Energy Principle." In *Neuroimage*. vol. 86: 514–24. doi: https://doi.org/10.1016/j.neuroimage.2013.10.035.

Malabou, Catherine. 2008. *What Should We Do with our Brains?* New York: Fordham University Press.

Malabou, Catherine. 2014. "Foreword: After the Flesh." In *Plastic Bodies: Rebuilding Sensation After Phenomenology*, edited by T. Sparrow, 13–21. UK: Open Humanities Press.

Malabou, Catherine and Adrian Johnston. 2013. *Self and Emotional Life: Philosophy, Psychoanalysis, and Neuroscience*. New York: Columbia University Press.

Malraux, André. 1978. *The Voices of Silence*. Princeton University Press.

Mandik, Pete. 2010. *Key Terms in Philosophy of Mind*. London: Continuum Press.

Mandrigin, Alisa and Thompson Evan. 2015. "Own-Body Perception." In *The Oxford Handbook of Philosophy of Perception*, edited by Mohan Matthen, 1–19. Toronto. Oxford University Press.

Manney, Patricia J. 2008 "Empathy in the Time of Technology: How Storytelling is the Key to Empathy." In *Journal of Evolution and Technology* – Vol. 19 Issue 1 – September 2008 – p. 51–61.

Manovich, Lev. 2001. *The Language of New Media*. Cambridge, MA: MIT Press.

Marcel, Gabriel, Michael A. Machado and Henry J. Koren. 1967. *Presence and Immortality*. Pittsburgh: Duquesne University Press.

Martiny, K. M. 2015. "How to develop a phenomenological model of disability." In *Med Health Care and Philos* (2015) 18: 553. https://doi.org/10.1007/s11019-015-9625-x

Masson, J.M. 1985. (Ed.) "The complete letters of Sigmund Freud to Wilhelm Fliess", 1887–1904. Cambridge: Harvard University Press.

Massumi, Brian. 1992. *A User's Guide to Capitalism and Schizophrenia: Deviations from Deleuze and Guattari*. London: The MIT Press.

Massumi, Brian. 1996. "The Bleed: Where the Body Meets Image." In *Rethinking Borders*. John C. Welchman (ed):18-40. UK: Palgrave Macmillan Publishing.

Massumi, Brian. 2002. *Parables for the Virtual: Movement, Affect, Sensation*. North Carolina, USA: Duke University Press.

Massumi, Brian. 2011. *Semblance and Event: Activist Philosophy and the Occurrent Arts*. London: The MIT Press.

Matthen, Mohan. 2015. "The Individuation of the Senses." In *The Oxford Handbook of Philosophy of Perception*, p. 567–587. Edited by Mohan Matthen. Toronto: Oxford University Press.

McLuhan, Marshall. 1994. Understanding Media: The Extensions of Man. Cambridge: The MIT Press.

McNamara, Patrick. 1996. "Bergson's 'Matter and Memory' and Modern Selectionist Theories of Memory." April 1996, in *Brain and Cognition Journal* 30(2):215-31.

Mellard, James M. 2006. *Beyond Lacan*. New York: SUNY Press.

Merleau-Ponty, Maurice. (1942) 1963. *The Structure of Behavior*. Translated by Alden Fisher, Boston: Beacon Press.

Merleau-Ponty, Maurice. 1968. *The Visible and The Invisible*. Translated by Alphonso Lingis. New York: Northwestern University Press.

Merleau-Ponty, Maurice. (1945) 2002. *Phenomenology of Perception*. London: Routledge Press.

Metzinger, Thomas. 2003. *Being no one: The self-model Theory of Subjectivity*. London: The MIT Press.

Metzinger, Thomas. 2018. "Why is VR interesting for Philosophers?" In *Front. Robot. AI*, 13 September 2018 | https://doi.org/10.3389/frobt.2018.00101.

Mohan Matthen. 2015. "Introduction." In *The Oxford Handbook of Philosophy of Perception*, Oxford University Press; Auflage: 1 (2. September 2015), pages 1–19. Edited by Mohan Matthen.

Mori, Masahiro. 2012. "The uncanny valley." Translated by MacDorman, K. F.; Kageki, Norri. In *IEEE Robotics and Automation*. 19 (2): 98–100.

Moss, David. 1996. "Memories of Being. Orlan's Theatre of the self." In *Journal Art + Text*, no. 54, 67–72.

Murphy, Jennifer., Brewer, Rebecca., Catmur, Caroline., and Bird, Geoffrey. 2017. "Interoception and psychopathology: A developmental neuroscience perspective." In *Dev. Cogn Neurosci*. 2017 Feb;23:45-56. doi: https://doi.org/10.1016/j.dcn.2016.12.006.

Murray, Craig D., Pettifer, Stephen. Caillette, Fabrice and Patchick, Emma. 2008. "Immersive Virtual Reality as a Rehabilitative Technology for Phantom Limb Experience: a Protocol." In *Cyberpsychol Behav*. 2006 Apr;9(2):167-70. doi: https://doi.org/10.1089/cpb.2006.9.167. PMID: 16640472.

Nagel, Thomas. 1974. "What Is It Like to Be a Bat?" In *The Philosophical Review*, Vol. 83, No. 4 (Oct., 1974), pp. 435–450, New York: Duke University Press.

Nast, Heidi J. and Pile, Steve. 1998. "Introduction: MakingPlacesBodies." In *Places through the Body, Bodies-Cities*, ed. Heidi J. Nast and Steve Pile, 1–15. London: Routledge.

Nikolajsen. L. and Jensen, T. S. 2001. "Phantom Limb Pain." In *British Journal of Anaesthesia* 87(1): 107–116. doi: https://doi.org/10.1093/bja/87.1.107.

Noë, Alva. 2005. *Action in Perception*. London: The MIT Press.

Noë, Alva. 2009. *Out of Our Heads: Why You are not Your Brain and Other Lessions from the Biology of Consciousness*. New York: Hill and Wang Press.

North, Max M., North, Sarah M. Joseph R Coble. 1997. "Virtual Reality Therapy: An Effective Treatment for Psychological Disorders." In IOS Press Studies in *Health Technology and Informatics*, p. 59–70. Volume 44, doi: https://doi.org/10.3233/978-1-60750-888-5-59.

Obrist, Marianna, Subramanian, Sriram & Carter, Thomas. 2015. "Emotions Mediated Through Mid-Air Haptics." From CHI '15: *Proceedings of the 33rd Annual ACM Conference on Human Factors in Computing Systems*, April 2015, Pages 2053–2062. https://doi.org/10.1145/2702123.2702361.

O'Callaghan, C. 2014. "Speech Perception." In *The Oxford Handbook of Philosophy of Perception*, 475–495. Edited by Mohan Matthen. Toronto: Oxford University Press.

O'Dea, John. 2011. "A Proprioceptive Account of the Senses." In *The Senses: Classical and Contemporary Philosophical Perspectives*. Fiona Macpherson (ed.). Oxford: Oxford University Press.

Oliveira, Elen. et al., "Virtual Body Swap: A New Feasible Tool to Be Explored in Health and Education," in *XVIII Symposium on Virtual and Augmented Reality (SVR)*, 2016, pp. 81–89, doi: https://doi.org/10.1109/SVR.2016.23.

O'Regan, J. Kevin & Noë, Alva. 2001. "A sensorimotor account of vision and visual consciousness." In *Behavioral and Brain Sciences* 24 (5), 939–973. doi: https://doi.org/10.1017/S0140525X01000115.

Pan, Xueni and Hamilton, Antonia F. de C. 2018. "Why and How to use Virtual Reality to study Human Social Interaction: The Challenges of Exploring a New Research Landscape." In *British Journal of Psychology*, Volume109, Issue3 August 2018, Pages 395–417.

Panksepp, Jaak. 1998. *Affective Neuroscience: The Foundations of Human and Animal Emotions*. USA: Oxford University Press.

Peters, Dorian and Calvo, Rafael A. 2014. "Compassion vs. Empathy: Designing for Resilience." In *Interactions*, volume 21. Issue October 2014, pp 48–53 https://doi.org/10.1145/2647087

Peters, Dorian & Calvo, Rafael A., 2014. *Positive Computing: Technology for Wellbeing and Human Potential*. London: The MIT Press.

Petersen, Sibylle. von Leupoldt, Andreas. Van den Bergh, Omer. 2015. "Interoception and the uneasiness of the mind: affect as perceptual style." In *Front. Psychol.*, 17 September 2015 | https://doi.org/10.3389/fpsyg.2015.01408.

Petkova, Valeria and Ehrsson, H. Henrik. 2008. "If I Were You: Perceptual Illusion of Body Swapping." In *PLoS ONE* Journal, 3(12): e3832. https://doi.org/10.1371/journal.pone.0003832).

Polanyi, Michael. 1967. *The Tacit Dimension*. New York: Anchor Books.

Posner, M.I., Nissen, M.J., Klein, M. 1976. "Visual Dominance:An Information Processing Account of its Origins and Significance." In *Psychological Review*, 83(2):157-171, https://doi.org/10.1037/0033-295X.83.2.157.

Poster, Marc and Aronowitz, Stanley. 2001. *Information Subject*. London: Routledge.

Price, Cedric. 1960. *Technology Is the Answer, But What Was the Question?* From Audiobook. World Microfilms Publications Ltd, London (1 Dec. 1979).

Proske, Uwe and Gandevia, C. Simon. 2012. "The Proprioceptive Senses: Their Roles in Signaling Body Shape, Body Position and Movement, and Muscle Force." In *Physiological Reviews*, doi: https://doi.org/10.1152/physrev.00048.2011.

Radák, Zsolt. 2018. "Fundamentals of Strength Training." In *The Physiology of Physical Training*. Editor(s): Zsolt Radák, Pages 55–80. London: Academic Press.

Ramachandran, V. S. 1999. *Phantoms in the Brain: Human Nature and the Architecture of the Mind*. New York: William Morrow Paperbacks.

Ramachandran, V. S. 2012. *The Tell-Tale Brain: A Neuroscientist's Quest for What Makes Us Human*. London: Norton Press.

Ramachandran, V. S. 2019. "Computational models of multisensory integration." In *Multisensory Perception: From Laboratory to Clinic*. Edited by K. Sathian V.S. Ramachandran, Pages 157–178. London: Academic Press.

Ramachandran, V. S., Stewart M, Rogers. 1992. "Perceptual correlates of massive cortical reorganization." In *Neuroreport*. 1992 Jul;3(7):583-6. doi: https://doi.org/10.1097/00001756-199207000-00009.

Revonsuo, Antti. 2005. *Inner Presence, Consciousness as a Biological Phenomenon*. London: The MIT Press.

Revonsuo, Antti. 2010. *Consciousness, The Science of Subjectivity*. New York: Taylor and Francis Group, Psychology Press.

Richardson, Ingrid and Harper, Carly. 2002. "Corporeal Virtuality: the Impossibility of a Disembodied Ontology." In *BST Body, Space and Technology* Journal 2. doi: http://doi.org/10.16995/bst.243.

Riemer, Kai and Johnston, Robert B. 2017. "Clarifying ontological inseparability with heidegger's analysis of equipment." In *MIS Quarterly*, volume 41, 4, pages 1059–1081. doi: https://doi.org/10.25300/MISQ/2017/41.4.03.

Ritchie, J. Brendan and Peter Carruthers, Peter. 2015. The Bodily Senses. In *The Oxford Handbook of Philosophy of Perception*, 353–371, edited by Mohan Matthen. Toronto: Oxford University Press.

Roe, Anna W. Pallaq, Sarah L, Young H. Kwon, Young. and Mriganka Sur. 1992. "Visual Projections Routed to the Auditory Pathway in Ferrets: Receptive Fields of Visual Neurons in Primary Auditory Cortex." In *The Journal of Neuroscience*, September 1992, 12(g): 3651–3664.

Rorty, Richard. 2008. *Philosophy and the Mirror of Nature*. Princeton: Princeton University Press.

Rötzer, Florian. 2000. "Vom zweiten und dritten Körper oder: Wie es wäre, eine Fledermaus zu sein oder einen Fernling zu bewohnen?" In *Medien Computer Realität, Wirklichkeitsvorstellungen und Neue Medien*, 152–169. Herausgegeben von Sybille Krämer. Berlin: Suhrkamp Taschenbuch Wissenschaft.

Russell, James A. & Barrett, Lisa Feldman. 1999. "Core affect, prototypical emotional episodes, and other things called emotion: Dissecting the elephant." In *Journal of Personality and Social Psychology*, 76(5), 805–819, https://doi.org/10.1037/0022-3514.76.5.805.

Salamin, Patrick & Thalmann, Daniel. 2006. "The Benefits of Third-Person Perspective in Virtual and Augmented Reality" From the Conference: *Proceedings of the ACM Symposium on Virtual Reality Software and Technology*, VRST 2006, Limassol, Cyprus, November 1–3, 2006 doi: https://doi.org/10.1145/1 180495.1180502.

Sanchez-Vives, MV. and Slater, Mel. 2005. "From presence to consciousness through virtual reality." Nat Rev Neurosci 6, 332–339 (2005). https://doi.o rg/10.1038/nrn1651.

Santiesteban, I. et al. 2012. "Training social cognition: From imitation to Theory of Mind." In Cognition 122, 228–235 (2012). doi: https://doi.org/10.1016 /j.cognition.2011.11.004.

Saygin, Ayse P., Chaminade, Ishiguro, Driver, & Frith. 2012. "The thing that should not be: predictive coding and the uncanny valley in perceiving human and humanoid robot actions." Social cognitive and affective neuroscience, 7(4), 413–422. https://doi.org/10.1093/scan/nsr025.

Schechtman, M. 2011. "The Narrative Self." In *The Oxford Handbook of the Self*, Ed. S. Gallagher (394–416). Oxford: Oxford University Press.

Schilder, Paul. 1935. *The Image and Appearance of the Human Body: Studies in the Constructive Energies of the Psyche*. New York: Heritage Bookseller

Schmitz, Hermann. 1980. *Neue Phänomenologie*. Bonn: Bouvier Verlag.

Scott, Wayne. Stevens, Jennifer. Binder–Macleod, Stuart A. 2001. "Human Skeletal Muscle Fiber Type Classifications." In *Physical Therapy*, Volume 81, Issue 11, 1 November 2001, Pages 1810–1816, https://doi.org/10.1093/ptj/81. 11.1810

Seyfert, Robert. 2012. "Beyond Personal Feelings and Collective Emotions: Toward A Theory of Social Affect." In *Sage Journals Theory, Culture and Society*, Volume: 29 issue: 6, page(s): 27–46. https://doi.org/10.1177/02632764124385 91.

Sfez, Lucien. 1990. *Critique De La Communication*. Paris: Seuil Press.

Shaviro, Steven. 1995. "The Cinematic Body." In *Cultural Studics*, Bd. 2, 1995: 5, second edition, Minneapolis, London.

Siewert, Charles. 2015. "Phenomenological Approaches." In *The Oxford Handbook of Philosophy of Perception*, 136–153. Edited by Mohan Matthen. Toronto: Oxford University Press.

Slater Mel, Frisoli A, Tecchia F, Guger C, Lotto B, et al. 2007. Understanding and Realizing Presence." In the *Presenccia Project*. IEEE Comput Graph Appl 27: 90–93.

Slater, Mel, Spanlang, B. Sanchez-Vives, M. V., and Blanke, O. 2010. "First person experience of body transfer in virtual reality." PLoS ONE 5(5): e10564. https://doi.org/10.1371/journal.pone.0010564.

Sobchack, Vivian. 2000. *Electronic Media and Technoculture (Depth of Field Series)*. Edited by John Thornton Caldwell. New Jersey: Rutgers University Press.

Sobchack, Vivian. 2004. *Carnal Thoughts: Embodiment and Moving Image Culture*. Berkeley: University of California Press.

Sobchack, Vivian. 2010. "Living a 'Phantom Limb': On the Phenomenology of Bodily Integrity." In *Sage Journals, Body & Society*. Volume: 16 issue: 3, page(s): 51–67. https://doi.org/10.1177/1357034X10373407.

Sobchack, Vivian. 2016. "The Scene of the Screen: Envisioning Photographic, Cinematic, and Electronic 'Presence'." In *Post-Cinema. Theorizing 21st-Century Film*. Shane Denson, Julia Leyda (Hg.): Falmer: REFRAME Books 2016, S. 88–128. doi: https://doi.org/10.25969/mediarep/13484.

Sparrow, Tom. 2014. *The End of Phenomenology: Metaphysics and the New Realism*. Edinburgh: Edinburgh University Press.

Spinoza, Benedictus de. 1994. *A Spinoza Reader: The Ethics and Other Works*. Translated and edited by Edwin M. Curley. Princeton and Chichester: Princeton University Press.

Spinoza, Benedictus de. (1677) 2001. Ethics (Wordsworth Classics of World Literature). Translated by W.H. White and A.H. Stirling. London: Wordsworth Editions Ltd.

Stein, Edith. (1916) 2010. *Gesamtausgabe.: Zum Problem der Einfühlung – Gesamtaufgabe*. Freiburg: Herder GmbH Verlag.

Stivale, Charles J. 2004. "Intersections of Science, Sensation, and Culture." In *Materia Media Criticism*: Vol. 46: Iss. 1, Article 8. Wayne State University.

Stone, Allucquere Rosanne. 1992. "Will the Real Body Please Stand Up? Boundary Stories about Virtual Cultures." In M. Benedickt (ed.) *Cyberspace: First Steps*, 81–118, 111. Cambridge: The MIT Press.

Stone, Allucquère Rosanne. 1995. *The War of Desire and Technology at the Close of the Mechanical Age*. Cambridge: The MIT Press.

Sur, Mriganka, Anna W. Roe, Pallaq, Sarah L, Young H. Kwon, Young. 1992. "Visual Projections Routed to the Auditory Pathway in Ferrets: Receptive Fields of Visual Neurons in Primary Auditory Cortex." In *The Journal of Neuroscience*, September 1992, 12(g): 36513664.

Taiple, Joona. 2014. *Phenomenology and Embodiment: Husserl and the Constitution of Subjectivity*. Illinois: Northwestern University Press.

Takagi, A., Ganesh, G., Yoshioka, T. et al. 2017. "Physically interacting individuals estimate the partner's goal to enhance their movements." In *Nat Hum Behav* 1, 0054 (2017). https://doi.org/10.1038/s41562-017-0054.

Tsakiris, M., Tajadura-Jimenez, A., Costantini, M., 2011. "Just a heartbeat away from one's body:Interoceptive sensitivity predicts malleability of body-representations." In *Proceedings of the Royal Society Biological Sciences* 278(1717): 2470–6, doi: https://doi.org/10.1098/rspb.2010.2547.

Turkle, Sherry. 2015. *Reclaiming Conversation: The Power of Talk in a Digital Age.* London: Penguin Press.

Van Den Eede, Yoni. 2017. *Postphenomenology and Media: Essays on Human-Media-World Relations (Postphenomenology and the Philosophy of Technology).* Washington DC: Lexington Books.

Van Pelt, Tamisa. 2000. *The other Side of Desire, Lacan's Theory of the Registers.* New York: SUNY Press.

Varela, Francisco J. 1993. *Embodied Mind, A Fundamental Circularity: In the Mind of the Reflective Scientist.* Cambridge: MIT Press.

Varela, Francisco J. 1996. "Neurophenomenology, A Methodological Remedy for the Hard Problem." In *Journal of Consciousness Studies*, 3, No. 4, 1996, pp. 330.

Varela, Francisco J. Depraz, Nathalie. 2000. "At the source of time: valence and the constitutional dynamics of affect." In *Journal of Consciousness Studies* 12 (No. 8–10):61-81.

Varela, Francisco J., Rosch, Eleanor and Thompson, Evan. 1992. *The Embodied Mind, Cognitive Science and Human Experience.* Cambridge: The MIT Press.

Vasseleu, Cathryn. 1998. *Textures of Light: Vision and Touch in Irigaray, Levinas and Merleau-Ponty.* London: Routledge.

Vintges, Karen. 1996. *Philosophy as Passion: The Thinking of Simone De Beauvoir.* Bloomington: Indiana University Press.

Virilio, Paul. 1994. *The Vision Machine (Perspectives).* Bloomington: Indiana University Press.

Virilio, Paul. 1996. *Politics of the Very Worst: An Interview with Philippe Petit.* Edited by Sylvère Lotringer, translated by Michael Cavaliere. Cambridge: The MIT Press.

Von Foerster, Heinz. 1989. "Wahrnehmung." In *Philosophien der neuen Technologie. Philosophien der neuen Technologien,* ed. ARS ELECTRONICA, 27–41. Berlin: Merve Verlag.

Waldenfels, Bernhard. 2000. "Experimente mit der Wirklichkeit." In *Medien Computer Realität, Wirklichkeitsvorstellungen und Neue Medien,* 213–244.

Herausgegeben von Sybille Krämer. Berlin: Suhrkamp Taschenbuch Wissenschaft.

Waldenfels, Bernhard. 2011. *Phenomenology of the Alien*. New York: Northwestern University Press.

West, Geoffrey B., Brown, James H. and Enquist, Brian J. 1997. "A General Model for the Origin of Allometric Scaling Laws in Biology." In *Science Journal* (New York, N.Y.). 276. 122–6. 10.1126/science.276.5309.122.

Winkler, Sean. 2016. *The Conatus of the Body in Spinoza's Physics*. Bucharest: Editura Universităţii Vasile Goldiş Press.

Wiseman, Rachel. 2016. *Routledge Philosophy GuideBook to Anscombe's Intention*. London: Routledge.

Wittgenstein, Ludwig. 1958. *Philosophical Investigations*. Translated by G. E. M. ANSCOMBE. Oxford: Basil Blackwell Ltd.

Wittgenstein, Ludwig. 1961. *Notebooks/1914-1916*. Edited by G. H. von Wright and G. E. M. Anscombe, English translation by G. E. M. Anscombe. Chicago: University Of Chicago Press.

Wittgenstein, Ludwig. 1972. *On Certainty*. Edited and translated by G. E. M. Anscombe and G. H. von Wright. New York: Harper & Row Press.

Zahavi, Dan. 2003. *Husserl's Phenomenology*. California: Stanford University Press.

Zahavi, Dan. 2018. *Phenomenology: The Basics*. London: Routledge.

Zwier, Jochem., Vincent, Blok., and Pieter, Lemmens. 2016. "Phenomenology and the Empirical Turn: a Phenomenological Analysis of Postphenomenology." Philos. Technol. 29, 313–333 (2016). https://doi.org/10.1007/s13347-016-0221-7.

Online Media

BeAnotherLab. "Aims of the MachineToBeAnother (MTBA)." June, 2018. https://www.beanotherlab.org

Bogost, Ian. "The New Aesthetic Needs to Get Weirder." *The Atlantic*, April 2012. https://www.theatlantic.com/technology/archive/2012/04/the-new-aesthetic-needs-to-get-weirder/255838/.

Clariana, Antony., Jasper, Verbon., Burgess, Richard. "Hærfest.", November 2009. https://www.mobygames.com/game/hrfest.

Dimitri Ginev. Review of "Husserl's Missing Technologies." May, 2016. https://ndpr.nd.edu/news/husserls-missing-technologies/.

Ehrsson, Henrik. "Out of Body Experiences (OBE)." October, 2017. http://www
.ehrssonlab.se/henrik.php.

Fraunhofer Institute. "Vision and Imaging Technologies." April, 2019, https://
www.hhi.fraunhofer.de/en/departments/vit/research-groups/immersive
-media-communication/research-topics/3d-human-body-reconstruction
-for-virtual-reality.html

Gandevia, Simon and Uwe Proske. "Proprioception: The Sense Within." July 25,
2018. *The Scientist.* https://www.the-scientist.com/features/proprioceptio
n-the-sense-within-32940.

Hansen, Maggie. "Theorizing Media since 2003." *The Chicago School of Media Theory.* April 2019. https://lucian.uchicago.edu/blogs/mediatheory/keywords
/bodyembodiment/.

Holland, Norman N. *The Trouble(s) with Lacan.* May, 2020. http://users.clas.ufl.
edu/nholland/lacan.htm.

Manovich, Lev. "From DV Realism to a Universal Recording Machine." June,
2019. http://manovich.net/content/04-projects/031-reality-media/28_arti
cle_2001.pdf.

Massumi, Brian. "The Thinking-Feeling of What Happens A Semblance of a
Conversation." May, 2008, http://inflexions.org/n1_The-Thinking-Feeling
-of-What-Happens-by-Brian-Massumi.pdf. Université de Montréal.

O'Shaughnessy, Brian. "Consciousness and the World." November 2003. Published to Oxford Scholarship Online: https://oxford.universitypressschola
rship.com/view/10.1093/0199256721.001.0001/acprof-9780199256723.

Smith, David Woodruff, "Phenomenology", The Stanford Encyclopedia of Philosophy (Summer 2018 Edition), Edward N. Zalta (ed.), URL = <https://pla
to.stanford.edu/archives/sum2018/entries/phenomenology/>.

Turkle, Sherry. "Interview Sherry Turkle." September, 2009. https://www.pbs.
org/wgbh/pages/frontline/digitalnation/interviews/turkle.html.

Interviews

Kristeva, Julia. 1988. "Interview with Kristeva: Cultural Strangeness and the
Subject in Crisis." In *Women Analyze Women.* September, 1991. edited by E.
Baruch and L. Serrano. New York: New York University Press. https://ww
w.jstor.org/stable/41389174.

Massumi, Brian. 2008. "The Thinking-Feeling of What Happens" In the interview *How is Research-Creation?* Inflexions 1.1 (May 2008) https://www .inflexions.org.

Sobchack, Vivian. "The journeys of a film phenomenologist: An interview with Vivian Sobchack on being and becoming." Interview by Julian Hanich, December 2017. https://necsus-ejms.org/vivian-sobchack-interview/

Conferences (Unpublished)

Gallese, Vittorio. "Inhabiting Paralel Worlds: Mirror Neurons, the Brain and the Body." Conference at UDK, in Berlin, 2. May 2019, organized by Einstein Foundation.

Tacikowski, Pawel. "Merging of self-concept and friend-concept during illusory ownership of friend's body: Updating of beliefs during illusory ownership of friend's body." In The "Open Self, Investigating the Boundaries of the Self: Bodily, Social and Technological" Conference in Berlin, June 2018. https://openself2018.com/.

Cultural Studies

Gabriele Klein
Pina Bausch's Dance Theater
Company, Artistic Practices and Reception

2020, 440 p., pb., col. ill.
29,99 € (DE), 978-3-8376-5055-6
E-Book:
PDF: 29,99 € (DE), ISBN 978-3-8394-5055-0

Markus Gabriel, Christoph Horn, Anna Katsman, Wilhelm Krull,
Anna Luisa Lippold, Corine Pelluchon, Ingo Venzke
**Towards a New Enlightenment –
The Case for Future-Oriented Humanities**

October 2022, 80 p., pb.
18,00 € (DE), 978-3-8376-6570-3
E-Book: available as free open access publication
PDF: ISBN 978-3-8394-6570-7
ISBN 978-3-7328-6570-3

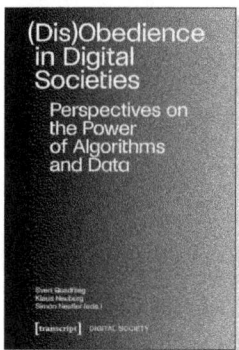

Sven Quadflieg, Klaus Neuburg, Simon Nestler (eds.)
(Dis)Obedience in Digital Societies
Perspectives on the Power of Algorithms and Data

March 2022, 380 p., pb., ill.
29,00 € (DE), 978-3-8376-5763-0
E-Book: available as free open access publication
PDF: ISBN 978-3-8394-5763-4
ISBN 978-3-7328-5763-0

**All print, e-book and open access versions of the titles in our list
are available in our online shop www.transcript-publishing.com**

Cultural Studies

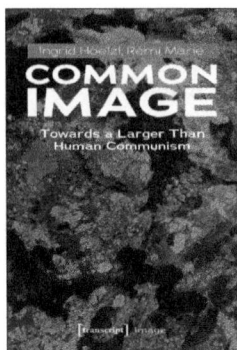

Ingrid Hoelzl, Rémi Marie
Common Image
Towards a Larger Than Human Communism

2021, 156 p., pb., ill.
29,50 € (DE), 978-3-8376-5939-9
E-Book:
PDF: 26,99 € (DE), ISBN 978-3-8394-5939-3

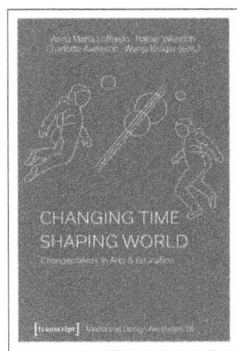

Anna Maria Loffredo, Rainer Wenrich,
Charlotte Axelsson, Wanja Kröger (eds.)
Changing Time – Shaping World
Changemakers in Arts & Education

September 2022, 310 p., pb., col. ill.
45,00 € (DE), 978-3-8376-6135-4
E-Book: available as free open access publication
PDF: ISBN 978-3-8394-6135-8

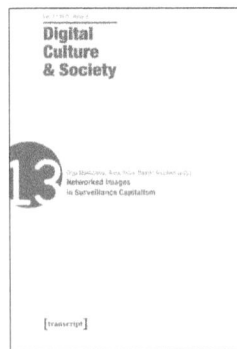

Olga Moskatova, Anna Polze, Ramón Reichert (eds.)
Digital Culture & Society (DCS)
Vol. 7, Issue 2/2021 –
Networked Images in Surveillance Capitalism

August 2022, 336 p., pb., col. ill.
29,99 € (DE), 978-3-8376-5388-5
E-Book:
PDF: 27,99 € (DE), ISBN 978-3-8394-5388-9